Farming and Gardening in the Bible

FARMING and GARDENING in the BIBLE

Alastair I. MacKay

MARIST COLLEGE   POUGHKEEPSIE, NEW YORK

The frontispiece is from an engraving of
the Creation found in an old German Bible

This book is dedicated to my father and
mother, whose lifelong practice of morning
and evening reading of a chapter of the
Bible, often followed by broad-minded
discussion of the subject matter,
laid a sound foundation for my
scriptural education.

ACKNOWLEDGMENT

"Render to Caesar the things that are Caesar's, and to God the things that are God's." So Jesus ruled on acknowledgment. Research is a dignified word, and in any field of inquiry conscientious research involves painstaking and time consuming attention to detail, and the overhauling and inspection of a large mass of extraneous matter in order to discover the desired nuggets. Literary research exacts a full quota of time and labor, but it must be admitted frankly that much literary research is unoriginal, and consists to a large extent in tapping and collating the mental contributions of earlier workers in the field. Search is the primary producer, and takes precedence over the copy-work and synthesis of research.

Probably more than any other subject, the Bible has been examined and cross-examined, investigated and analyzed, interpreted and misinterpreted, sifted and scrutinized. Anyone and everyone, irrespective of qualifications, may expound the meaning of the Scriptures, or parts thereof, and get an audience. Many self-appointed authorities claim divine guidance and spiritual intelligence for their version of God's meaning, and no man can say they are wrong, nor can any man prove they are right. "Ye shall know them by their fruits."

This book owes its existence, and frankly acknowledges it, to the search and research of thousands of men and women who have passed on, and to a few who are contemporary. The author's original contributions are very minor, and purely speculative. The last writings in the Bible were completed before 100 A.D. and this volume is confined to the agricultural background of the peoples of the Bible prior

[7]

to that date. Modern customs in Bible lands, and modern modifications of ancient usages, are occasionally mentioned but only incidentally so. Archaeological findings are limited to a few instances of supplementary data confirming scanty or circumstantial biblical evidence.

To single out by name the multitude of students and writers, spread out over thousands of years, who have contributed to our modern knowledge of the customs of the peoples of the Bible, and the flora and fauna of Bible lands, is impossible even if desirable; nearly all are buried in anonymity. To single out a few known names, and ignore the unknown contributors, would not be impartial.

This book has been written deep in the country, forty-five miles from the nearest reference library. Accordingly it is ninety-nine per cent the product of the books in the author's possession, or loaned to him, and it is these books and their authors which will be singled out for mention. The main source books are all encyclopedias. Most helpful has been *The Treasury of Bible Knowledge* by the Rev. John Ayre, M.A., published by Longmans Green and Co., London, 1866. This valuable work was kindly loaned by Mrs. Henry Bayley, to whom the author is very grateful. Next is the *Bible Dictionary* by Wm. Smith, LL.D., revised and edited by Rev. F. N. and M. A. Peloubet, published by John C. Winston Co., Philadelphia, 1884. This book was presented to the writer by Mrs. Stuart Mulligan, and is cordially acknowledged. The third source book is *A Biblical Encyclopedia* by John Eadie, D.D., LL.D., published by The Religious Tract Society, London, 1877.

Equally important with the foregoing is the *Analytical Concordance to the Bible,* by Robert Young, LL.D., published by Funk and Wagnalls Co., New York (undated).

The *Encyclopedia Britannica* published by Encyclopedia Britannica Inc., Chicago, 1947, and *Everyman's Encyclopedia* published by J. M. Dent and Sons Ltd., London, 1913, have made many contributions to the secular side of the book.

From the foregoing volumes the author has compiled the greater part of his text. The following books were not obtained until much of the first draft of the volume had been written, and their influence has been inspirational in enlarging and correcting some of the original subject matter. Probably the best modern treatment of Bible times is *Encyclopedia of Bible Life* by Madeleine S. and J. Lane Miller, pub-

[8]

lished by Harper and Bros., New York, 1944. This book offers a fund of unbiased information on the peoples and lands of the Bible. Another very interesting book is *Gospel Light* by George M. Lamsa, published by A. J. Holman Co., Philadelphia, 1939. Mr. Lamsa was born and brought up in the land that was once Assyria, where Aramaic is still spoken and the customs of the Bible were preserved intact until the First Great War introduced the benefits of modern civilization. I am indebted to Miss Elizabeth Monsarrat and Miss Millicent Brennen, who kindly presented me with *Gospel Light*. My thanks are due to Major H. A. H. Rice for loan of *The Bible Handbook* by Joseph Angus, M.A., D.D., published by the Religious Tract Society, London, 1908. Miscellaneous Bible documents of historical interest are in my possession through the courtesy of Mrs. R. Wainman-Wood, Mr. C. A. Bowman, and Mr. K. Beauchant.

The editorial staff of Rodale Press have been most helpful and encouraging. Mr. J. I. Rodale inspired me to write this book and he has been a most understanding and patient publisher, and I take this opportunity to publicly acknowledge my deep appreciation. Dr. Heinrich Meyer, Ph.D., formerly with Rodale Press, has furnished both literary contributions and expert advice. Dr. Wm. H. Eyster, Managing Editor of *Organic Gardening*, has kept supplying me with relevant clippings, as well as the very informative booklet, *Plants of the Holy Scriptures* by Eleanor King, adapted from the research of Dr. H. N. Moldenke, and published by the New York Botanical Garden.

As a long-time student both of the Bible and of nature I have accumulated a lot of miscellaneous data, both memorized and written, from sources which have been forgotten or not recorded. Some such items may have found their way into the book, and if so I render acknowledgment to the originators.

Writing a factual book requires more than research, stringing words together, and pounding a typewriter. The author has to live in the meantime. Twelve months ago the Rehabilitation Branch, Department of Veterans' Affairs, of the Canadian Government, was good enough to assess my literary ability as a major factor in my post-war rehabilitation, and each month since then a check has arrived from D. V. A. Without such financial assistance this book, in its present form, could not have been written. I am deeply grateful to the people and government of Canada for their far-sighted provisions for the future of veterans, and to the local officials of D. V. A. for their continued courtesy and their friendly understanding of an unusual type of application for assistance. I hope I have merited their confidence.

Last, but by no means least, I pay tribute to my wife. Without her unselfish and spontaneous shouldering of many of my regular farm chores, her efficient efforts to insulate me from interruptions and distractions, her warm encouragement of my efforts and her blindness to my composing temperament and writing idiosyncrasies, the writing of this book would have been a much more difficult and drawn-out task.

A. I. M.

Maple Bay,
Vancouver Island.
Canada.   29th May 1948.

Table of Contents

[11]

Farming and Gardening in the Bible

"Wisdom is the principal thing; therefore
get wisdom: and with all thy getting get
understanding."   *Proverbs 4/7*

CHAPTER 1

The Bible

THE ORIGINS of agriculture and horticulture are lost in the mists of antiquity. The Bible opens on a fully developed garden. It was the Lord God, the Creator, and not Adam, the created, who "planted a garden eastward in Eden." The unfortunate First Family, expelled from that cool and pleasant domain, pitched right into cultivating the soil and raising sheep; there is no mention of the beginner's discoveries and disappointments, of trial and error during initiation into these skilled functions.

It is not only the sacred history of Christendom, Jewry, and Islam, which neglects to tell us of the primitive inception of agriculture. The earliest preserved records of ancient China and India, Egypt and Babylon throw no more light than does *Genesis*. In the Western hemisphere Inca and Aztec chronicles are equally vague. All accept agriculture as a *fait accompli*. Only in mythology do we find the gods teaching the people the rudimentary principles of plant growth and domestication of animals. Perhaps legendary Atlantis or Lemuria held the secret of man's earliest and most important conquest of nature, and the account of it has been forever lost beneath the waves.

What the Bible lacks in record of agricultural beginnings, it compensates for in wealth of reference to plant and animal life and associated rural husbandry in the Holy Land and adjacent terrain. The Children of Israel were a pastoral and agricultural people; they counted their assets in flocks and herds, vineyards and olive trees. "And Judah and Israel dwelt safely, every man under his vine and under his fig tree, from Dan even to Beer-sheba, all the days of Solomon" (1 *Kings* 4/25). That was the ancient counterpart of our chicken in every pot and car in every garage. Trade and commerce were incidental to farming. The walled cities of the Bible corresponded to the stockades and forts of the early American settlers, defenses behind which farmers and their families could protect themselves against enemy raids.

[15]

Prophets, footloose and fearless, in their spiritual fervor neglect-
ful of food and shelter, symbolized and lent force to their preachings
by blending them with the simple truths of plant and animal life
known to even the youngest in their audiences, skilfully associating
promises and warnings with familiar and accepted natural processes.
None of the great orators of scripture attempted to talk over the heads
of their listeners. Some of the loveliest prose in the Bible, indeed in
any literature, owes its beauty to the rapture of a garden lover. "I am
the rose of Sharon, and the lily of the valleys. As the lily among
thorns .... as the apple tree among the trees of the wood, so is my
beloved .... For, lo, the winter is past, the rain is over and gone; the
flowers appear on the earth; the time of the singing of birds is come
.... the fig tree putteth forth her green figs, and the vines with the
tender grape give a good smell." Solomon, in his *Song of Songs*, could
find no greater inspiration to glorify his love than his own gardens
and orchards afforded.

Time and again Jesus went to nature and to the familiar plants
of the countryside to adorn and garnish his parables and drive home
his precepts, so that even the most illiterate peasant could readily
grasp the allegory, even though the spiritual interpretation remained
esoteric. Along dirt roads, on hillside pastures and clearings, and by
the beaches, He spoke to the people in their own tongue, in the everyday language of the farmer and the shepherd. To most of us, even to
the countrymen among us, the familiar parables, "Consider the lilies
of the field," "A sower went forth to sow," "Behold the fig tree," fail
to arouse the interest that a deeply familiar analogy always excites.
Our attitude towards the living soil is too mechanized, too pseudo-
scientific. But to the multitudes who thronged around Jesus, He spoke
their blunt language and demonstrated His familiarity with their
rural labors and rewards.

The Bible can be all things to all men. To the theologian it is an
inspired spiritual document, to be emphasized in one part and slurred
over in another, interpreted or expounded in the light of the school
of belief to which he adheres. To the scholar it is a record of fragmentary archives, some skilfully and smoothly woven into a fabric of continuity, while others jar in incongruity. The spiritual fervor and
dogmatic drive which sustains the theologian is absent from the
groping research of the scholar. A spade wielded by an Arab fellah

[16]

may uncover new evidence sufficient to wreck the patient work of years of study.

The ordinary man and woman, neither theologian nor scholar, commonly reads the Bible, or listens to its reading, without much analysis or even consciousness of the myriad segments of daily life, and evidences of the periodic and seasonal routine of a remarkable people. Several factors contribute to this seeing without perception, this hearing without awareness, limitations which Jesus criticized in his audiences two thousand years ago. The artificial intonation with which the Scriptures are so often droned from pulpit or lectern is partly responsible. The familiar, richly resonant lines of the Authorized Version of the Bible, most common of editions, dramatic and inspiring as they are, for this very reason tend to obscure the wealth of detail and pattern to which practically every chapter contributes its quota. The arbitrary division into chapter and verse, often without literary or factual continuity, further accentuates the part at the expense of the whole. Even the potent force of tradition and veneration with which Bible study is surrounded plays its part in blurring the design of the tapestry of seedtime and harvest, desert and sown field, out of which ancient Hebrew life was largely fashioned.

There is a modern trend to arrange and present the Bible so that its literary qualities, its drama, and its poetry, are offered to better advantage than in the conventional black-bound copy of Holy Writ. While such innovations may displease the rigid fundamentalist, it seems probable that the Bible is thus introduced to a wider and more unorthodox audience, and also that many who had regarded the Bible as a sacred but rather dull book are inspired to read its pages with new and enhanced appreciation.

The treatment of the Bible in this volume is a simple respectful effort to screen the words and phrases pertaining to agriculture, gardening, and animal husbandry, from the body of the text; then to arrange them in an orderly and natural sequence, as one would plan the layout of a balanced and diversified farm. Where detail is given in Holy Writ, vineyards and threshing floors will be reconstructed so that we may visualize them as we would a country property described to us by its owner. When no better evidence is available, it is assumed that frequent repetition indicates common use or native habitat, rarity the unusual or foreign. In general, the Bible has been allowed

[17]

to speak for itself and scriptural information has been given priority over that furnished by non-biblical sources. The literal meaning of the text has been accepted in most instances as the basis from which to commence research and build data, for the critics (and they are many) who dispute the literal meaning seldom agree on a substitute.

The author is neither a professional nor an expert in Bible knowledge, or in farming and gardening, but he is an enthusiastic amateur in both fields. His knowledge of Hebrew and Greek, languages from which the better known English versions of the Bible are translated, is negligible. Yet much of the record hinges on the relation between the original tongues and our modern equivalent, so Young's *Analytical Concordance of the Bible* has been adopted as the medium of exchange. Here may be found the English translation or translations of each Hebrew and Greek word, as well as the many instances where one English word translates several different words in the original language. These multiple cross-connections in comparative philology open up a wide field of research and speculation, so involved that the author is conscious of the enforced limitations of his presentation in this volume. Only in a textbook or encyclopedia could the ramifications be given adequate coverage, and this book aims at being a popular treatise rather than an erudite study. Yet the vast majority of the facts herein are supported by documentary evidence, while speculation is labelled as such. Practically everything can be verified by reference to Young's *Concordance* and a few good Bible encyclopedias; more than one are necessary, for different commentators have different views and interpretations, and in most disputed cases no finite and conclusive proof is available. The Authorized or King James Version of the Bible, in the Canadian "Gideon" edition with marginal notes, has been used as the source Bible, with the Revised Version, British edition, and the Moffat translation of the New Testament as supplementary references.

A farmer is not only a specialist in plants and the soil and domestic animals; he is also a human being in the frame of contemporary society, with its political and economic and metaphysical components. He usually has a family and has known romance and perhaps tragedy. His religion and his philosophy and his folklore influence his life and his actions, extending to his celebrations and even his travels. He buys and sells in the marketplace, and rubs shoulders and ideas with strangers and foreigners as well as with neighbors. He pays taxes and may be conscripted for war or participate in rebellion against injustice. If crops fail, or rulers oppress, or a wave of history overtakes him, he may emigrate to another country. So, the husbandmen of this book are treated as people whose human interests extend beyond and beside their fields and flocks. Also, most of the pertinent facts associated with the title of this volume are buried in religious and historical passages; sometimes one chapter or even one verse may suggest more farm data than a scriptural book. Taking words and sentences out of context is like pulling up a plant by the roots to see how well it is growing. Preserving a minimum of context makes a certain amount of repetition unavoidable, for sometimes a heterogeneous collection of rustic lore is found lumped together, and both agricultural and spiritual significance suffer if rigid classification is adopted.

While Palestine remains the focal area, the agricultural influences of surrounding countries and peoples are also examined. The rivers of Eden flowed far distant from the Jordan, Noah landed the ark on Mount Ararat in Armenia. The Children of Israel knew the servitude of Egypt, Babylon, and Assyria, as well as that of Rome. Baal, the nature god of Canaan, strove on many a hill against Jehovah for homage as the lord of fertility and the giver of a bounteous harvest. But, in the main, it is the produce and cultivation of Palestine's fields and gardens, and the livestock that cropped her verdant pastures, which we shall examine in the following pages.

CHAPTER 2

Foreign Influences

No RACE and no country has a pure unmixed culture and civilization. The customs of contiguous nations and tribes, the innovations introduced by travellers, traders, and captives, the New Order imposed by conquerors, the agricultural heritage derived from earlier inhabitants, all contribute to the alloy of the melting pot.

Of foreign influences, those of Egypt and Babylon must be considered outstanding in their effect on the agricultural practices of the Israelites, while that of the dispossessed Canaanites, whose farms and gardens the conquering Chosen People moved into, inevitably set the pattern for land cultivation by the newcomers. It is still the soundest of agricultural advice that the new farmer follow the type and technique of farming which has a record of success on the other landholdings in the district, until mature judgment based on experience is attained.

Accordingly we shall take a look at the agronomies of Egypt and Babylon, with a briefer glance at the other kingdoms of Mesopotamia, as well as the later influence of Persia, Rome, and Greece, before moving over to the land flowing with milk and honey, the land of Canaan.

More than six hundred references to Egypt occur in the Bible; the first is in the 12th chapter of *Genesis*. There the patriarch Abram, accompanied by his nephew Lot, journeyed progressively westward from his native Ur, in Mesopotamia, towards Canaan, where he settled until one of the recurrent crop failures imperiled the lives of his cattle and made their survival dependent on reaching the rich pastures and grain fields of Egypt. The 13th chapter tells of the departure of Abram and Lot from Egypt, "very rich in cattle, in silver, and in gold." They trekked towards Canaan but found that the grazing lands of the more northerly region provided scant fodder for their augmented herds, "for the land was not able to bear them. " Wisely, they decided to part company.

From the Highlands of Gilead a camel caravan set out, laden with spices and precious ointments for the luxury trade of Egypt. Soon after crossing the Jordan, a band of sheep-tending Nomads hailed the traders; after a brief pause, the caravan wended its way south, its membership increased by a good looking young slave (*Genesis* 37/25-28). So, Joseph reached Egypt and his fantastic career there. Came another famine, and Israel, his family and his flocks left Canaan and took up domicile in the fertile valley of the Nile.

The Children of Israel dwelt in Egypt for four hundred and thirty years; during that period Jacob's family and their children's children grew into a nation. At the Exodus there were "about six hundred thousand on foot that were men, beside children. And a mixed multitude went up also with them" (*Exodus* 12/37-38). When we consider that it will be more than one hundred years hence before the descendants of the Pilgrim Fathers have the same length of tenure in North America as the Israelites had in Egypt, and that for the greater part of their stay there is nothing to indicate that the Hebrews were not treated with consideration by the native Egyptians, it is logical to assume that the settlers shared and even accepted as their own way of life many of the practices of the Egyptians, including the arts of agriculture and horticulture in which the Nile dwellers excelled. That Pharaoh recognized his guests' ability in cattle raising is shown by his choice of Israelites to manage his own herds.

All the might of Egypt was tied to the rich silt of the Nile. Egyptian mythology recognized its debt to agriculture, many of the deities having connection with fertility and irrigation. According to Diodorus Siculus, the god Osiris discovered agriculture in Egypt and later travelled far abroad teaching others the art. His wife Isis was the first to identify barley growing beside the Nile, and she domesticated it and brought it under cultivation. The god Tybi, under his alternate name Shefbodet, meant "sprouting of the grain", and his image was depicted holding a growing ear of corn. Some of the most important national festivities of Egypt were agriculturally significant, coinciding with critical dates in irrigation, planting and harvesting.

The Land of Goshen, where the Israelites settled (*Genesis* 47/6) is believed to have been the northeastern delta of the Nile, a fertile territory where the practice of good delta farming would soon be the accepted custom of the later generations of Hebrews. The original ones, Jacob and his sons, were essentially cattlemen and shepherds, and their descendants retained their interests in flocks and herds, as

[21]

well as adapting themselves to the intensive cultivation of the soil. The Hyksos or Shepherd Kings had been defeated and expelled by the reigning dynasty, according to some historians, and sheepmen were ostracized by the public. *Genesis* (46/34) tells us, "Every shepherd is an abomination unto the Egyptians."

The story of Joseph is equally the story of corn. (The biblical corn denotes cereal grain in general). The 47th chapter of *Genesis* tells how Joseph, acting as Pharaoh's corn controller, used his monopoly to strip the Egyptians progressively of their money, their cattle, and their land, and finally reduced them to the status of serfs. All that the Egyptians got in return was sufficient grain to eke out an existence for themselves and their families. Probably the seeds of their hatred of the Israelites may be traced to Joseph's hard bargaining.

From Egyptian records we learn that wheat, barley, millet, emmer and lentils were grown. So profitable was this cereal trade that it largely displaced the growing of grass. Even cattle were stall-fed with loaves of bread, to fatten them. Other domestic animals included sheep and goats, gazelles and pigs, the last being regarded as unclean. The injunction against the use of swine's flesh in the Mosaic Law may stem from the Egyptian taboo.

A wide variety of fruit was cultivated, including apples, pears, peaches, apricots, cherries, melons, grapes, olives, figs, dates, lemons and pomegranates. Amongst the vegetables were peas, asparagus, cabbage, celery, leeks, onions, cress, radishes and garlic. Flowers were much admired and roses, chrysanthemums, lilies, oleanders, narcissus, lotus, cornflowers and poppies flourished in Nile gardens.

Students of economics and politics may be interested to learn that probably the first comprehensive system of government control, and the establishment of a strong central government to plan and enforce such control, developed in ancient Egypt as a consequence of the necessity of regulating the periodic Nile overflows and floods, and administering an equable system of irrigation. Occasional high freshets would wash away banks and retaining walls, landmarks would disappear, and so a system of land measurement had to be devised; thus the rudiments of geometry came into being.

Ownership of land was vested in the crown, and farmed out under a type of feudal system. Rent was paid in cash or in kind, and the agricultural administration was organized with a bureaucratic system of licences and permits, inspectors and fines. The 47th chapter of *Genesis*, verses 20-26, tells us of enforced collective farming, while the evidence of priestly prerogative and double tithing may be considered to have influenced comparable edicts in the later Mosaic Law. "And Joseph bought all the land of Egypt for Pharaoh; for the Egyptians sold every man his field, because the famine prevailed over them: so the land became Pharaoh's. And as for the people, he removed them to cities from one end of the borders of Egypt even to the other end thereof. Only the land of the priests bought he not; for the priests had a portion assigned them of Pharaoh, and did eat their portion which Pharaoh gave them: wherefore they sold not their lands. Then Joseph said unto the people, Behold, I have bought you this day and your land for Pharaoh; lo, here is seed for you, and ye shall sow the land. And it shall come to pass in the increase, that ye shall give the fifth part unto Pharaoh, and four parts shall be your own, for seed of the field, and for your food, and for them of your households, and for food for your little ones.... And Joseph made it a law over the land of Egypt unto this day, that Pharaoh should have the fifth part; except the land of the priests only, which became not Pharaoh's."

Joseph issued seed for only the initial sowing; succeeding plantings were to be furnished from the farmer's crop. Pharaoh claimed one fifth, which was a double tithe, but he probably allocated half of this, one tenth of the total, to the priesthood. In this way the priests remained subservient to Pharaoh and dependent on his bounty. Moses later stipulated that one tenth of the produce of the land should go directly to the priestly Levites, thus divorcing them from the control of the secular ruler.

The children of Israel did not take kindly to regimentation, and as Canaan had no irrigation system nor indeed much need of one, it is unlikely that the complicated regulations governing Nile farming had much influence in the agricultural development of the Promised Land. At least some of the tribes of the Exodus had retained their old nomadic attachment to flocks and herds; their leader, Moses, had spent years tending the flocks of his father-in-law, Jethro, while a fugitive from Pharaoh. Accordingly, the Egyptian influence would be found more in animal husbandry, breeding and types of livestock, than in intensive cultivation of the soil and crop specialization. However, farming techniques and plant cultivation practiced in Egypt were transferred in some degree when the Hebrews finally settled down in Canaan, for only the tribes of Reuben, Gad and part of Manasseh chose to become full time stockmen. (*Numbers 32*)

Becoming nauseated with the monotony of manna, the people cried to Moses, "Who shall give us flesh to eat? We remember the fish, which we did eat in Egypt freely; the cucumbers, and the melons, and the leeks, and the onions, and the garlick" (*Numbers 11/4-5*); and again, "Would to God we had died by the hand of the Lord in the land of Egypt, when we sat by the flesh pots, and when we did eat bread to the full; for ye have brought us forth unto this wilderness, to kill this whole assembly with hunger" (*Exodus 16/3*). Their appetites and desires sharpened by the hardships of the desert, many of the weary Israelites must have planned a "little Egypt" farm in some sheltered valley of the Promised Land. That they did so seems probable, for the influence of Egypt was not left behind at the Red Sea. During the centuries of Bible history, Palestine and Egypt were allied by treaty and torn by war. In 320 B.C. about 100,000 Jews settled in Egypt. Each country provided a means of refuge for citizens of the other who had incurred the displeasure of the authorities, the best known example being the flight of Joseph and Mary with the infant Jesus to temporary safety in Egypt (*Matthew 2/13-15*).

There can be little doubt of the agricultural influence of Egypt on the Holy Land. Anyone who knows the farming practices of the Pennsylvania Dutch can trace the close ties with the proven methods of their German ancestors. The introduction (perhaps re-introduction would be more correct) of oriental composting methods to the English-speaking world by Sir Albert Howard and J. I. Rodale, and of European bio-dynamic soil treatment by E. Pfeiffer demonstrates the powerful and far reaching results of the efforts of a few able men.

Equally important, though documented less orderly than that of Egypt, was the agricultural heritage first derived from, and later imposed by, the countries of the Mesopotamian plains and foothills. Under a variety of names and alliances these nations flowed and ebbed around the nucleus of the Tigris and Euphrates. Here lay the Garden of Eden; above these inundated plains floated Noah in his ark; this was home to Abram's father and home to Abram for the first three-quarter century of his life, and the beauty and virtue of its women impelled Isaac and Jacob to seek wives there.

To the inhabitants of Sumer and Accad, cities giving their names to districts and peoples of the plain, modern civilization acknowledges its debt for some of the founding records of historical progress. The earliest preserved inscriptions featuring skilled agriculture are Accadian.

The Bible tells of various nations who developed this fertile alluvial soil. Sometimes different names describe the same territory and race, such as Babylonia and Chaldea, famous for intellectual leadership. *Genesis* (10/10) mentions the cities of the old land of Shinar, and the succeeding chapter describes the rise and fall of the Tower of Babel there. Elam was once a great nation whose shores were washed by the Persian Gulf. Further north the dreaded Assyrians held sway. Mesopotamia, a Greek rendering of the native Aram Naharaim, lay between the higher reaches of the Tigris and the Euphrates, northwest of Chaldea.

The dwellers in Palestine lumped these countries together as the land of the people of the East. These nations fought among themselves and against Israel with varying fortunes, interspersed with periods of peace and friendship. In 721 B.C. Samaria capitulated to the armies of Sargon, the Kingdom of Israel collapsed, and its people disappeared from history, leaving only the standard of Judah to maintain the prestige of the race. Isaiah, writing shortly after the catastrophe, indicates how widespread was the foreign settlement of Hebrews, many of whom had emigrated or been taken captive prior to the Assyrian debacle: "The Lord shall set his hand again the second time to recover the remnant of his people, which shall be left, from Assyria, and from Egypt, and from Pathros, and from Cush, and from Elam, and from Shinar, and from the islands of the sea" (*Isaiah* 11/11).

Emigrants and immigrants, conquerors and captives, bring more to their new homes than their persons, their families and their goods. Their native culture is transplanted, and some takes root even in the most inhospitable soil. Folklore and country superstition often outlast more cultivated ideas. "We didn't do it that way back home," may be fighting words in new surroundings, but methods thrive long

[25]

after tactlessness has been forgotten. Carefully preserved seeds and plant slips may be unknowing hosts to unwanted weeds and pests.

The Babylonian Captivity was comparatively brief compared with the sojourn in Egypt; its duration was little more than fifty years. Yet that half century allowed two new generations to attain maturity with only hearsay evidence of the farms and gardens of their homeland. It was long enough to kill the Hebrew language as the spoken tongue of the masses, to the extent that paraphrases of the Hebrew Scriptures had to be translated into Aramaic, the speech of the conquerors, in order that the fate of the language should not overtake the religion. Even the most race-conscious minority group feels this conformity pressure in a foreign country, and while the immigrant generation is usually immune, the succeeding native-born children are increasingly orientated towards the outside world. It is too early to estimate the influence which the British and European children, evacuated to this continent during the recent war, have taken back with them to their native lands, but there is no doubt that many of the rural-domiciled older boys and girls will introduce American farm practices taught them by their hosts. The Jews of the Exile, freed by Cyrus about 536 B. C., returned to rebuild the temple and restock the ruined farms of their ancestors, and seed, plants, animals and husbandry native to the valley of the Euphrates were transplanted to Palestine.

What the bamboo is to China, the date palm was to the Babylonian Empire. According to Gibbon, no less than three hundred and sixty uses were credited to this tree. It was a source of bread and syrup, vinegar and wine. Herodotus confirms the manufacture of date wine in Babylon and also refers to the importation of grape wine, carried by river boats from Armenia. Even the stones of the dates were processed and fed to cattle and sheep to fatten them.

The Babylonians knew and practiced the art of fertilizing female plants with pollen from the male. In the British Museum is a sculpture portraying a Babylonian priest or ruler shaking a male cone over the female flower. We still use this hand fertilization, notably with marrows.

Beer was brewed from barley and from wheat, and could be purchased only by surrendering an amount of grain equal to that consumed in its manufacture. Heavy penalties were attached to in-

[26]

fringement of this regulation, which was enforced to maintain an adequate supply of grain for food. The idea might commend itself to modern temperance advocates.

Apples, figs, apricots and grapes were grown, also almonds and pistachio nuts. Plane, cypress and acacia trees were common.

Both white and black goats, and white and black sheep, were raised for food and for their fleece, the white wool bringing premium prices. Cattle and pigs were fattened for the market. While the horse and the ass were extensively used for transportation, there is no record of their being hitched to the plow. Babylonian archives are singularly lacking in portrayal or description of agricultural implements and practices, but they are much more informative on regulations governing farming and the marketing of food. The Babylonians had legal minds and were thorough bureaucrats; the famous Code of Hammurabi (called Amraphel in *Genesis* 14/1) covered the widest range of social and economic conduct and transactions, including the legal and business aspects of farming and the buying and selling of produce. Each city had public markets with stalls assigned to the venders of cereals and herbs, fruit and vegetables, meat and poultry. Records of apiculture date from 8th century B. C. Dogs assisted the shepherds with their flocks, which included gazelles as well as sheep and goats.

The hanging gardens of Babylon were one of the Seven Wonders of the ancient world. The great Sargon I. had been a famous gardener and gardening was a popular hobby. Unlike Egypt, shepherds followed a respected calling in public regard.

According to the 10th chapter of *Genesis,* Nimrod, "the mighty hunter before the Lord," was the founder of Babylon; a marginal note in the same chapter credits Nimrod with also building Nineveh, the Assyrian metropolis, although the text gives the honor to Asshur. Assyria, watered by the Tigris, specialized in war rather than in peaceful agriculture. Like the U.S.S.R., Assyria enforced mass transfers of population as national policy. Her absorption of the majority of the Israelites and their replacement in Palestine by Assyrians and Assyrian satellites had more far-reaching consequences on the destiny of the Hebrew race than any previous or subsequent event. Unfortunately, details of the agricultural implications are unobtainable.

From a farmer's viewpoint, the Assyrian rural scene had much

[27]

GARDENING IN THE BIBLE

in common with the Babylonian one. The story of Jonah and his
famous gourd which came up in a night and, blighted by a worm,
withered in a night, is the best known biblical reference to the plant
life of Nineveh; from the final words of the Book of *Jonah* we learn
that the Assyrian capital contained "much cattle." Its massive walls
enclosed an urban area of about 250 square miles, and the raising of
herds of livestock within the city limits was probably a defense precaution of the war-minded Assyrians.

A gap of four centuries occurs in Old Testament history and
records, bridged only by fragmentary prophecies. Nehemiah is the
last biblical historian, Malachi the last prophet, preceding the Christian era.

Only a small minority of the Jews took advantage of the proffered
liberty to return to their devastated homeland. Most of them preferred the easier and accustomed life of Babylonia and Persia, where
opportunity for material advancement and reward was greater. The
Books of *Daniel* and *Esther* are segments from the lives and fortunes
of these willing exiles.

This scriptural gap is historically documented by secular texts.
The Holy Land remained under Persian domination for a century
after Nehemiah, until the overthrow of the Empire by Alexander the
Great in 330 B.C. From that date until 167 B.C. Graeco-Macedonian
sovereignty ruled Judea. Antiochus IV (Antiochus Epiphanes) went
to great extremes to Hellenize the Jews, finally provoking the revolt
of the Maccabees, which succeeded in establishing virtual indepen-
dence by 141 B.C. Unfortunately, internal dissension encouraged the
intervention of Pompey the Great, who captured Jerusalem after a
three month siege in 63 B.C., and the rest of the country was later
subjugated by the Romans. Herod the Great, Roman puppet king,
ruled from 73-4 B.C. In New Testament times, Judea was an imperial
province of Rome, ruled by a procurator or governor, but permitted
a large degree of local autonomy or home rule.

The agricultural effects of these national changes must have been
considerable. The Persian influence was largely a continuation of
Babylonian practices, but Greece and Rome represented a new type
of civilization, with all that that involves. In its simplest terms it
meant that new and hardier varieties of cattle and plants were introduced by the occupying power. Western farmers too were hardier

[28]

and not limited by the age-old and age-sanctified rural customs of the East. Pre-Christian Greece and Rome had highly developed agricultural and horticultural knowledge and practices, and much current literature is available on these subjects.

In the New Testament we find a few clues. Absentee ownership was common: "A certain man planted a vineyard, and let it forth to husbandmen, and went into a far country for a long time" (*Luke* 20/9). Great estates had been broken up together with ancestral holdings and given to court favorites or collaborationists: "A certain nobleman went into a far country to receive for himself a kingdom, and to return" (*Luke* 19/12). The Moffat Edition substitutes "royal power" for "kingdom." Farm labor had become a commercial commodity, rather than the outcome of a family or personal contract. Jesus speaks of the use of salt in composting, the first Biblical mention of this. In *Luke* (13/8) a gardener asks permission to use a Roman technique on an unproductive fruit tree. Paul, a great traveller and observer, addressing himself to Gentile converts in Rome, writes with professional knowledge of the grafting of olive trees, perhaps basing his choice of simile on a practice the Romans may have introduced into Palestine, although the Babylonians practiced grafting the male spathe of the date palm into the female spathe to ensure fertilization.

Specifically, Greece is credited with the introduction of the domestic hen into Palestine. Archaeological discoveries dating back to 200 B.C. depict fowls, and the accompanying inscriptions are in Greek.

Roman documents tell of grants of farms and small landholdings to war veterans, settlers in conquered provinces including Palestine. Pliny writes of the balsam plantations of the Holy Land, a Roman monopoly and highly esteemed both for its natural properties and as a source of wealth. Insurgent Jews sometimes sabotaged the Roman protected balsam groves. The most important and best effect of the Roman occupation was the *Pax Romana*, which allowed the peasants of Palestine to till their acres in peace.

CHAPTER 3

The Promised Land

"FOR THE Lord thy God bringeth thee into a good land, a land of brooks of water, of fountains and depths that spring out of valleys and hills; a land of wheat, and barley, and vines, and fig trees, and pomegranates; a land of oil olive, and honey; a land wherein thou shalt eat bread without scarceness, thou shalt not lack anything in it; a land whose stones are iron, and out of whose hills thou mayest dig brass .... a land that floweth with milk and honey. For the land, whither thou goest in to possess it, is not as the land of Egypt, from whence ye came out, where thou sowedst thy seed, and wateredst it with thy foot, as a garden of herbs: but the land, whither ye go to possess it, is a land of hills and valleys, and drinketh water of the rain of heaven .... I will give you the rain of your land in his due season, the first rain and the latter rain, that thou mayest gather in thy corn, and thy wine, and thine oil. And I will send grass in thy fields for thy cattle, that thou mayest eat and be full."

Such is the glowing picture of the Promised Land as set forth in the Fifth Book of Moses (*Deuteronomy* 8/7 ff.). In less descriptive language the pledge of a new homeland recurs in many scriptural passages; common to most of them is the familiar phrase, "A land of milk and honey." *Ezekiel*, in his 20th chapter, avers that the glory of all lands is to flow with milk and honey!

As we read the opening citation, the emphasis on water cannot be overlooked. Anyone who has had to endure long periods with scanty or uncertain water supply, and has had to share what little there was with his animals and perhaps with the thirsty plants in his garden, develops the deepest respect for abundant water. To the parched tribes wandering in the desert south of Canaan, inured to brackish and far-apart oasis wells, water galore meant more than the most tempting of food; for food, whether animal or vegetable, was directly dependent on water supply. The Israelites may have been remiss in their duty towards Jehovah in religious matters but they were ever grateful for the plenteous water He provided. Numerous passages testify to this: "He shall be like a tree planted by the rivers of water, that bringeth forth his fruit in due season; his leaf also shall not wither" (*Psalms* 1/3). The term "living waters" used in the Scriptures emphasized the difference between the bubbling brooks and gushing springs of Canaan, and the stagnant desert wells and dull ditch water of the Nile irrigation canals. Another reference to Egyptian irrigation practices was, "where thou sowedst thy seed and wateredst it with thy foot, as a garden of herbs." Foot-propelled water wheels and treadmills fed water to irrigation ditches, a method still followed in the East.

Canaan means "low" or "flat," and the original land of Canaan was a level coastal strip bordering the Mediterranean. Its early history is vague. The 10th chapter of *Genesis* traces the genealogy of Canaan and the boundaries of the family holdings. "Now these are the generations of the sons of Noah; Shem, Ham, and Japheth.... and the sons of Ham; Cush, and Mizraim, and Phut, and Canaan.... And Canaan begat Sidon his firstborn, and Heth, and the Jebusite, and the Amorite, and the Girgasite, and the Hivite, and the Arkite, and the Sinite, and the Arvadite, and the Zemarite, and the Hamathite: and afterwards were the families of the Canaanites spread abroad. And the border of the Canaanites was from Sidon, as thou comest to Gerar, unto Gaza; as thou goest, unto Sodom, and Gomorrah, and Admah, and Zeboim, even unto Lasha." The 15th chapter of *Genesis* replaces some of these names with others, whilst *Deuteronomy* (7/1) reduces the Canaan tribes to seven, "seven nations greater and mightier than thou." Bordering races at the time of the Israelite occupation were the Ammonites, the Amalekites, the Edomites, the Midianites, the Moabites and the Philistines. The Israelites infiltrated in some districts and occupied others by force of arms, but the population remained heterogeneous. As the Hebrew conquest progressed, the territory occupied by the twelve tribes became known as the land of Canaan, although its boundaries extended beyond the original area from which it derived its name.

In the 34th chapter of *Numbers* the borders of the Holy Land are defined, and the River Jordan, with its connecting inland seas or lakes, is established as the eastern limit. At the height of their power, under David and Solomon, the Israelites were in possession of much vaster territory than their biblical heritage. "From Dan even unto

Beer-sheba" is the expression quoted several times in the Bible as the north-south limits, a stretch of about one hundred and forty-five miles. Another encompassing phrase was "from the entering in of Hamath to the river (or brook) of Egypt." This was a considerable extension of the Dan-Beer-sheba axis; the river of Egypt was not the Nile, but a stream, the Wady el-Arish, entering the Mediterranean about 40 miles beyond Gaza.

At its upper extremity the country was little more than twenty miles wide, while the southern end of the Dead Sea, at the Wilderness of Zin, was but seventy-five miles from the Mediterranean. In size and shape it roughly resembled New Hampshire. Within this small area lay a wide variety of topography and climate.

The general contour of the Holy Land runs north and south, the Jordan almost directly so, the Mediterranean coastline about north-north-east south-south-west. East of the Maritime Plain rises the Shepelah (low hills), which in turn climb to the Central Range. These mountains drop sharply to the low sunken Jordan Valley, their sides furrowed by gullies down which torrents roar in spring, subsiding to a trickle in late summer. Beyond the Jordan rises the Eastern Range.

The low coastal plain is elevated in one section by a transverse spur from the Central Range, terminating in Mt. Carmel on the Mediterranean shore. The Central Range is broken by the Plain of Esdraelon, or Jezreel, which divides the mountains of Galilee from those of Ephraim.

The coastal flats may be divided into three sections. Stretching from a little south of Gaza to Joppa is the Philistine plain, averaging sixteen miles in width and noted for its fertility. The light loamy brown soil was virtually stoneless in Bible days; the whole region was a wheat belt, but the absence of trees to act as a windbreak allowed the sand of the beaches to encroach inland. Wells were abundant and good. North of Joppa the plain narrows to a ribbon ten miles or so in width; mountains rise abruptly from the eastern edge of the Plain of Sharon, which stretches as far as Mt. Carmel. This was a richly fertile region in ancient times, wooded in the north, and dotted with date groves, gardens and wheat fields further south. We remember Solomon's "I am the rose of Sharon." North of Carmel the land falls away to the Plain of Acre (Accho), until the mountains

[32]

finally shut in to the sea just north of Ach-zib. Beyond lay Phoenicia with its famous ports of Tyre and Sidon.

The Shepelah, an undulating moorland with hills of limestone and chalk, was the no-man's land between the Israelites and the Philistines. A series of valleys lie parallel with the Central Range, and five transverse depressions wind between the low hills, connecting coastal towns with interior ones. This country was mainly given over to grazing flocks of sheep and goats.

Beyond the Shepelah lay the highlands of Judea, sloping towards the wilderness of the south and east. South of Hebron the territory was known as the Negeb, or land of dryness. Much of Judea was stony and infertile, where shepherds guarded their flocks against wolves. Spring rain and sunshine covered even the bare hills with verdure but in a few months they were dry and brown again. Further north, and towards the sea, cultivation and fertility increased. In Samaria, the central province, the natural aspects were more open and pleasing and the soil lent itself to more intensive cultivation. The rainfall was heavier, assuring better returns to the husbandman. Cultivated fields were larger and country living easier and more productive than in the Judean hills.

Samaria ended at the Plain of Esdraelon, rich pastureland all too often trodden down not by cattle but by opposing armies on the famous battlefield of Megiddo (Armageddon of *Revelation*). Northward lay Galilee, divided into Upper and Lower districts; Lower Galilee was the richest and most fertile farmland in Palestine. The Rev. Selah Merrill describes it: "Such is the fertility of the soil that it rejects no plant, for the air is so genial that it suits every variety. The walnut, which delights above other trees in a wintry climate, grows here luxuriously, together with the palm tree which is nourished by heat. It not only possesses the extraordinary virtue of nourishing fruits of opposite climes, but also maintains a continuous supply of them. Here were found all the productions which made Italy rich and beautiful. Forests covered its mountains and hills, while its uplands, gentle slopes and broader valleys were rich in pasture, meadows, cultivated fields, vineyards, olive groves and fruit trees of every kind." Upper Galilee shared the bounties of the southern section, with the modification in vegetation due to its greater height above sea level, its higher hills and more rugged terrain. Its northern boundary lay

[33]

under the shadow of majestic Mount Hermon (9166 ft.) and lesser mountains of the Lebanon Range.

Here, on the western slopes of Mt. Hermon is the watershed which drains into the beginnings of the River Jordan, joining with other streams from the hills of Antilebanon to form the only river of any consequence in the Holy Land. The Jordan Valley and the Dead Sea rift into which the Jordan flows constitute one of the most remarkable phenomena known to geologists. It has aptly been termed the world's deepest ditch. The Jordan proper may be considered to start at the ancient Waters of Merom (Lake Huleh), a lush marshy depression, home of innumerable wildfowl and teeming with fish. For a couple of miles beyond Merom it winds through rich meadowland, then roars down a long narrow series of gorges for ten miles distance and six hundred feet drop, to enter the Sea of Galilee (known also in the Bible as the Sea of Chinnereth, Gennesaret or Tiberias). From the Sea of Galilee until the river empties into the Dead (Salt) Sea is but sixty-five miles as the crow flies, but the Jordan being earthbound follows its tortuous river bed for two hundred miles and is precipitated through twenty-seven rapids in its course. At its junction with the Dead Sea it lies more than thirteen hundred feet below sea level.

From an agricultural standpoint the Jordan valley has little significance. Josephus speaks of the Jordan as flowing through a desert. While there were many small patches of very fertile land, they were early abandoned to natural vegetation rather than being kept under cultivation. High spring freshets were a recurrent menace, and the climate was enervating and unhealthy. Jericho, in the lower Jordan valley, experiences shade temperatures of 130°F. with little relief at night. The only biblical evidence of the Jordan valley being an attractive pastoral district occurs in the 13th chapter of *Genesis*, where, prior to the destruction of Sodom and Gomorrah, Lot considered its fertility comparable to the land of Egypt. It is an interesting speculative point whether the brimstone and fire which destroyed Sodom and Gomorrah may have been accompanied by seismic fissure which changed the bed and course of the Jordan.

Geologically, the hills of Palestine are preponderantly hard limestone. The limestone is frequently overlaid with softer chalky deposit, with coral, shells, and marine remains to indicate that at one era parts of the Holy Land lay below the waters of the Great Sea. In

[34]

this soft calcareous rock, caves, both natural and handhewn, were numerous. It was a logical setting for permanent wine and olive presses, and grain and other food were stored in subterranean cellars chiselled from the easily worked stone; the excavating of family tombs or sepulchres was a recognized practice. Near the Dead Sea and the Sinai Peninsula granite formations are predominant, with bituminous shale and slate in the former region. Around Cana and Galilee basaltic rocks are evident. Signs of former volcanic action are widespread, the hot springs of Tiberias furnishing evidence of underground energy. The pillar of cloud by day and of fire by night (*Exodus* 13/22) aptly describes the emanations of an active volcano whose crater lay just below the horizon of the observer.

From the eternal snows of Mt. Hermon to the ultra-tropic heat of the lower Jordan lay the widest variety of climate and temperature, with resultant diversification of flora and fauna. The husbandman who was dissatisfied with the temperature, the humidity, the rainfall or the length of growing season at his homestead need only travel a few miles to find different meteorological conditions. Probably no country in the world of equal size has such a variety of climate. The lower Jordan depression has a mean temperature of about 75°F.; the plains rising from sea level to a few hundred feet average 68°; the elevated tablelands two or three thousand feet above the sea record a mean of 60°-62°, while the Lebanon above 4000 ft. drops to an annual mean of 35°. Two main factors influence the varied Palestine climate. One is the pronounced range between elevation and depression, the extremes of Mt. Hermon and the lower Jordan lying over ten thousand feet apart. The other big factor is the variation caused by proximity to desert or sea. South and east lie the hot desert sands, while the western frontier is the cool, moist Mediterranean.

The agricultural processes of Egypt were synchronized to the Nile levels rather than to climate and weather progression. Except on the Mediterranean coast, rain is infrequent and scanty. Alexandria, on the sea, has about 10 inches annually, Cairo (close to the Biblical Memphis or Noph) but 2 inches.

Amongst the many changes which Canaan developed in Hebrew mentality was meteorological observation and forecasting; this was necessarily of local character, conditioned by the topography and proximity to sea, mountain or desert, although some of the atmos-

[35]

pheric sequences and relationships were national. The incidence of
locality may explain some discrepancies between cause and effect
in the lore of the old weather prophets, but even in this era of
scientific meteorology mistakes are common.

Solomon poked gentle sarcasm at the weather expert of 1000 B.
C.: "He that observeth the wind shall not sow; and he that regardeth
the clouds shall not reap" (*Ecclesiastes* 11/4). The man who waited for
perfect conditions, meanwhile passing up suitable if less favored ones,
would find that his procrastination had ruined his crop prospects.

Probably most of the weather lore was learned from the aborig-
inal inhabitants, and the influence of Chaldean astronomers and
astrologers must also be recognized. Yet Hebrew intellect and the
unbiased observation of nature inherent in monotheism doubtless
contributed to a more scientific appraisal of weather probabilities.

Though the husbandman incorporated half a dozen seasons in
the agricultural year, the climate was popularly regarded as having
but two phases—wet and dry, cold and heat, winter and summer;
spring and fall were evanescent. "The former and the latter rain"
is a well known Biblical expression. In late October or early November the former rain arrived, the first showers quickly vanishing in the
parched soil. December to February was mid-winter, with intermittent rain and hail on the lower levels and snow on the highlands. In
March came the heavier latter rain; by mid-April the dry season had set
in, to continue till October, with cloudless blue skies the rule, and
rain of rare occurrence. The precipitation of the wet season fell in
sharp heavy showers or rainstorms, with dry periods of bright sunshine intervening; continuous rain or drizzle was uncommon.

Amos (4/7) tells of the vagaries of the weather, which he attributes to divine intervention. "I have witholden the rain from you,
when there were yet three months to the harvest: and I caused it
to rain upon one city, and caused it not to rain upon another city:
one piece was rained upon, and the piece whereupon it rained not
withered. So two or three cities wandered unto one city, to drink
water; but they were not satisfied." Presumably their reception was
chilly. Solomon, a much married man, uses an apt comparison: "A
continual dropping in a very rainy day and a contentious woman are
alike" (*Proverbs* 27/15). Other observations of this versatile monarch
are factual as well as allegorical: "The wind goeth toward the south,

[36]

and turneth about unto the north; it whirleth about continually, and the wind returneth again according to his circuits" (*Ecclesiastes* 1/6). The prevailing winds of Palestine followed a definite cycle: wet westerlies brought the rains of winter, followed by east winds from February to June; from summer to autumn equinoxes, north winds prevailed, backing in late September to northwest and settling in the west in November. More of his weather observations may be found in *Proverbs* (25/14): "Whoso boasteth himself of a false gift is like clouds and wind without rain." And *Proverbs* (25/23): "The north wind driveth away rain," which a marginal notation and the Revised Version text change into "The north wind bringeth forth rain." A weather rhyme, credited by the modern as well as by the ancient mariner, says:

> "Red sky at morning, sailors take warning;
> Red sky at night, sailors' delight."

Jesus quoted the same lore when the Pharisees and the Sadducees asked him for a sign from heaven, in the opening verses of the 16th chapter of *Matthew*. "When it is evening, ye say, It will be fair weather; for the sky is red. And in the morning, It will be foul weather to-day, for the sky is red and lowring. O ye hypocrites, ye can discern the face of the sky; but can ye not discern the signs of the times?" In *Luke* (12/54-55) Jesus continues: "When ye see a cloud rise out of the west, straightway ye say, There cometh a shower; and so it is. And when ye see the south wind blow, ye say, There will be heat; and it cometh to pass." Interesting confirmation of the rain presaged by westerly clouds is found in 1 *Kings* (18/42-45). After a long and particularly severe drought, Elijah was divinely advised that rain was due. When sceptical King Ahab doubted this forecast, Elijah and his servant climbed Mt. Carmel (1810 feet) and eagerly scanned the far sea horizon westward. Six times the servant climbed the highest crag and returned to the praying prophet to say that only blue sky met his gaze. "And it came to pass at the seventh time, that he said, Behold, there ariseth a little cloud out of the sea, like a man's hand. And he said, Go up, say unto Ahab, Prepare thy chariot, and get thee down, that the rain stop thee not. And it came to pass in the meanwhile, that the heaven was black with clouds and wind, and there was a great rain." Elijah knew his weather!

[37]

Dew condenses on plants during calm nights under cloudless skies, and the precipitation of dew was unusually heavy in the otherwise dry Palestine summer. Were it not for its welcome moisture, plant life would have been scantier and less productive. The Hebrews had a tender affection for the dew, and it sparkles from some beautiful scriptural passage. Its importance may be gauged from Isaac's inclusion of it in the blessings on both his sons, Jacob and Esau. To the former he said: "See, the smell of my son is as the smell of a field which the Lord hath blessed. Therefore, God give thee of the dew of heaven, and the fatness of the earth" (*Genesis* 27/27-28). Esau got a similar blessing. Moses opens his song in *Deuteronomy* (32): "My doctrine shall drop as the rain, my speech shall distil as the dew." David, bitterly mourning the death of Saul on Mt. Gilboa cries: "Ye mountains of Gilboa, let there be no dew, neither let there be rain, upon you." (2 *Samuel* 1/21). Solomon adds his testimony, "The king's wrath is as the roaring of a lion; but his favor is as dew upon the grass" (*Proverbs* 19/12). *Hosea* (14/5-7), prophesying for Jehovah, declares, "I will be as the dew unto Israel; he shall grow as the lily .... shall revive as the corn .... the scent thereof shall be as the wine of Lebanon."

Such was the land of Canaan as the Israelites found it. The original inhabitants were good farmers and skilled fruit growers, and harvested heavy crops, as the Hebrew spies discovered. The Canaanites were strong lusty men and women, worshipping Baal and Ashtaroth, god and goddess of fertility. They were not foreigners like the Egyptians but kin to the Israelites, and spoke the same language in different dialect, as the Tel el Amarna tablets have proven. Canaan had been home to Abraham, to Isaac and to Jacob, and many of the patriarchs' direct descendants still farmed the fields and grazed their flocks on their native hills. Naturally they resented the armed invasion of what they considered to be self-appointed men of destiny, demanding an early version of *Lebensraum* from a country their ancestors had forsaken four centuries earlier, and to which they had contributed nothing since.

The Canaanites lost most of their land but won much of the battle of ideology, as subsequent Bible history and the discouragement of the prophets reveal, for only a minority carry the standard of the One God through the pages of Scripture.

CHAPTER 4

Gardens

THE OPENING CHAPTERS of *Genesis* unfold the first garden and the first lesson in botany: "Let the earth bring forth grass, the herb yielding seed, and the fruit tree yielding fruit after his kind, whose seed is in itself, upon the earth." In the last chapter of the last book, *Revelation,* the tree of life, eternal perennial, makes its final appearance in Holy Writ, gracing the banks of the river of water of life: "It bare twelve manner of fruits, and yielded her fruit every month; and the leaves of the tree were for the healing of the nations."

Lying between this biblical Alpha and Omega are hundreds of references to all those things which make up a garden. A history written in our times, whether sacred or profane, would show little of the love for gardening and familiarity with the simple things of the soil which the men of old demonstrated; and such a history would be a more mechanical, more material, less impressive and less inspiring record than the timeless chronicles of the ancient prophets, priests and scribes, whose first hand knowledge of growing plants illumines and embellishes so many of the books of the Bible.

The gardens of Babylon, Assyria and Egypt, and more distant Persia and India, excelled in splendor the gardens of Israel; however, those nations had a head start for they were established horticulturists long before the Chosen People gave up their nomadic wanderings. It was not until the time of Saul and David, in the Books of *Samuel,* that the Hebrews are depicted as settling down to cultivation. Such being the case, the glories of the gardens, vineyards and orchards of David's son Solomon show that he lost no time in keeping up with the regal Joneses of the Nile, the Tigris and the Indus.

The garden of Eden and the botanical specialization shown in the first chapter of *Genesis,* denote a skilled and professional knowledge of the science of plants which was unknown to, or lost by, the patriarchs. The ark safely moored, Noah wasted no time in establishing a vineyard and celebrating his survival. The art of vine culture

[39]

and fermentation of the grape is far advanced from the crude beginnings of agriculture and nomadic desert wanderings.

While the Scriptures abound in references to plants and their
growth processes, and the simile of a well-watered or parched garden is frequently used, yet specific gardens identified by name or
location are very few. The garden of Eden, the King's garden (of
Jerusalem), the garden of Uzza, also owned by the Kings of Judah,
Naboth's vineyard converted into Ahab's herb garden, the Persian
garden of King Ahasueres, and Solomon's famous gardens complete
the Old Testament list. The New Testament has only two, Gethsemane and the garden of Joseph of Arimathea.

To us, a garden commonly brings to mind a small plot of land
on which we may grow flowers and fruit, vegetables and herbs; a
place to walk through along narrow paths, and look down on nature's
beauty and bounty. To the ancients, a garden was predominantly a
garden of trees, a place of shade from the heat of the sun, refreshed
by brooks or fountains. The social aspects sometimes outweighed
the horticultural; gardens were the scenes of feasts and receptions,
religious saturnalia or austere prayer meetings, sanctums for quiet
meditation, and finally burial grounds for the owner and his family.
Accordingly, as we visualize the gardens of the Bible we should depict
something different from our modern flower and vegetable patches;
trees and a protected water supply should be foremost in the mind's
eye; a sub-tropical botanical garden would be a modern equivalent.

Gardening was the hobby and the pride of kings and princes,
an ornament of splendor and luxury as well as horticultural skill
and good taste. These were formal gardens, still cultivated in the
East and often the motif for oriental carpets and tapestries. The
pattern has persisted to near-contemporary times and Christian kings
vied with Moorish infidels in landscaped magnificence. Economic
pressure and the march of events has practically eliminated the class
of people who had the wealth, the pride and the love for such monu-
ments of natural display, and in our democratic times gardens in
most instances means backyard plot or allotment.

Eden is commonly regarded as being synonymous with the garden of the Lord and man's first earthly paradise. *Genesis* (2/8, 10)
tells us: "The Lord God planted a garden eastward in Eden .... and
a river went out of Eden to water the garden," so we deduce that

[40]

Eden was a district or territory of which the famous garden occupied only a small part. When Adam and Eve were expelled, they were free to wander through the remainder of the land of Eden as well as beyond its boundaries, and it is reasonable to suppose that the pastoral and agricultural interests of the first family restricted their roving to the valley of the river of Eden, or one of its branches. The tropical nature of Eden is evident from the comfortable nudity of our first parents. It was modesty or prudishness, rather than low temperatures or chilly winds, which inspired the apron of fig leaves. The coats of skins later donated by Jehovah were probably meant for protection against thorns and briers rather than for warmth.

Let us study that most famous of gardens. Usually the spotlight of attention is focused on Adam and Eve and the Serpent. For a change we will concentrate on the garden, as described in *Genesis*. Note the emphasis on trees. "And the Lord God planted a garden eastward in Eden .... and out of the the ground made the Lord God to grow every tree that is pleasant to the sight, and good for food; the tree of life also in the midst of the garden, and the tree of knowledge of good and evil .... And the Lord God took the man, and put him into the garden of Eden to dress it and to keep it. And the Lord God commanded the man, saying, Of every tree of the garden thou mayest freely eat: but of the tree of the knowledge of good and evil, thou shalt not eat of it: for in the day that thou eatest thereof thou shalt surely die .... Now the serpent .... said unto the woman, Yea, hath God said, Ye shall not eat of every tree of the garden? And the woman said unto the serpent, We may eat of the fruit of the trees of the garden: but of the fruit of the tree which is in the midst of the garden, God hath said, Ye shall not eat of it, neither shall ye touch it, lest ye die. And the serpent said unto the woman, Ye shall not surely die: for God doth know that in the day ye eat thereof, then your eyes shall be opened, and ye shall be as gods, knowing good and evil. And when the woman saw that the tree was good for food, and that it was pleasant to the eyes, and a tree to be desired to make one wise, she took of the fruit thereof, and did eat, and gave also unto her husband with her; and he did eat. And the eyes of them both were opened, and they knew that they were naked; and they sewed fig leaves together and made themselves aprons. And they heard the voice of the Lord God walking in the garden in the cool of the day: and Adam and his wife hid themselves from the presence of the Lord God amongst the trees of the garden. And the Lord God .... said .... Hast thou eaten of the tree? .... and the man said, The woman .... she gave me of the tree, and I did eat .... And the Lord God said .... unto Adam .... Because .... thou hast eaten of the tree, of which I commanded thee, saying, Thou shalt not eat of it; cursed is the ground for thy sake; in sorrow shalt thou eat of it all the days of thy life; thorns also and thistles shall it bring forth to thee; and thou shalt eat the herb of the field; in the sweat of thy face shalt thou eat bread .... Therefore the Lord God sent him forth from the garden of Eden, to till the ground from whence he was taken."

We observe then that the garden of Eden was a garden of trees, watered by streams which flowed four ways, a symbol typical of the gardens of the East. It was a garden of shade trees and fruit trees, together with the metaphysical tree of life and the tree of the knowledge of good and evil. The tree of life is glorified in many religions, but only those who attribute man's sorrowful state to the fall of Adam give precedence to the tree of discrimination. In the East practically all trees were held sacred to a greater or lesser extent. Assyrian sculpture depicts Asshur, founder of the Empire, as a tree-god, and tree-worship claimed a leading role in Assyrian religion. Most primitive worship revered trees, regarding them as symbols or even temple dwellings of the gods of fertility, their grandeur, their protective shade, and their long life calling forth adoration and gratitude. The location of Eden has never been satisfactorily established but most evidence places it in the Mesopotamian plain, where sacred trees studded mythology. The father of the Hebrew race, his early life imbued with reverence for trees, brought his ideas to distant Canaan: "Abraham planted a grove in Beer-sheba, and called there on the name of the Lord, the everlasting God" (*Genesis* 21/33).

Adam was placed in the garden of Eden to dress it and to keep it. In the rich virgin soil and semi-tropical conditions of the sacred garden the duties intended for Adam presumably were light and pleasant. Weeds, blight, and caterpillars, if they existed, were beneficent rather than harmful. The low regard in which herbs of the field — probably cereal grains, vegetables and edible herbs—were held is evident in Adam's expulsion sentence: "Cursed is the ground for thy sake; .... thorns also and thistles shall it bring forth to thee; and thou shalt eat the herb of the field; in the sweat of thy face shalt thou eat bread." The contempt of the lordly keeper of the garden for the lowly serf clearing thickets of weeds, and laboriously tilling the soil with inadequate primitive implements, dependent on scanty rain while the well situated garden is irrigated or fed from a constant spring, the delectable ripening fruit requiring no drawn out processing —all this is implicit in the curse on poor Adam.

Later in *Genesis* (13/10) Lot, impressed by his first vista of the then fertile Jordan valley, observed it to be well watered "like the garden of the Lord." The importance of water recurs again and again, the abundantly watered garden being lauded as a thing of beauty and joy, while the garden deficient in moisture was a symbol of waste and despair. Living waters were glorified: "A fountain of gardens, a well of living waters, and streams from Lebanon" (*Song of Solomon* 4/15).

Ahab's covetous desire for Naboth's vineyard, which he wished to convert to a garden of herbs, resulted in Naboth's being murdered at the instigation of Ahab's wife. The resulting feud brought violent death to Jezebel and to her son, King Ahaziah, who attempted to flee the avengers "by way of the garden house" (2 *Kings* 9/27). Here is the first mention of this addition to the utility garden. The ancient scribes feature this garden of the Kings of Judah as an escape route, from internal enemies as in the instance just quoted, and through the besieging army of Nebuchadnezzar, Emperor of Babylon, for the starving garrison of King Zedekiah, last of the Kings of Judah (2 *Kings* 25/4). This garden is identified in *Nehemiah* (3/15) as being by the Pool of Siloah (Siloam), at the junction of the valleys of the Kidron and Hinnom, the gullies of which would provide cover for escapees. The garden of Uzza, adjacent to the palace of Manasseh, was another royal garden originally privately owned. Manasseh and his son Amon were buried in it (2 *Kings* 21/18, 26). While there is no scriptural confirmation, it is believed that other Hebrew monarchs found their last resting place in the King's Garden. Regretably, the Bible gives no clue to the landscaping nor the plants of the imperial gardens. The only other Bible reference to garden interment concerns the sepulchre in which Jesus was laid, in a garden close by his crucifixion tree.

"The king made a feast unto all the people that were present in Shushan the palace, both unto great and small, seven days, in the

[43]

court of the garden of the king's palace; where were white, green, and blue, hangings, fastened with cords of fine linen and purple to silver rings and pillars of marble; the beds were of gold and silver, upon a pavement of red, and blue, and white, and black, marble. And they gave them drink in vessels of gold, (the vessels being diverse one from another), and royal wine in abundance." Such was the fabulous palace garden of Shushan, the oriental splendor of which is briefly glimpsed in the drama of *Esther,* biblical Cinderella who later won the beauty contest which crowned her queen and consort of King Ahasueres (Xerxes) of Persia. Unfortunately it was the architecture and man-made splendor of the garden court which caught the attention of this early society reporter, and no botanical detail is given.

This feast was a proletarian affair, to whip up patriotic support for the invasion of Greece. It followed a six month diplomatic entertainment of the princes and ruling classes of the empire, and no doubt potential allies were lavishly courted. With palace favorites crowding the court of the garden during this bacchanalian windup, we may infer that the populace did their celebrating in the vast garden grounds where their noisy merry-making would not disturb the court. We know that Persian rulers landscaped their hunting grounds into parklike domains, and Shushan (Susa) being the capital city and seat of the throne, it is likely that the king's hunting parks adjoined and formed extensions to the palace garden proper, so that a large concourse of people could revel there for a week without disturbing the aristocracy in the palace.

The Greek invasion ended in ignominious disaster, and the king returned to drown his sorrows in debauchery. To divert popular resentment into political channels the king's advisers counselled the age-old propaganda, "Blame the Jews" (*Esther* 3/8-9). The plan backfired, and later in the tale it was to the quiet solitude of the palace garden that the perplexed monarch retired, to cool his wrath and plan appropriate action on court intrigue.

The Jews of the Exile, taken captive by Nebuchadnezzar to Babylon, were very familiar with the world-famous hanging gardens of their capturer's palace; they probably helped to construct some of the features which gave it the rating of one of the seven wonders of the ancient world. After a series of victories in Syria, Palestine, and Egypt, the victorious king returned to Babylon and remodeled much of the city, building himself an ornate new palace in the architecture of which he incorporated the hanging gardens. 2 *Kings* (24/14, 16) tells that Nebuchadnezzar deported from Jerusalem "all the craftsmen and smiths . . . one thousand . . . to Babylon." *Jeremiah* (24/1; 29/2) confirms this, substituting carpenters for craftsmen. The Bible makes no mention of this renowned garden.

To some of the scribes and historians whose combined literary testaments we term the Holy Bible, gardens were of documentary interest only insofar as they served as scenes of action for historical people or events. The garden lover who finds more inspiration in the rhythmic processes of nature than in man's materialism is indebted to Solomon, who may justly be termed the gardening king. Solomon considered beautiful and bountiful gardens a more enduring tribute than victory in war. Not only did he plant and develop gardens and orchards whose fame spread to distant countries, but in some of the richest prose in the Bible he glorified love in terms redolent with the perfume and natural beauty of his flowers, fruits and spices. In *Ecclesiastes* (2/4 ff.) he declares: "I planted me vineyards; I made me gardens and orchards, and I planted trees in them of all kind of fruits: I made me pools of water, to water therewith the wood that bringeth forth trees: . . . also I had great possessions of great and small cattle above all that were in Jerusalem before me." In succeeding verses he proves that his gardens and flocks were not just a rich man's whim. He writes as though he shared in the manual labor and displays epicurean pleasure in the good things which his gardens and his cattle furnished to his table. "There is nothing better for a man, than that he should eat and drink, and that he should make his soul enjoy good in his labor. This also I saw, that it was from the hand of God. For who can eat, or who else can hasten thereunto, more than I? . . . Moreover, the profit of the earth is for all: the king himself is served by the field."

Solomon was acclaimed a great botanist. In his *Song of Songs* there are over seventy references to plants, a miniature herbal in itself. In passionate and emotional language, Solomon reveals a deeply sensuous appreciation of the glory of the garden which remains unequalled in literature. How he must have loved the rich mellow earth and nature's bounty growing therefrom! It is in Solomon's Song, and only there, that the Bible becomes a garden ode. Here is no garden of paradise, of mystical trees, talking serpents, and fallen Man. Man, is here, and woman too, but they are as contemporary and understandable as other great lovers. There are no forbidden fruits in this garden: "A man hath no better thing under the sun, than to eat, and to drink, and to be merry; for that shall abide with him of his labor the days of his life, which God giveth him under the sun." This, of course, is too often misconstrued and should not be taken out of the context of Solomon's advice which repeatedly condemns gluttony, drunkenness and debauchery as severely as any hair-shirted prophet. The good husbandman, then or now, raising the bounty of the fruitful earth with his own labor and planning, according justice and kindness to his associates, his servants, his animals and even his plants, can and should eat, drink and be merry with a good conscience.

The true garden lover will find pleasure and profit in accompanying Solomon "down into the garden of nuts to see the fruits of the valley, and to see whether the vine flourished, and the pomegranates budded . . . to the beds of spices, to feed in the gardens, and to gather lilies." Solomon's gardens are believed to have lain in a valley (Wady Urtas) between Bethlehem and Hebron, irrigated by water from Solomon's Pools. These reservoirs, three in number, were huge cisterns with walls of stone and masonry bonded to the rock foundations. Their total capacity is estimated to have been a hundred million gallons. Underground conduits from an ever-flowing fountain, also walled in, carried the water which helped replenish the Pools. It is this water system and the gardens it irrigated which is believed to be referred to in *Song of Solomon* (4/12): "A garden inclosed . . . a spring shut up, a fountain sealed."

From non-biblical sources we learn that many gardens lay outside the city walls of Jerusalem, in what we should now term suburban areas. One garden flourished within the city walls from the time of the prophets; it was a rose garden and lay west of the Temple. The prohibition against gardens in the city proper was principally for sanitary reasons connected with the fertilizing process common in the East. Congested housing left little room for gardens. In the better class homes, built around spacious courtyards, choice plants were sometimes grown in the open space. This custom is alluded to in *Psalms* (128/3): "Thy wife shall be as a fruitful vine by the sides of thine house; thy children like olive plants round about thy table."

Among the Canaanites and other pre-Israelite inhabitants of Palestine, varied images of the great nature god Baal were set up in gardens, and worshipped there under sacred trees. In their periodic backsliding the Hebrews sometimes forsook the austere worship of the invisible Jehovah and lapsed into the emotional and sensual adoration of Baal and his feminine counterpart Ashtaroth. In his last two chapters *Isaiah* denounces this idolatry: "I have spread out my hands all the day unto a rebellious people . . . . a people that provoketh me to anger continually to my face; that sacrificeth in gardens, and burneth incense upon altars of brick . . . . they sanctify themselves, and purify themselves in the gardens behind one tree in the midst, eating swine's flesh, and the abomination, and the mouse." Modern garden statuary, although purely ornamental in function and purpose, nonetheless is a direct link with the sacred gardens of Canaan, dominated by pagan images.

Christianity reacts to the garden of Gethsemane in sorrow and sadness; there Jesus, the Exemplar of quiet confidence and divine assurance, slumped momentarily into human nervousness as the shadow of betrayal and torture crept inexorably towards him: "My soul is exceedingly sorrowful, even unto death." Jesus and his disciples held many happy memories of the old garden, adjoining an olive grove, for it was a favorite haunt of theirs, as *John* (18/1, 2) tells: "Jesus . . . went forth . . . over the brook Cedron, where was a garden, into the which he entered, and his disciples . . . for Jesus ofttimes resorted thither with his disciples." Jesus loved the friendly earth, and the poignancy of approaching death in this garden of happier times swept over him. Gethsemane lay at the foot of the Mount of Olives, nearly a mile beyond the city walls of Jerusalem.

A few hours later, the tortured body of the Master found earthly rest in an unfamiliar garden. "Now in the place where he was crucified there was a garden; and in the garden a new sepulchre, wherein was never man yet laid. There laid they Jesus . . . " (*John* 19/41, 42). From *Matthew* (27/57-60) we learn that this garden was owned by Joseph of Arimathea, a wealthy and influential Jew and a secret disciple of our Lord. Such a well-to-do citizen probably owned a garden in keeping with his position, and evidently he em-

[47]

ployed a professional gardener. "Many stood without the sepulchre, weeping ... and ... she turned ... and saw Jesus standing, and knew not that it was Jesus. Jesus saith unto her, Woman, why weepest thou? whom seekest thou? She, supposing him to be the gardener, saith unto him, Sir, if thou have borne him hence, tell me where thou hast laid him, and I will take him away. Jesus saith unto her, Mary ... " (*John* 20/11-16).

CHAPTER 5

Herbs

"BETTER IS a dinner of herbs where love is, than a stalled ox and hatred therewith," wrote King Solomon, satiated with luxury and vexed with court intrigue. Herbs were the staple food of the poor man, yet they attained royal splendor in the establishments of the Kings of Israel and Judah. Solomon's herb gardens lay south of Bethlehem, and the Queen of Sheba was proud to contribute exotic specimens to their variety. One of the most famous tragedies of the Bible developed from the simple, and originally honest desire of one man to purchase from or exchange with a neighbor a small plot of land for use as an herb garden. One man, Ahab, was King of Samaria; the other, Naboth, just a vine grower. Yet the commoner might have lived to retain his inheritance had not Queen Jezebel, who came from a land where kings ruled by divine right and exercised royal domain, stepped in and in true totalitarian fashion liquidated the rugged democrat. Ahab acquired his blood-stained herb garden at the price of death and a curse. Hezekiah, King of Judah, counted spices and oils derived from herbs of equal importance with gold and silver and other precious belongings, and enshrined them together in the King's Treasury.

The word "herb" has both a popular and a botanical meaning which do not always coincide. Strictly speaking, an herb is a plant which dies to the roots annually, as distinct from one with a woody stem which survives from year to year. However, popular usage has a habit of unobtrusively yet effectively impressing its own stamp of authenticity on words whose origin lies outside the pale of the dictionary. Nowadays herbs are commonly considered to include those plants which contribute culinary flavoring and seasoning, or possess medicinal properties, irrespective of their botanical genus.

Naturalists as well as archaeologists have waged wordy warfare, and the loose scriptural use of the various words translated uniformly into English as herb adds nothing to the botanist's peace of mind.

Young's *Concordance* lists six Old Testament Hebrew words, and two New Testament Greek ones, all rendered as the one English word "herb." Even the accompanying scriptural text is little help. The first chapter of *Genesis*, dealing with the Creation, divides plant life into three types—grass, herb-yielding seed, and fruit whose seed is in itself. Two chapters later, with Paradise lost, the Adamic curse condemns man to eat the herb of the field, indicating its lowly status in the scheme of creation. Elsewhere, the frailty of man and his uncertain life span is compared to the ephemeral and hazardous growth of herbs, exposed to the drought and hail of Palestine.

Jesus, whose teachings are so colorfully interspersed with His intimate knowledge of the plant life of His native land, refers on two occasions (*Matthew* 23/23; *Luke* 11/42) to the Pharisees' tithing of herbs—anise, and mint, and rue, and cummin—and scornfully rebuked such punctilious observation of inconsequential values while they "omitted the weightier matters of the law, judgment, mercy and faith." These two verses contain the only biblical mention of anise, mint and rue. *Isaiah,* in his 28th chapter, describes how cummin seeds were threshed out with a stick, a practice still followed in Mediterranean lands. Cummin was found in a wild state, as well as under cultivation. Its seeds, similar to caraway but larger, were bitter but aromatic, and were used both as spices and for medicinal purposes, being regarded as a specific for colic and flatulency. It belongs to the order *Umbelliferae*. The biblical anise is authoritatively believed to have been dill, a member of the parsley family, growing a couple of feet high. Its aromatic seeds were used for sour condiments and in seasoning cakes, while its medicinal properties were similar to those of cummin. It was one of the commonest of garden herbs in Bible times. The mint of the New Testament is supposed to have been one of three varieties, *Mentha sativa, M. sylvestris* or *M. arvensis,* all common in the Levant. On account of its pleasant aroma the Jews scattered it on the floors of their houses and synagogues, and used it freely in cooking and seasoning. It was one of the herbs to be tithed, and was subject to the ban on sowing and gathering every seventh year. According to the *Talmud,* rue, while a kitchen herb, was not liable to tithe, as it was not regularly cultivated in gardens. In the time of Jesus it appears to have been a garden plant and accordingly tithable. Rue, *Ruta graveolens,* was a shrubby plant, yellowish-

[50]

green in color, with numerous small transparent spots, containing a volatile oil having strong stimulant, anti-spasmodic and tonic qualities. The plant had a pungent aromatic odor, its leaves being very bitter. Its common name, *Herb o' Grace*, probably derives from scriptural sanctity.

The parable of the mustard seed must have impressed the disciples, for Matthew, Mark and Luke all recount it. Matthew sows it in the field, Luke in the garden, while Mark merely puts it in the earth. As in the case of so many other Bible plants, botanists have varied theories as to the species meant. Modern opinion tends to identify it with black mustard, *Sinapis nigra*. It has been observed growing wild to a height of twelve feet, so the cultivated variety may have been as sturdy as Jesus describes. The minute mustard seed, while not the smallest known to the Jews, was however the tiniest sown by the husbandman, and the disparity between the little seed grains and the large mature plants was noteworthy.

St. Paul, in an able plea for tolerance and consideration towards the beliefs of others, makes a telling reference to a vegetarian diet: "For one believeth that he may eat all things; another, who is weak, eateth herbs. Let not him that eateth despise him that eateth not; and let not him which eateth not judge him that eateth: for God hath received him" (*Romans* 14/2-3). The lesson is as needful to-day as when it was written.

Coriander seed is mentioned twice in the Old Testament, but merely for its earthly similarity to the heaven bestowed manna. This herb is an annual of the parsley family, common in Palestine and Syria; it has a tall stalk with small white flowers. The plant itself emits a disagreeable odor. The seeds are globular, light gray in color, and their aromatic flavor is prized in seasoning and cooking; they also have medicinal properties.

In *Numbers* (11/5), just two verses prior to the second mention of coriander, may be found a lone nostalgic reference to garlic. Egyptian garlic is specified, but the strongly flavored bulb was grown in the Holy Land where it was much esteemed and used both for culinary purposes and medicinal ones. The antiseptic nature of its juice was demonstrated during the First World War.

"Purge me with hyssop and I shall be clean," sang the Psalmist (51/7). Hyssop takes precedence among Bible herbs for background interest. Many centuries ago St. Augustine contended that students of the Scriptures who were ignorant of the nature of hyssop thereby lost the real meaning of the various Bible passages which mention it. He described the plant as a short stemmed one with roots penetrating the spaces between rocks and the interstices of stone walls, and attributed purgative qualities to it. That great botanist, Solomon—"He was wiser than all men; . . . and he spake of trees, from the cedar tree that is in Lebanon even unto the hyssop that springeth out of the wall" (1 *Kings* 4/31-33)—considered hyssop a rock-loving plant. In St. John's story of the Crucifixion, he relates that a sponge soaked in vinegar was put upon hyssop and held to Jesus' mouth; in parallel passages, St. Matthew and St. Mark omit reference to hyssop and say the sponge was put on a reed.

Biblical students cannot agree whether the hyssop referred to was indeed a long reed (hardly consistent with the plant's being a lowly rock species) or if the cleansing, antiseptic, aromatic properties of hyssop were added to the vinegar. There is enough Bible evidence to indicate that the word translated into English as hyssop may not have consistently designated the same plant. Hyssop is first mentioned in *Exodus* (12/22); there the Israelites were ordered to dip a bunch of hyssop in the blood of the paschal lamb, and mark their doorways therewith. It must have been of a bushy nature to serve as a sprinkling medium, and presumably its purifying and aromatic qualities were transferred in part to the liquid clinging to its leaves. In two of the most important purification ceremonies of the Mosaic Law, the cleansing of leprosy (*Leviticus* 14) and from defilement by the dead (*Numbers* 19), hyssop was a mandatory agent. Thus in Egypt, in the arid desert, and on Palestine hillsides, hyssop must have made a hardy growth.

As we so commonly and regrettably find in Bible research, no positive identification can be given to many of the plants mentioned by the ancient scribes. Hyssop is no exception. The famous Swedish botanist Celsius, who specialized in study of Bible plants in the 17-18th centuries, lists no less than eighteen different identifications of hyssop, and modern research has done little to clarify the type. Amongst the best documented are rosemary, thyme, marjoram, caper, sorghum and our modern hyssop, *Hyssopis officinalis*. The latter is a shrub, almost evergreen, and popular for low hedges. The flowers are commonly blue, but sometimes pink or white. Medicinally it is claimed to be helpful as a cathartic and for inducing perspiration. The essential oil is used in the manufacture of chartreuse and absinthe, and in toilet water.

While hyssop furnishes us with an historical and ritualistic element, mandrake supplies an erotic touch in the Bible herbal. "And Reuben went in the days of wheat harvest, and found mandrakes in the field, and brought them to his mother Leah. Then Rachel said to Leah, Give me, I pray thee, of thy son's mandrakes. And she said unto her, Is it a small matter that thou hast taken my husband? and wouldest thou take away my son's mandrakes also? And Rachel said, Therefore he shall lie with thee to-night for thy son's mandrakes." From the rest of the story in the 30th chapter of *Genesis* we may infer the great value attached to the power of the mandrake by the ancient Hebrews. The scene of this drama lay in Padan-Aram, "the tableland of Syria," believed to have been in the vicinity of the Euphrates. The month was May, the time of wheat harvest. The rarity of the plant in this district is evident by its bargaining value. That it also grew in Palestine is shown by a romantic allusion to it in the closing lines of the seventh chapter of the *Song of Solomon*. Naturalists are in general agreement that the scriptural mandrake is the same as our modern variety, *Atropa mandragora,* closely allied to the deadly nightshade as well as to the highly edible tomato. This relationship of the tomato, together with its old fashioned name of love apple, furnishes interesting speculation. The fruit of the mandrake, which ripens in May, is similar in size to a tomato, but yellow in color; its appearance, its smell, and its taste, are all pleasant. Arabs call it the devil's apple, from its aphrodisiac reputation. The mandrake has strong thick taproots, large dark green leaves, with small pale green or purple flowers.

The *Song of Solomon,* in a verse (4/14) pungent with perfume and spice, includes the sole scriptural mention of saffron. The word derives from the Arabic *zafran,* yellow. The ancients valued it for its delicate perfume, and pot-pourri was made from it. The saffron crocus, *Crocus sativus,* is a member of the iris family. Saffron is prepared by plucking the three stigmata, together with a portion of one style, from the flower, as soon as the calyx is fully opened. Some idea of the tedious work involved may be furnished by the fact that it takes four thousand stigmata to make one ounce. The stigmata are

[53]

dried in the sun, or in a kiln. In the Levant saffron is used, as in olden time, for condiment purposes or as a medical stimulant. Modern industry utilizes it as a coloring extract, and it is one of the "must" ingredients in the famous French dish *bouillabaisse*.

The Hebrew word translated into English as wormwood is also rendered as hemlock, while hemlock in turn is used as a variant of the word we call gall. Most people associate gall with a bitter internal secretion, but with a divergence of opinion which would match a Big Four conference, there are Bible students who claim gall was a bitter or poisonous herb, or even serpent venom. All scriptural usage of wormwood is symbolic, denoting bitterness or despair, and it is usually coupled with gall for emphasis. In the New Testament, written in Greek, *apsinthos* is the original word translated in *Revelation* (8/11) as wormwood. When we look up the botanical name of the modern wormwood plant we find *Artemisia absinthium,* and further investigation discloses that it is one of the chief ingredients from which absinthe was made. Absinthe, once a popular alcoholic drink in France and Switzerland, has had its manufacture prohibited for a number of years because of the harmful effect on its addicts. There are several species of wormwood, most of them bitter. *Artemisia absinthium* is a tall perennial, with silky leaves and an abundance of small yellow flowers.

The foregoing covers what are generally regarded as the herbs of the Bible. With the modern flexibility applied to herb classification, and the lack of agreement among botanical students of the Bible, it is difficult to draw a definite line including all herbs and excluding non-herbs. The inspiring words of the Psalmist lift us above man-made rules: "He causeth the grass to grow for the cattle, and herb for the service of man; that he may bring forth food out of the earth."

CHAPTER 6

Trees of the Forest and the Field

"WHERE there is no vision, the people perish," warned Solomon. His broad statement may serve as an introduction to this chapter, with particular reference to land conservation and reforestation, not only thousands of years ago in distant Bible lands, but also to-day and here in North America. In the United States, for an example, eight hundred million acres of virgin forest have been reduced to a hundred million or so, most of this reserve lying in comparatively inaccessible reaches of the Pacific coast. Reforestation and land conservation are relatively new words in the language, and their effective application to repair man's ravages is newer still. People who think and plan in long range terms are always a small minority, but to those few people of vision, some private citizens and some government agents, who are endeavoring to stem and to repair our ruthless forest waste, we, and our children's children, will owe a debt of gratitude.

Starving China and starving Europe are not altogether the victims of man's inhumanity to man; part of their plight is the end result of man's inhumanity to trees. Forests are cut down or negligently burnt; windbreaks, slowly and painstakingly nurtured by some provident ancestor, are slashed for quick money or industrial development. The soft humus, now unprotected against winter rainstorms, washes away and the residue bakes hard under summer sun. Water is no longer absorbed and held in the spongy mould, but streams across adjacent cultivated fields, and sheet erosion degenerates into gully erosion; crop yields diminish, and the standard of living falls. The rich get rich and the poor get children, but neither the rich nor the poor attempt to grow new trees or otherwise conserve the soil, and down the slope of diminishing returns the nation slides towards famine.

We are told that one issue of a big Sunday newspaper requires more than fifty acres of forest to feed its presses. Yet without benefit of Sunday papers, *sans* power-saws and bull-dozers, the people of the Scriptures hewed down forests and trees with unintelligent fervor, and of course suffered nature's consequences. Fortunately for the well being of mankind, there are a few wise men in every age, and the sacred esteem with which trees were almost universally regarded throughout the East, and thus protected against destruction, was probably due to a far-sighted high priest or religious leader who realized that only by raising trees to divine or sacred stature could they be protected against man's insensate destruction. A biblical instance of this protection for certain trees is found in *Deuteronomy* (20/19-20): "When thou shalt besiege a city a long time, in making war against it to take it, thou shalt not destroy the trees thereof by forcing an ax against them: for thou mayest eat of them, and thou shalt not cut them down (for the tree of the field is man's life) to employ them in the siege. Only the trees which thou knowest that they be not trees for meat, thou shalt destroy and cut them down; and thou shalt build bulwarks against the city."

This declaration, "The tree of the field is man's life," brings to mind the more widely known "All flesh is grass" (*Isaiah* 40/6). These statements are not only comparative, they are absolute. The vegetarian will need no convincing, the meat-eater need only visit a farm or consult a book on livestock feeding to find irrefutable proof. Without plant growth there would be no fish in the sea nor birds in the air, nor their man-made rivals, ships and planes. Our atomic civilization is as firmly tied to plant growth as was the primitive husbandry of the patriarchs. Even water, so essential to man's existence, would lie in stagnant pools beneath a cloudless sky, were the transpiration systems of plants to cease functioning.

It was around trees which produced edible food, such as fruit and nuts, that the Bible wrapped its protective ordinance. What we may term the secondary effects of trees, such as anchoring soil on hillsides, creating humus, retention of water, windbreaks, natural reseeding and other factors inherent in good land management, were presumably disregarded by the people of the Bible.

The veteran leader of the Israelites, who paid this homage to the tree of the field, had a profound appreciation of the importance of the date palm, characteristic jewel of the desert oasis. Under its shade and refreshed and fortified by its fruit, his unruly charges found intermittent solace during their long trek towards the Promised Land. In Egypt where Moses grew up, the date palm, with its myriad services to man, was the most valued tree, and it is fair to assume that it was to this emblem of the arid field that Moses paid tribute rather than to one of the numerous types of fruit trees which required fertile soil and ample water.

In several passages of the Gospels, Jesus, like Moses, appears to evaluate trees in terms of their fruit rather than for their less observable benefits to man, and the rigorous culling of unproductive specimens is skillfully woven into parable fabric.

From the opening verses of the seventh chapter of *Revelation* may be deduced the great importance which the mystical author accorded trees. There on two occasions trees are given the same emphasis as the basic constituents of our world, the earth and the sea.

Trees have been worshipped or held sacred throughout the ages and in all parts of the world, the veneration of the oak and its parasite the mistletoe by the ancient Druids of Britain being one of the better known examples. Scriptural commentary on *Genesis* (12/6), and *Judges* (9/37), translates the place-names mentioned as the oak, or grove of the teacher, and of the diviner, respectively. "Abraham planted a grove in Beer-sheba, and called there on the name of the Lord." This precedent by one of the most venerated men in Jewish history must have been a source of great annoyance to later prophets, faced with the recurrent task of preventing the Israelites from imitating or collaborating in the neighboring heathen practices of Baal worship, in shady groves which provided the environment conducive to orgiastic rites. As we turn the pages of the Bible we find injunctions to destroy the groves of the Canaanites, and then in *Deuteronomy* (16/21) comes the ban: "Thou shalt not plant thee a grove of any trees near unto the altar of the Lord thy God."

However, the story of the kings of Judah and Israel is equally the story of tree planting and grove worship by one king and his subjects, and the uprooting of the groves and desecration of the idols therein by a successor, to be followed by another swing of the pendulum. King Josiah was particularly thorough in his grove destruction: "He brought out the grove from the house of the Lord, without Jerusalem, unto the brook Kidron, and burned it at the brook Kidron, and stamped it small to powder, and cast the powder thereof upon the graves of the children of the people. And he brake down the houses of the sodomites, that were by the house of the Lord, where the women

[57]

wove hangings for the grove" (2 *Kings* 23/6-7). Primitive man did not approve of the idea of shutting up his god within walls, and groves of trees suggested a natural setting for early temples.

We usually associate parables with the teachings of Jesus, and in his famous allegories we find not only spiritual treasures but also a wealth of information on the agricultural practices of the Holy Land. How many can identify the first parable in the Bible, even with the clues that it is found in the *Book of Judges,* was related by Jotham, youngest son of Gideon, most famous of the Judges, and that trees were the allegorical symbol? "The trees went forth on a time to anoint a king over them; and they said unto the olive tree, Reign thou over us. But the olive tree said unto them, Should I leave my fatness, wherewith by me they honor God and man, and go to be promoted over the trees? And the trees said to the fig tree, Come thou, and reign over us. But the fig tree said unto them, Should I forsake my sweetness, and my good fruit, and go to be promoted over the trees? Then said the trees unto the vine, Come thou, and reign over us. And the vine said unto them, Should I leave my wine, which cheereth God and man, and go to be promoted over the trees? Then said all the trees unto the bramble, Come thou, and reign over us. And the bramble said unto the trees, If in truth ye anoint me king over you, then come and put your trust in my shadow: and if not, let fire come out of the bramble, and devour the cedars of Lebanon" (*Judges* 9/8-15).

The variety of trees outnumbers all other plant groupings in the Bible. We shall never attain final botanical classification of Bible plants, so the names, accurate or otherwise, given by the editors of the King James Version are those used as the basic list in this book. The Bible has seven flowers, seven vegetables and seven weeds but no less than thirty-seven differently named trees. In some instances the same tree was known by two or more names, and loose translation has further confused identification. This should not surprise us, for our own nomenclature of trees is ambiguous. For example, the plane tree is also known as the buttonwood and the sycamore, while a variety of maple is also called sycamore; arbutus and madrona, linden and basswood and dozens of others come to mind. Only single mention is accorded a dozen or so of these Bible trees, while others. notably the cedar, are common. While scant mention does not

[58]

necessarily denote rarity or insignificance, the converse may be accepted
as proof of widespread growth and familiarity.

The author of the Book of *Job,* in grim pessimistic mood, considered a tree's chance of survival better than a man's. "Man that
is born of a woman is of few days, and full of trouble. He cometh
forth like a flower, and is cut down . . . . For there is hope of a tree,
if it be cut down, that it will sprout again, and that the tender
branch thereof will not cease. Though the root thereof wax old in
the earth, and the stock thereof die in the ground; yet through the
scent of water it will bud, and bring forth boughs like a plant. But
man dieth, and wasteth away: yea, man giveth up the ghost, and
where is he?" (*Job* 14/1 ff.).

The cedars of Lebanon! What reader of the Bible has not shared
in some degree the sense of majesty and grandeur which this phrase
and the picture it invoked brought to the Israelites. "Come with me
from Lebanon, my spouse, with me from Lebanon," sang Solomon,
"from the top of Amana, from the top of Shenir and Hermon, from
the lions' dens, from the mountains of the leopards." Solomon must
have visited the Lebanon mountains often during the many years'
logging operations which he carried out there in partnership with
Hiram, King of Tyre. The fifth chapter of 1 *Kings,* and with slight
variations the second chapter of 2 *Chronicles* tell of this large scale
lumber project, which in man power and commissariat dwarfs our
most ambitious forest felling.

"And Solomon determined to build an house for the name of
the Lord, and an house for his kingdom ... And Solomon sent to
Huram the king of Tyre, saying, As thou didst deal with David my
father, and didst send him cedars to build him an house to dwell
therein, even so deal with me. Behold, I build an house to the name
of the Lord my God ... And the house which I build is great: for
great is our God above all gods ... Send me now ... cedar trees, fir
trees, and algum trees, out of Lebanon: for I know that thy servants
can skill to cut timber in Lebanon; and, behold, my servants shall
be with thy servants, even to prepare me timber in abundance: for the
house which I am about to build shall be wonderful great. And, behold,
I will give to thy servants, the hewers that cut timber, twenty thousand
measures of beaten wheat, and twenty thousand measures of barley, and
twenty thousand baths of wine, and twenty thousand baths of oil.

[59]

Then Huram the King of Tyre answered in writing . . . Now therefore the wheat, and the barley, the oil, and the wine, which my lord hath spoken of, let him send unto his servants: and we will cut wood out of Lebanon, as much as thou shalt need; and we will bring it to thee in flotes by sea to Joppa; and thou shalt carry it up to Jerusalem. And Solomon numbered all the strangers that were in the land of Israel . . . and they were found an hundred and fifty thousand and three thousand and six hundred (153,600). And he set threescore and ten thousand (70,000) of them to be bearers of burdens, and fourscore thousand (80,000) to be hewers in the mountain, and three thousand and six hundred (3,600) overseers to set the people a work."

Summarizing the foregoing reveals that Solomon impressed the original Canaanite population still resident in Palestine into forced labor battalions—"but of the children of Israel did Solomon make no servants for his work; but they were men of war" (2 *Chronicles*: 8/9) —to work alongside Huram's (Hiram's) lumberjacks. There is no mention of the food requirements of Solomon's serfs, but Huram's gangs were supplied from the agricultural resources of Palestine with nearly half a million bushels of grain, and two hundred thousand gallons of wine, and of oil, annually (Josephus' scale of measurement). This was the first large commercial venture in Jewish history. It took Solomon seven years to build the temple and thirteen more to complete his own palace. We are also told of the construction of a huge treasure house called the house of the forest of Lebanon, and of a palace for Pharaoh's daughter, one of Solomon's wives. In all of these Lebanon cedar was the principal building material. We have no record of the number of lumbermen Huram furnished, but twenty thousand is probably a very conservative estimate. Taking that figure, we get a timber crew of one hundred thousand fallers and buckers working for approximately twenty-five years in the Lebanon forests. The destruction of standing timber must have been so great that most of the good stands would be wiped out. The method of sea transport, by flotes (floats) to Joppa, port of Jerusalem, remains standard procedure. Floats, or rafts and booms as they are known on the Pacific coast, are used to freight millions of feet of lumber from the beach nearest the logging grounds to the sawmill perhaps hundreds of miles distant.

A very subdued echo of the great log rolling days of Solomon

[60]

and Hiram is sandwiched into the 3rd chapter of *Ezra*. The Jews
who returned from the Babylonian Captivity to settle and rebuild
Jerusalem, under the patronage of Cyrus, Emperor of Persia, found
the city in ruins and the residents hostile. "The children of Israel ...
gathered themselves together as one man to Jerusalem ... for fear was
upon them because of the people of those countries. . . . From the first
day of the seventh month began they to offer burnt offerings unto the
Lord. But the foundation of the temple of the Lord was not yet laid.
They gave money also unto the masons, and to the carpenters; and
meat, and drink, and oil, unto them of Zidon, and to them of Tyre, to
bring cedar trees from Lebanon to the sea of Joppa, according to
the grant that they had of Cyrus king of Persia."

Not only was cedar used in building construction in Jerusalem
and other cities, it was also a favored plank for ship construction.
Choice logs of the aromatic wood were carefully seasoned and carved
by craftsmen into idols. The Egyptians used it for coffins and mummy
cases. Cedar has a high resistance to moisture rot, and insects are
repelled by its smell and its taste. The Mosaic Law prescribed cedar
in purification ritual, in conjunction with hyssop and scarlet (*Leviticus*
14/4).

Less dramatized than cedar but of great natural and commercial
importance were the firs which graced the slopes of Lebanon and
elsewhere. Fir wood was deemed worthy of inclusion in the temple.
"Solomon ... covered the floors of the house with planks of fir ... and
the two doors were of fir tree...and he carved thereon cherubims
and palm trees and open flowers" (1 *Kings* 6/15, 34, 35). "And the
greater house he ceiled with fir tree" (2 *Chronicles* 3/5). The opening
verses of the 27th chapter of *Ezekiel* describe in detail the materials
used for shipbuilding in the great seaport of Tyre. The hull was
fir: "They have made all thy ship boards of fir trees of Senir." Senir
was Mt. Hermon, or part of it. From *Nahum* (2/3) we infer that
fir was formed into weapons of war, possibly spear shafts or battering
rams. A great musician as well as a famous warrior, "David and all
the house of Israel played before the Lord on all manner of instruments
made of fir wood, even on harps, and on psalteries, and on timbrels,
and on cornets, and on cymbals" (2 *Samuel* 6/5).

We associate pine with cedar and fir, but there is scant mention
of biblical pine, and some authorites claim that the words translated

[61]

pine refer to another type of tree. *Isaiah* (60/13, also 41/19), writing three hundred years after Solomon and Hiram had virtually deforested the great timber stands of Lebanon, speaks as though the once famous cedars were negligible: "The glory of Lebanon shall come to thee, the fir tree, the pine tree, and the box together, to beautify the place of my sanctuary." The Revised Version substitutes a marginal "plane" for "pine," and in *Nehemiah* (8/15) uses "wild olive" where the Authorized Version says "pine." This last reference denotes a different type of tree from *Isaiah's* Hebrew variety, the *Nehemiah* original suggesting an oil tree in literal translation; pitch or resin may be inferred.

The two *Isaiah* verses listed in the preceding paragraph contain the only mention of the beautiful evergreen box tree, but the authors of the Revised Version expand the ivory of *Ezekiel* (27/6) into ivory inlaid in boxwood.

Another tree which gets brief mention is the algum, called almug in the 1 *Kings* 10 version of Solomon's timber deal. When he first approached Hiram, the Jewish ruler asked for "cedar trees, fir trees, and algum trees, out of Lebanon." More than twenty years later we read of Hiram's navy bringing Solomon algum trees from Ophir. "And the king made of the algum trees terraces to the house of the Lord, and to the king's palace, and harps and psalteries for singers; and there were none such seen before in the land of Judah" (2 *Chronicles*: 9/11). We may infer, then, that the original algum trees from the Lebanon mountains were small, with wood of mediocre quality, but that Solomon liked the wood so well that he imported much superior algum from Ophir, an unplaced region believed to have been southern Arabia or even India. Some Bible authorities consider that this latter algum was the odorous red sandalwood.

"Make thee an ark of gopher wood," God commanded Noah (*Genesis* 6/14). No positive identification has yet been given the structural material of this first ship of the Bible, but cypress is considered the most likely timber. The Assyrians and Egyptians used it for their largest vessels. Cypress occurs only once in the Authorized Version (*Isaiah* 44/14), and in the Revised Version cypress is supplanted by holm wood, better known as holly or ilex. Yet cypress forests were common in ancient Palestine and the wood had high commercial value. Like cedar, it was fashioned into idols and used for coffin cases; mummies discovered in recently explored Egyptian tombs were found to be encased in cypress wood, showing that its great durability was known and esteemed thousands of years ago. The Egyptians tied soul survival to the duration of mummy preservation.

According to modern classification the juniper is a conifer resembling the cedar, but the juniper of the Bible is believed to have been a species of broom. The Hebrew word used in the text, *rethem,* corresponds to the Moorish *retama,* by which desert dwellers designate broom. A few years prior to Naboth's murder at the instigation of Jezebel, the great prophet Elijah had run afoul of the Queen: "And Ahab told Jezebel all that Elijah had done, and withal how he had slain all the prophets (of Baal) with the sword. Then Jezebel sent a messenger unto Elijah, saying, So let the gods do to me, and more also, if I make not thy life as the life of one of them by tomorrow about this time. And when he saw that, he arose, and went for his life, and came to Beer-sheba, which belongeth to Judah, and left his servant there. But he himself went a day's journey into the wilderness, and came and sat down under a juniper tree: and he requested for himself that he might die; and said, It is enough . . . and as he lay and slept under a juniper tree, behold, then an angel touched him, and said unto him, Arise and eat. And he looked, and, behold, there was a cake baken on the coals, and a cruse of water at his head. And he did eat and drink, and laid him down again" (1 *Kings* 19/1 ff.). *Job* (30/4) disparagingly refers to the roots of juniper as being eaten by the lowest class of people; a marginal alternative in the Revised Version offers, "The roots of the broom are to warm them." This substitution of fuel for food is supported by *Psalms* (120/4): "Sharp arrows of the mighty, with coals of juniper." Wood for fuel was very scarce in the desert, and juniper-broom supplied the traveller's need.

"I have seen the wicked in great power, and spreading himself like a green bay tree," confesses *Psalms* (37/35). The evergreen mountain laurel is supposed to have been the prototype for this seeming prosperity of evil. A marginal alternative gives "a green tree that groweth in his own soil," and the Revised Version supports this rendering (i.e., not transplanted nor domesticated, but showing the virility of an evergreen tree growing naturally in its native habitat). The *laurus nobilis* is indigenous to the slopes of Palestine; its leaves have culinary value while its roots and bark are used medicinally.

[63]

Esther, the exiled orphan maid who rose to be queen of the far-flung Persian empire, is curiously associated with the myrtle tree. *Esther* (2/7) tells us, "Mordecai ... brought up Hadassah, that is, Esther." The latter name was her Persian title, a tribute to her beauty, for Esther was the Persian goddess and planet Venus, the Ishtar of Babylonia-Assyria, Ashtaroth of Canaan, called Astarte by the Romans. The Greeks held the myrtle sacred to Venus. Her native name, Hadassah, was Hebrew for myrtle, and is familiar to us as the title of a benevolent association of Jewish women. The myrtle tree of Scripture is accepted by Bible students as the same beautiful evergreen which we admire today under that name. It was highly esteemed by *Isaiah,* "'Instead of the brier shall come up the myrtle tree" (55/13), and from the promulgation of the Mosaic Law to modern times, myrtle boughs continue to adorn the celebration of the Feast of Tabernacles. Its known affinity for hillsides and bottomland is confirmed by biblical references. *Nehemiah* (8/15) sent the Israelites to nearby Mt. Olivet to collect myrtle branches, while *Zechariah* (1/8) had a vision of an angel on horseback "among the myrtle trees that were in the bottom." In Palestine the myrtle blooms in May, with sweet scented reddish-white flowers. From the succeeding black berries both oil and wine were prepared.

Forecasting the destruction of mystical Babylon with all its splendor and wealth, the author of *Revelation* (18/12) gives the only biblical mention of the wood of the thyine tree. The thyine is believed to have been a conifer, related to our pine or arbor vitae. The Bible text indicates that thyine was a valuable article of commerce; a marginal note reveals its sweet odor.

The cedar was monarch of the evergreens; the oak held pride of place among the deciduous trees. Isaiah, Amos, and Zechariah, all bracket the strong oak with the towering cedar. Bashan was the ancestral home of the oak, a region occupying the foothills south of Mt. Hermon, and northeast of the Sea of Galilee. Many nations regard the oak as a synonym for sturdiness, and the Hebrews used the same word for oak and might. Man has always paid tribute to strength, so it was but natural that the oak tree should be deified. The Druid priests of ancient Britain and Gaul worshipped in oak groves, and held sacred the tree and its fruits. The early Prussians believed that their gods resided in oak trees. The oldest of the Greek oracles, at Dodona, revealed the mysteries through the rustling of the leaves of the sacred oak, which was tended by priests who slept on the ground at its base. Oak wood fed the perpetual holy fires of the Aryans. *Ezekiel* (6/13) denounced the pagan worship of the Israelites "under every thick oak, the place where they did offer sweet savor to all their idols."

The first Bible oak is connected with Jacob. The 35th chapter of *Genesis* tells us how the Patriarch, prior to setting out to build an altar to the Lord in Bethel, collected the idols and amulets of his household and prudently hid them beneath an oak. His faith in Jehovah was perhaps not quite strong enough to risk destroying the former gods, so he buried them in the sacred ground beneath an oak, just in case.... Four verses later, we read of the death of Deborah, Rebekah's faithful old nurse, "and she was buried beneath Bethel under an oak; and the name of it was called Allon-bachuth" (*i.e.* oak of weeping). Saul, first king of Israel, also was buried beneath an oak, following the defeat of his army by the Philistines. An oak tree brought lingering death to Absalom, David's much-loved but rebellious son; fleeing on a mule with the remnants of his vanquished army Absalom's long tresses caught in the branches of a great oak; stunned and weighted by his armor he dangled in agony until finished off by Joab. David's anguish was heartbreaking: "O my son, Absalom, my son Absalom! would God I had died for thee, O Absalom, my son, my son!"

The Hebrew word *elah* is translated variously as oak (freq.), teil (*Isaiah* 6/13), and elm (*Hosea* 4/13). In the Revised Version the terebinth tree is used, either directly or alternately, to designate the foregoing trio. Hosea, deploring the idolatry of the Israelites, gives a practical explanation of the vogue of sacrificing to idols under the *elah* trees. Discounting any particular sanctity attached to the tree, he tells us, "They sacrifice... and burn incense... under oaks and poplars and elms, because the shadow thereof is good." The Valley where David slew Goliath was named Elah, presumably because of the prevailing type of tree growing there. Isaiah uses the power of the teil (or terebinth) and the oak to put forth new stems and buds after the original tree had been felled, to symbolize the eventual restoration of the power of the Chosen People. Only single reference is given to the teil and the elm. The associated terebinth tree is referred to in the Apocryphal Book of *Ecclesiasticus* (24/16) as the turpentine tree. This tree is common throughout the Mediterranean area and a resinous extract known as Chian, Scio or Cyprus turpentine is tapped from its trunk.

The poplar tree, bracketed by Hosea with the oak and elm, as quoted in the preceding paragraph, is also mentioned in *Genesis* (30/37), where it is identified with miraculous fertility rites: "And Jacob took him rods of green poplar, and of the hazel and chestnut tree; and pilled white strakes in them, and made the white appear which was in the rods. And he set the rods which he had pilled before the flocks in the gutters in the watering troughs when the flocks came to drink, that they should conceive when they came to drink. And the flocks conceived before the rods, and brought forth cattle ringstraked, speckled and spotted." The Revised Version gives this variation: "And Jacob took him rods of fresh poplar (marginal alternative: 'storax tree') and of the almond and of the plane tree; and peeled white strakes, etc. . . ."

This parallel passage is a good example of the uncertain and contradictory botanical classification and identification which confront the Bible student. The storax tree of the Revised translation is *Liquidambar orientalis,* native to the Levant. The modern storax is more of a shrub than a tree, a beautiful plant with its dark green leaves, silvered underneath, and its clusters of delicate white flowers: it yields an aromatic balsam, used medicinally as an ointment in some parasitic skin diseases, and as an expectorant when taken internally. Tradition makes it more exciting: Moses' staff is said to have been a storax branch, and some authorities claim that *stacte,* one of the ingredients of the sacred perfume of Jehovah, was the gum of the storax tree. Even in this material age the people of the East accord the storax respect and immunity from destruction. The value of some plants as aphrodisiac or fertility mediums was commonly accepted in Jacob's time, and it is in this same 30th chapter of *Genesis* that we find the account of Reuben's mandrakes as well as Jacob's magic wands.

The chestnut tree, or plane tree according to the Revised Version, part of the components of the fertility charm of Jacob, gets its only other mention in *Ezekiel* (31/8), where it is lauded along with the cedar and the fir as one of the glories of the garden of God. In contemporary times Longfellow has immortalized it in "The Village Blacksmith."

[66]

In *Isaiah* (44/14), where we find so many names of trees, occurs the sole reference to the ash. As far as is known the ash was never native to Palestine, and botanists consider that the Aleppo pine is indicated. Isaiah's fine irony is tellingly directed at idol worship, and the more intelligent of his pagan audience must have felt doubts sweep over them as the great prophet's sarcasm struck home: "He planteth an ash, and the rain doth nourish it. Then shall it be for a man to burn: for he will take thereof, and warm himself; yea, he kindleth it, and baketh bread; yea, he maketh a god, and worshippeth it; he maketh it a graven image, and falleth down thereto. He burneth part thereof in the fire; with part thereof he eateth flesh; he roasteth roast, and is satisfied: yea, he warmeth himself, and saith, Aha, I am warm, I have seen the fire: and the residue thereof he maketh a god, even his graven image; he falleth down unto it, and worshippeth it, and prayeth unto it, and saith, Deliver me; for thou art my god . . . . And none considereth in his heart, neither is there knowledge nor understanding to say, I haved burned part of it in the fire; yea, also I have baked bread upon the coals thereof; I have roasted flesh, and eaten it; and shall I make the residue thereof an abomination? shall I fall down to the stock of a tree?" The tree referred to was apparently quick growing, furnished good fuel for heating and cooking purposes, and could be satisfactorily worked up as idol-wood.

Ezekiel devotes his twenty-seventh chapter to the luxury imports of the great port of Tyre, which had continued to maintain its trading supremacy down the centuries separating it from its earlier commercial importance in the Solomon-Huram era. To read this chapter and to visualize the harbor and the market place, the arrogant mercenary troops and the sweating slaves, the clamor in the narrow streets and the decadent luxury of the merchant princes and their women, conveys a sharper and more realistic picture than pages of modern description and cataloguing. Side by side with exotic imports we find the produce of farm, forest, and pasture ground. Here, tucked away among more common woods is the lone mention of ebony, coupled with ivory as a contribution of the men of Dedan in the Persian Gulf. Then as now, the best ebony came from India and Ceylon. What traveller to the East has not been tempted to buy a miniature elephant, carved from ebony and fitted with ivory tusks, or the cheaper imitation made from black-stained wood and bone. Ebony, susceptible to high polish,

[67]

was used for carvings, decorative trimmings and musical instruments.

Balaam, popularly associated with his talking ass, tells of "trees of lign-aloes which the Lord hath planted." This reference in *Numbers* (24/6) is the only one to lign-aloe, but the word "aloe" or "aloes" occurs elsewhere in both the Old and New Testaments. By modern classification the aloe and lign-aloe are quite separate. The aloe is a shrub of the family *Liliaceae*, used both for its ornamental value and for the medicinal juice extracted from its leaves. This extract has purgative properties. It is considered that all the biblical aloes are lign-aloes, the abbreviated form of the word being commonly used. Lign-aloe itself is a diminutive of the Latin *lignum-aloe;* the Hebrew name, as well as the context, supports the view that lign-aloe is the correct species throughout Scripture text. The lign-aloe, known also as *Agallochum, Agila, Eagle Wood, Paradise Wood and Calambac,* is not native to Palestine but thrives in more tropical regions of Asia. The tree is a large one, its height exceeding a hundred feet. From the heartwood the extract was obtained, which in ancient times was more valuable than its weight in gold. It was a favorite perfume of David and Solomon. After the crucifixion of Jesus, His follower Nicodemus anointed the body with "a mixture of myrrh and aloes, about an hundred pound weight" *(John* 19/39).

Shittim-wood was divinely specified for the construction of the ark of the covenant and other furnishings of the tabernacle. Shittim is the plural form of shittah, the tree from which the wood was cut, but only in *Isaiah* (41/19) do we find the tree itself mentioned. Isaiah wrote nearly eight hundred years after Moses supervised the making of the tabernacle, but the shittah tree continued to be esteemed, being classed with the cedar, the myrtle and the oil. The Revised Version of the Bible translates shittim and shittah uniformly as acacia, several varieties of which are found in Asia Minor. From one of these the substance known as gum arabic is obtained, but there is no evidence that the ancient Jews knew of or used this exudation. The Septuagint uses "incorruptible wood" instead of shittim; the wood is close grained and hard, and suitable for fine furniture. Our mimosa tree is comparable to the Bible shittah.

The weeping willow still grows green by the banks of the Euphrates, but though it bears the Latin title *Salix babylonica,* it is not the willow on which the Jew of the Exile hung his harp and nostalgically mourned the glory that was Jerusalm. *S. babylonica* came from China, after Babylon had fallen. Two different Hebrew words are translated "willow," one of which is restricted to *Ezekiel* (17/5). The willows of Babylon, immortalized in the 137th *Psalm,* are thought to have been aspens or oleanders. Whatever the identity of the Bible willows, they were all stream-loving plants, for each of the five references connects them with streams and water courses.

CHAPTER 7

Fruit and Nut Trees

IN THE FIRST volume of the *Encyclopedia Britannica,* illustrating the Adam reference, is a reproduction of an old Venetian woodcut dated 1492. Here are depicted Eve's temptation of Adam and the subsequent expulsion from the garden of Eden. The tree from which Eve has plucked the forbidden lure is certainly not an apple tree, but the fruit she proffers to her somewhat embarrassed lord and master might pass for an apple. Somewhere in the long stretch of history popular tradition has identified the apple with the forbidden fruit of the tree of the knowledge of good and evil, although there is nothing in the Bible to suggest this. Scriptural experts argue that the tree and the fruit translated in both the Authorized and the Revised Versions as the apple is properly the quince, or the orange, or the citron, or the apricot. The apple tree has its defenders too, for the apple grew, and grows, in Palestine, but the native species has degenerated from that lauded by Solomon. When we consider how a neglected apple orchard can retrogress in a few years, we have little basis to conclude that the comparative absence of thriving apple trees in modern Palestine is proof that there were no prosperous apple orchards there three thousand years ago.

"The righteous shall flourish like the palm tree," sang the Psalmist, going on to pay further tribute to this tree noted for its utility, its beauty and its persistence; "They shall still bring forth fruit in old age; they shall be fat and flourishing" (*Psalms* 92/12, 14). There are many species of palm trees but it is to the date palm that the Bible refers in its numerous mentions. The date palm was prolific in the lands of the Near East, and the tree and its fruit filled many requirements of the natives, an age-old service which shows no signs of declining. The fruit ripened progressively, so the harvesting was spread over an extended season. Skilled gatherers climbed the trees to pluck the dates, but much ripe fruit could be obtained by shaking the tree and catching the falling dates in nets rigged underneath.

Some of the fruit was eaten fresh but most was sun-dried and processed for future use; pressing the dates yielded a rich syrup; the residue was steeped in water and later strained, furnishing a pleasant refreshing drink. Date wine was noted for its potent qualities, and some authorities believe that the "strong drink" of Scriptures was the fermented juice of the date. Vinegar was a by-product. Date honey was a delicacy and the marginal note against 2 *Chronicles* (31/5) refers to this confection. Even the stones were utilized, being dried and ground in hand mills and fed to camels and cattle, or made into charcoal for the forges of the metal smiths. The largest leaves were used for roofing, the smaller woven into mats, baskets, bags and coverings. The shoots, cut each year from the base of the tree, were worked into hats, sandals, baskets, fans and ropes. The fibers became pliable cordage for the running rigging of ships, the finer ones being converted into thread and twine. From the branches, fences and cages were constructed. The wood was used for building, for masts, and as fuel. The sweet sap was drunk as tapped, and also distilled into alcohol. Oil, wax and parchment were other by-products.

The weary desert traveller and his equally fatigued camel felt their spirits rise and new vigor strengthen them when the waving palm tops of a distant oasis were sighted; water, food, shade, and perhaps company, lay ahead. It was natural that palm branches should become the emblem of welcome, public homage and journey's end. Jesus, entering Jerusalem at the height of his fame, was greeted by the fickle populace who "took branches of palm trees, and went forth to meet him, and cried, Hosanna: Blessed is the King of Israel that cometh in the name of the Lord" (*John* 12/13). Palm branches were the conventional symbol of public approbation and welcome by eastern people to conquering heroes, and were strewn and carried in triumphal processions. *Revelation* (7/9) tells us, "Lo, a great multitude, which no man could number, of all nations, and kindreds, and people, and tongues, stood before the throne, and before the Lamb, clothed with white robes, and palms in their hands." The palm tree was embossed on ancient Hebrew coins, and the Romans celebrated the conquest of Judea by issuing a new coinage, still retaining the palm tree but with an added inscription announcing the victory.

The first biblical mention of palms is in *Exodus* (15/27). After the passage of the Red Sea the escaping Israelites journeyed three days, deep into the desert, before they found water; it proved bitter and undrinkable. Moses was divinely inspired to cast a tree into the pool, and the water became sweet. We are not told what type of tree accomplished this purification but evidently it grew in the vicinity of the well. Refreshed, the Hebrews continued to Elim, "where were twelve wells of water, and three score and ten palm trees." The name Elim means palm tree. Tamar is the more common Hebrew designation of the palm, and this was a popular name among Jewish girls. The city of Jericho was called "the City of Palm Trees," and is sometimes so referred to in the Bible without further ident-ification. Bethany meant "the house of dates." The valley of the Dead Sea was noted for its palm groves, some of which were twelve miles in extent. Two writers as diverse as Solomon and Jeremiah used the palm tree to symbolize straight stature. Palm trees figured prominently in the carved decorations of the temple, being usually associated with cherubim, lions, and open flowers. The symbolic sig-nificance trails back beyond recorded history.

The fig bears the distinction of being the first named plant of the Bible. It was of fig leaves that Adam and Eve made their first apron, or, more correctly, girdle, after falling from grace. Prudery was safe behind the garment, for some eastern fig trees have leaves several square feet in area. The fig was one of the commonest culti-vated fruit trees in Palestine, and to be able to relax under one's own vine and fig tree was the cherished desire of every countryman, for it meant an era of peace and prosperity. Mention of the fig tree, or its fruit, occurs more than sixty times in the Scriptures, and the associations make a colorful scenario. The glowing picture of the natural riches of the Promised Land, with which Moses encouraged the despondent tribesmen wandering in the arid desert, included figs as well as milk and honey. Factual confirmation was presented with the return of the spies laden with fig clusters, and other fruit.

As happens to-day, an alert wife saved a churlish husband from the consequences of his boorishness by quick thinking and action, plus a gift of homemade food which included two hundred cakes of dried figs. Abigail made such a good impression on David that when her husband conveniently died ten days later, David married her with-out delay. The tale is told in the twenty-fifth chapter of 1 *Samuel*.

Five chapters later we read of the Amalekites raiding David's headquarters during his absence, putting it to the torch and carrying off all the women, including Abigail. The vengeful David and his troop, pursuing hotfoot, found a straggler from the raider's band, sick and starving. Revived with a cake of figs and some raisins, he led them to the hideout of the unsuspecting brigands, whose drunken carousing left them at the mercy of the Israelites, and Abigail and another of David's wives were restored to the elated leader. Soon after David had been anointed king he celebrated his accession, entertaining his troops at a great military banquet lasting three days, and we read of cakes of figs being consumed along with other bounties of the land (1 *Chronicles* 12/40). A medical property of figs is related in 2 *Kings* (20/7), where Isaiah prescribed a fig poultice for the boils of the dying King Hezekiah; the treatment was so effective that he was restored to health and lived many more years. A very ancient remedy, syrup of figs, is still featured in modern drug stores.

An interesting parallel to some of the historical events of contemporary times may be found in the 24th chapter of *Jeremiah*. Nebuchadnezzar, having conquered Judea, deposed the ruling king and carried him, his princes, and his skilled craftsmen, to Babylon. A puppet king, Zedekiah, nephew of the defeated ruler, was set up in Jerusalem and a collaborationist regime established. The patriot Jeremiah, who may be compared to a resistance leader. denounced the renegade monarch, and prophesied the downfall of his administration and the eventual reestablishment of the deposed government. Two baskets of figs are used to represent the anti- and pro-Babylonian factions among the Jews. "One basket had very good figs, even like the figs that are first ripe: and the other basket had very naughty figs, which could not be eaten, they were so bad." We infer that the contrast between good and bad figs must have been very marked to justify use of this divinely inspired comparison to a divided kingdom.

Many good Christians have puzzled over Jesus' seemingly unreasonable condemnation of the fig tree, which, although in leaf, was without fruit (*Matthew* 21/18-20). The explanation is simple. Figs develop without preceding blossom, sometimes before the tree has come into leaf. Consequently on a fig tree in full leaf one expected

[73]

to find mature fruit; leaves without fruit indicated a sterile condition, a valueless tree. That the season was too early for normal
fig production was apparently irrelevant; the first figs of the season
were not usually ripe till May or June, and the cursing of the untimely fig tree occurred in April or even earlier. Possibly a warm
spring spell and a sheltered sunny location had tricked the unfortunate fig tree, a lone specimen, into premature and unbalanced
development.

The early figs were esteemed above all others as delicate and
choice, as we have seen from Jeremiah's political parable. *Hosea*
(9/10) acclaimed righteous Israel "as the first ripe in the fig tree
at her first time." As poets do each springtime, Solomon joyously
greeted the awakening of nature: "The winter is past .... the flowers
appear.... the fig tree putteth forth her green figs," and, in more
philosophical mood, "Whoso keepeth the fig tree shall eat the fruit
thereof: so he that waiteth on his master shall be honored" (*Proverbs*
27/18). The first tender figs were easily loosened from their stems,
and *Nahum* (3/12) used this simile to foretell the destruction of
Nineveh: "All thy strongholds shall be like fig trees with the first ripe
figs: if they be shaken, they shall even fall into the mouth of the eater."
Revelation (6/13) speaks of fig windfalls, "even as a fig tree casteth
her untimely [margin: green] figs, when she is shaken of a mighty
wind."

The fig tree was deservedly popular. As the first crop of early
figs reached maturity in June, the next growth - summer figs - began
to appear, and had ripened by August. This second installment was
most suited for drying and preserving. They were spread out on mats,
in the sun, pressed into moulds or pounded into a mass which sometimes was compounded with dates, then shaped into bricklike forms
and hardened in storage.

The winter figlets developed as the summer figs were harvested
and reached their fulness when the tree was once again bare of leaves
in late autumn. In mild winters some of the figs could be coaxed
along until early spring, furnishing an out-of-season delicacy. Winter
figs were the largest of the series, dark colored and oblong in shape.

The Jews, like other men of old, and a few countrymen in our
own time, kept nature's calendar rather than man's, and prepared
for seasonal farm labors in accordance with plant phenomena, move-

[74]

ments of migratory birds and animals, clouds and weather sequences. In each of the first three Gospels Jesus based a parable on the wide-spread belief that the leafing of the fig tree indicated summer weather was at hand. Another parable, of interest to the organic gardener, is recounted in *Luke* (13/6-9): "A certain man had a fig tree planted in his vineyard; and he came and sought fruit thereon, and found none. Then said he unto the dresser of his vineyard, Behold, these three years I come seeking fruit on this fig tree, and find none: cut it down; why cumbereth it the ground? And he answering said unto him, Lord, let it alone this year also, till I shall dig about it, and dung it: and if it bear fruit, well: and if not, then after that thou shalt cut it down." The absentee owner was impatient for results, while the patient husbandman who had tended the young tree for three years felt that in spite of the outward appearance of sterility, good cultivation and a dressing of organic matter might bring it into production.

Nathaniel, who under an alternate name is believed to have been the disciple Bartholemew, was seated under a fig tree when Jesus first spiritually discerned his saintly character. This demonstration of occult power amazed the good Nathaniel, and he willingly joined the devoted band of Jesus' followers (*John* 1/45-50).

Another man whom the Master honored was also associated with a tree. Zacchaeus (*Luke* 19/1-9) was short of stature, and climbed a convenient sycamore tree in order to see Jesus, obscured by the intervening crowd who thronged around him. This sycamore tree was more properly the sycamore fig, one of the varieties of the fig family common in Palestine and Egypt, and no relation to the sycamore maple or to the buttonwood. No other reference occurs in the New Testament, but the Old Testament gives us further information. Once in 1 *Kings* and twice in 2 *Chronicles,* Solomon is credited with having made the previously scarce cedar as plentiful as the sycamore which grew so prolifically in the valleys and plains. The tree was subject to frost damage, which accounted for its being grown in warm and sheltered fields, in contrast to hardier varieties of figs which thrived on rocky hillsides exposed to sea breezes. The fruit was considered of inferior grade and was consumed by the poorer classes, although in the time of David it was considered of sufficient importance to share, with the olive, the supervision of a

[75]

specially appointed minister of the crown (1 *Chronicles* 27/28). Sycomore figs grew in bunches, like grapes, both from twigs directly attached to the trunk and from the larger branches.

In the *Book of Amos* (7/14), the humble herdsman discounts his reputation as a prophet and says he is merely "a gatherer of sycomore fruit." A marginal note substitutes "wild figs" for "sycomore fruit." The Revised Version has Amos describing himself as a dresser of sycomore trees. His duty was to score the fig skins with a sharp instrument, for sycomore figs, in order to be edible, required to be punctured a few days before harvesting.

We are all familiar with the valuable contribution of the bee in pollinating flowers and fruit, but the benefaction of the fig wasp is less widely known. The relationship between plant and insect is lengthy and involved. The flowers of the fig are borne on the inside of a pear-shaped hollow receptacle, open at one end. Through this small channel climbs the tiny fig wasp, to lay her eggs in sterile flowers. In due course the eggs hatch into a small colony of wasps, the males fertilize the females and die within the fig, while the females crawl out of the fig through the still open channel. In so doing they brush against the male flowers and pollen sticks to their bodies. Entering inside other figs, this pollen fertilizes the female flowers there, and the transformation into fruit proceeds. The numerous seeds and seed coverings are the fruits of the flowers, the aggregate composing what we term a fig.

Sometimes identified with the sycomore tree is the sycamine, mentioned by Jesus (*Luke* 17/6) in a declaration of the power of faith over matter. Most authorities consider that the sycamine was of the mulberry family rather than that of the fig. Mulberry trees, which are referred to in parallel passages in 2 *Samuel* (5/23-24) and 1 *Chronicles* (14/14-15), are amongst those Bible plants on which no satisfactory identification has been reached. The Hebrew word used is similar to that signifying weeping, and weeping willows as well as balsam trees which exuded (wept) gummy substance have been suggested. Claims for the pear, aspen and poplar have also been advanced. Mulberry trees were common in the Holy Land but were cultivated for their fruit, which tasted something like raspberries, rather than for the leaf diet on which silkworms are raised.

[76]

We find the fig tree throughout the Bible books from *Genesis* to *Revelation,* and across this wide reach the olive also displays its homely figure. Noah welcomed the returning dove, carring an olive leaf in its beak, as a harbinger of peace and return to normalcy. The dove bearing the olive branch has been accepted as the symbol of peace throughout the ages, and as such flutters uneasily throughout myriads of newspaper cartoons in our troubled times.

With the fig and the vine, the olive made up the backbone of Hebrew horticulture. The fruit of the tree constituted an important dietary staple, as *Deuteronomy* (24/20) tells: "When thou beatest thine olive tree, thou shalt not go over the boughs again: it shall be for the stranger, for the fatherless, and for the widow." Proof that this provision was faithfully observed may be found in *Isaiah* (17/6) where the prophet, writing seven hundred years later, testifies: " Yet gleaning grapes shall be left in it, as the shaking of an olive tree, two or three berries in the top of the uppermost bough, four or five in the outmost fruitful branches thereof."

Beating and shaking of the olive tree was the harvesting method, the first step in the oil-extracting process. While the fruit was edible, it was to the production of oil that most of the commercial and communal olive yards were devoted. Olive oil was a culinary necessity to the housewife, a universal substitute for butter, yet having other unique uses. Its mercantile importance is attested, as early as Solomon's reign, by the quantity of olive oil sent King Hiram for his woodsmen. A good olive tree was expected to yield at least a thousand pounds of oil during its period of profitable production. Fruit was borne bi-annually rather than yearly, ten to twenty gallons of oil being the seasonal extraction from the fruit of healthy mature trees.

In *Exodus,* the Israelites were commanded to supply pure olive oil, specially refined and processed to ensure the unfailing burning of the sacred light before the altar; olive oil was a constituent of the oil of holy ointment with which the altar and other holy vessels of the ark of the tabernacle were anointed. Cruder grades of olive oil than those specified for the temple service were used in domestic lamps, and wick sputtering and failing must have been a common experience. The lamps of the ten virgins burnt olive, or other vegetable oil. Soap was one of the by-products: "For though thou wash thee . . . . and take thee much sope, yet thine iniquity is marked

[77]

before me" (*Jeremiah* 2/22). The efficacy of olive oil as a soap ingredient is attested by its inclusion in the name of a well known modern brand of toilet soap.

The Greek word translated oil throughout the New Testament is specifically olive oil, medicinal and cosmetic usage being reported. The apostles "anointed with oil many that were sick, and healed them" (*Mark* 6/13). The context suggests that spiritual or mental healing power was the dynamic therapeutic, the oil being soothing and perhaps symbolic, or a concession to more orthodox medical practice. This is borne out in *James* (5/14-15): "Is any sick among you? let him call for the elders of the church; and let them pray over him, anointing him with oil in the name of the Lord: and the prayer of faith shall save the sick, and the Lord shall raise him up." The good Samaritan treated the wounds of the traveler who fell among thieves by "pouring in oil and wine" (*Luke* 10/34). This application of olive oil and alcohol to open wounds was probably standard first-aid in Jesus' time. There are many references to the cosmetic use of olive oil throughout the Scriptures, some having added religious and symbolic meaning attached.

Olive harvesting was laborious and painstaking. The skins bruised readily, which impaired the value of the contents. The finest oil was extracted from fruit not quite ripe, the maturer berries giving an inferior grade. Contrary to other oil bearing plants, most of the oil was secreted in the outer pulp, and the first pressing, rather a gentle process, yielded the best quality oil. Second and third pressings followed, the oil progressively deteriorating, but being usable as soap base. The golden color of the oil is mentioned by *Zechariah* (4/12). Stone olive mills have been unearthed by archaeologists, with apertures allowing the expressed oil to run into stone receptacles. Foot presses were also used, as the allusion in *Micah* (6/15) reveals.

Traditionally, the olive likes sea air and occasional mist, and *Deuteronomy* (28/40) confirms this maritime compatibility: "Thou shalt have olive trees throughout all thy coasts"; yet it needs sunshine and protection from strong winds during its flower and fruit season, for the opening promise in the above quoted verse is offset in the conclusion, "but thou shalt not anoint thyself with the oil; for thine olive shall cast his fruit." In *Job* (15/33) retribution overtaking the wicked is compared to the olive casting its flowers; evidently the olive was chosen for this comparison as it is particularly profuse in its blooms, and so the ephemeral nature of wealth and material possessions is dramatized to poor Job by his sermonizing friend Eliphaz. However, it is the beneficence rather than the faults of the olive tree to which the Scriptures bear witness.

In the parable of the trees, quoted in the preceding chapter, it is the olive which is first offered the rulership, and in declining it boasts of its fatness, wherewith God and man is honored. Paul, in *Romans* (11/17), also pays tribute to the fatness of the olive. "The Lord called thy name, A green olive tree, fair, and of goodly fruit," *Jeremiah* (11/16) reminded the Jews, in recalling their heritage *Hosea* (14/6) too proclaimed Israel's true destiny: "His branches shall spread, and his beauty shall be as the olive tree." "But I am like a green olive tree in the house of God" rejoices David (*Psalms* 52/8), and again, in *Psalms* (128/3), he likens the children of the righteous man to olive plants growing around his table.

The olive was not spectacular nor majestic nor outwardly remarkable, but neither was the true purpose nor the destiny of the Chosen People. Much of the tragedy of the Jewish race, as the prophets constantly reiterated, came because they misinterpreted their spiritual role into worldly manifestation. The olive was productive rather than ornamental, throve in rocky soil where other plants could not grow, let alone produce a valuable crop. The trunk was gnarled and knotted, not towering like the cedar nor graceful like the palm. It matured slowly and seldom attained a height of thirty feet. Yet it had the constant charm of the evergreen, and its quiet olive-grey leaves set it apart from the lusher green display of other plants. Its longevity was proverbial. The Mount of Olives, so named for the trees which flourished there in Bible times, lay close to Jerusalem, and was much frequented by the Master. A few wizened old olive trees still cling to the sacred slopes.

In the herbal of *Isaiah* (41/19) we find the lone mention of the oil tree. In the original Hebrew, the same word is used in 1 *Kings* (6/23) and rendered into English as olive tree, with a marginal alternative, oily trees of oil. Again in *Nehemiah* (8/15) the Hebrew word is repeated, with the surprising translation as pine. Turning to the corresponding verses of the Revised Version, we find the

[79]

Isaiah reference given as oil tree, with a marginal choice of oleaster. 1 *Kings* becomes olive wood, while *Nehemiah's* pine is transformed into wild olive. This verse in *Nehemiah* mentions several other trees, including the (cultivated) olive, so whatever the tree was we may assume that it was not the orchard olive of commerce.

The last of the fruit trees is the pomegranate. The anglicized name comes from the Roman *pomum granatum,* grained apple. It is no relation of the apple but belongs to the myrtle family. The Hebrew term, *rimmon,* was also a common geographical place name, but is probably more familiar for its association with Naaman, commander of the Syrian armies, cured of leprosy by Elisha. Impressed by his healing, he accepted Jehovah as the true God, but apologetically asked for understanding of his political position, which required him to accompany the king of Syria into the house of his god Rimmon, and pay lip service to the idol. Hadad-rimmon was sun god of Syria, his emblem a pomegranate, symbol of fertility.

The Israelites acquired a taste for pomegranates during the Egyptian captivity and carried the memory into the arid desert; tantalizing thoughts of luscious Nile fruit and Egyptian comfort led the half-starved bands into near mutiny against Moses and Aaron. Plenteous pomegranates were pledged amongst the incentives of the Promised Land, to spur the Children of Israel onward, and the treasured fruit was amongst the samples which the spies brought back to assure the sceptics that Canaan was really worth fighting for (*Numbers* 13/23).

The Bible abounds with references to pomegranates, but most are artificial ones, embellishing sacred objects. The hem of the robe of the ephod had alternate pomegranates and golden bells, while pomegranates by the hundred ornamented Solomon's temple. The inclusion of pomegranate representations in the most sacred Jewish regalia and holy places denotes a sanctity connected with the pomegranate which is not explained in Bible literature, and was probably a relic of pagan belief, just as many of our modern celebrations and symbols are adaptations from more ancient religions. Solomon writes of his pomegranate orchards. From the context in the *Song of Solomon* it would appear that the pomegranates were grown in, or adjacent to, the grape vineyards. Both yielded wine and the monarch seems to have esteemed the spiced pomegranate wine (8/2).

On two occasions he poetically compares the temples (forehead) of his beloved to a piece of pomegranate (4/3, 6/7); the comparison is elusive to us.

The pomegranate tree, or bush, for it seldom reaches twenty feet, is thorny, with dark green leaves and remarkable bell-shaped crimson flowers. The orange-shaped fruit, green at first, darkens into a reddish hue by late August when it becomes ripe for plucking. The rind is hard but brittle, protecting the bright pink flesh, which is arranged sectionally like an orange; it is studded with little seeds and yields an abundance of bitter-sweet juice, very refreshing to tropical thirst. The seeds have medicinal properties; the rind is used in the native tanning of morocco leather.

Nut trees receive little notice in the Old Testament, none in the New, and with the exception of almonds there is difference of opinion as to the species' identification. *Genesis* (43/11) tells us that the patriarch Jacob sent a gift, including nuts and almonds, to the Governor of Egypt, who happened to be his missing and unrecognized son Joseph. The Revised Version, in a marginal note, identifies the nuts as pistachio; this is accepted by most Bible students. The pistachio nut was, and is, extensively cultivated in Palestine and Syria, but not in Egypt, hence Jacob's choice of this variety as an exotic to the recipient. The parent tree is a slim, multi-branched one, about twenty feet high, growing slowly and preferring a dry stony soil. April is blossom time and the tree covers itself with bunches of white flowers. The nut shells have a pleasant aroma, and the kernels, eaten fresh, are considered a delicacy. The dried pistachio nut of commerce is an export variety, regarded as insipid and stale by the native growers.

The account of Jacob's cattle fertility rites (*Genesis* 30/37) described in the preceding chapter, mentions rods of the hazel and the chestnut tree. The Revised Version substitutes "almond" for "hazel" and "plane" for "chestnut." However, the Hebrew word rendered hazel (or almond) is quite distinct from the word uniformly translated elsewhere in both Bible Versions as almond. This regular Hebrew word for almond has an associated sense of "wakener" or "hastener," the correspondence lying in the precedence of the almond tree's seasonal development over other fruit trees. The almond bloomed in January, the flowers developing on leafless branches,

[81]

and the nuts were harvested in April. This dual meaning explains an otherwise obscure passage in *Jeremiah* (1/11-12): "Jeremiah, what seest thou? And I said, I see a rod of an almond tree. Then said the Lord unto me, Thou hast well seen: for I will *hasten* my word to perform it."

Much speculation has been devoted to the meaning of *Ecclesiastes* 12/5, where feeble old age is symbolized by a series of references to its attendant circumstances. Here we find, "The almond tree shall flourish." It may signify the winter of life, the unusual feature of flowers growing on bare leafless branches representing the sparse gray hairs of age. One commentator, Gesenius, advances the theory that the almond tree shall flourish unharvested because the old man is toothless and cannot chew the nuts. To the ancient Hebrews, the almond had a mystical significance. It was Aaron's rod, alone among the rods of the tribes, which miraculously "brought forth buds, and bloomed blossoms, and yielded almonds" (*Numbers* 17/6-8). The golden candlesticks of the tabernacle had the bowls fashioned in the shape of almonds (*Exodus* 25/33). The rock crystals adorning modern candelabras still bear the trade name of almonds. Jewish housewives prized almond oil as a culinary flavoring.

Amongst Solomon's farms and orchards was a garden of nuts, lying in a valley (*Song of Solomon* 6/11). The Hebrew word for nuts in this text differs from the one used by Jacob, and Solomon's variety may have been walnuts. Walnuts were common in Palestine, and a dye was made from their shells.

CHAPTER 8

The Vine

"HE TOOK also of the seed of the land and planted it in a fruitful field; he placed it by great waters, and set it as a willow tree. And it grew, and became a spreading vine of low stature, whose branches turned toward him, and the roots thereof were under him: so it became a vine, and brought forth branches, and shot forth sprigs .... behold, this vine did bend her roots toward him, and shot forth her branches toward him, that he might water it by the furrows of her plantation. It was planted in a good soil by great waters, that it might bring forth branches, and that it might bear fruit, that it might be a goodly vine.... Yea, behold, being planted, shall it prosper? Shall it not utterly wither, when the east wind toucheth it? it shall wither in the furrows where it grew" (*Ezekiel* 17/5 ff.).

Thus Ezekiel described his observation of Babylonian viticulture, for the prophet, as he tells us in the introduction to his book, "was among the captives by the river of Chebar.... in the land of the Chaldeans." Lateral training of the vine is clearly indicated and was a Babylonian technique.

The whole range of Scripture is studded with references to vines and vineyards, vintage and wine, grapes and raisins. The concordance lists nearly five hundred texts enriched by the vine and its culture, a catalog which far surpasses that accorded any other Bible plant. In the Bible pages we find most of the flora of the Holy Land, but details of cultivation and gardening practices are few and far between. Fortunately viticulture is an exception and we are afforded some insight into the methods under which the grape was grown and its fruit fermented. The fifth chapter of *Isaiah* relates the vicissitudes of a Hebrew vinegrower on a terraced hillside in Canaan. Opening with language reminiscent of the *Song of Solomon*, the great prophet and orator begins, "Now will I sing to my well-beloved a song of my beloved touching his vineyard. My well-beloved hath a vineyard in a very fruitful hill: and he fenced it, and gathered out the stones thereof, and planted it with the choicest vine, and built a tower in the midst of it, and also made a winepress therein: and he looked that it should bring forth grapes, and it brought forth wild grapes. And now, O inhabitants of Jerusalem, and men of Judah, judge, I pray you, betwixt me and my vineyard. What could have been done more to my vineyard, that I have not done in it? wherefore, when I looked that it should bring forth grapes, brought it forth wild grapes? And now go to; I will tell you what I will do to my vineyard: I will take away the hedge thereof, and it shall be eaten up; and break down the wall thereof, and it shall be trodden down: and I will lay it waste: it shall not be pruned, nor digged; but there shall come up briers and thorns: I will also command the clouds that they rain no rain upon it."

Isaiah evidently blamed the soil, or the location, or the spirit of the place, for his disappointment, instead of the more obvious cause of sports developing from supposedly good domestic stock; even in this day of scientific horticulture, sports occasionally appear even in the best managed nursery. Vine growing was a skilled occupation, calling forth much preparatory work and then constant attention and vigilance. Unproductive or atypic vines were naturally a great disappointment, considering the output of labor, time, and expense involved, and they were ruthlessly destroyed by the emotional and hot-tempered Hebrews. The prophets, often speaking from bitter experience, used this convenient example to depict the fate of the unproductive and ungrateful man or nation.

The constant care demanded of the vine grower is evident in another passage from *Isaiah* (27/2-3): "A vineyard of red wine. I the Lord do keep it; I will water it every moment; lest any hurt it, I will keep it night and day." We are indebted to the same author for information on the large size of some vineyards: "... where there were a thousand vines at a thousand silverlings..." (7/23). A silverling was a piece of silver, probably a small part of a shekel.

Whatever the fortunes of the Children of Israel, the vine continued to flourish in the Holy Land, and a vineyard of Jesus' time was but a replica of the earlier culture of Isaiah. "There was a certain householder which planted a vineyard, and hedged it round about, and digged a winepress in it, and built a tower, and let it out to husbandmen, and went into a far country" (*Matthew* 21/33).

[84]

The pattern of the vineyard remains unchanged, but the decadence of absentee ownership has appeared.

Grapes were tempting to man and beast, hence the wall and hedge to discourage trespassers, with the tower a temporary shelter for the watchman during the vintage season. The peasant proprietor who had neither the means nor the inclination to hire a watchman, used the watch-tower for a family residence in the time of grapes. At harvest's end this rude structure was abandoned till the next season. Again we refer to *Isaiah* (1/8) for corroboration: "And the daughter of Zion is left as a cottage in a vineyard, as a lodge in a garden of cucumbers." The *Song of Solomon* (2/15) tells of "the foxes, the little foxes, that spoil the vines; for our vines have tender grapes," while the 80th *Psalm* describes worse depredations, through a broken down hedge: "All they which pass by the way do pluck her. The boar out of the wood doth waste it, and the wild beast of the field doth devour it." In *Proverbs* (24/30-34) that royal author and husbandman warns, not against the pillaging of others but against one's own neglect, in terms equally applicable to all eras of horti-culture: "I went by the field of the slothful, and by the vineyard of the man void of understanding; and, lo, it was all grown over with thorns, and nettles had covered the face thereof, and the stone wall thereof was broken down. Then I saw, and considered it well: I looked upon it, and received instruction. Yet a little sleep, a little slumber, a little folding of the hands to sleep: so shall thy poverty come as one that travelleth; and thy want as an armed man."

Good soil and adequate moisture are essential to successful vine culture, and Isaiah recognized these requirements just as the modern grape-grower does. Long before Isaiah, long before Israel and his children, the vine flourished. We have no record of the first beginnings of viticulture but it is as old as traditional man. Fossilized remnants of leaves, branchlets, and seeds, closely resembling current species of the grapevine, have been discovered in widely separated places, some as far north as Iceland. These evidences come from rocks of the Tertiary and Miocene periods of geological class-ification, antedating the ice age. We may assume that the original dis-covery of wine-making is equally far buried in the dim past.

When Noah was commanded to build an ark, Jehovah specified that male and female species of all animal, bird, and reptile life

[85]

should be preserved on board, together with adequate food. There is no mention of conservation of plant life. While the inundation was caused primarily by the downpour of (fresh) rain water, the rising seas encroaching on the land would result in plant roots and seeds being subjected to a saline soaking. Presumably sufficient plant life survived to reclothe field and forest.

From the account in the ninth chapter of *Genesis* we may deduce that Noah carefully preserved a choice vine slip along with his heterogeneous cargo. Stepping once more onto dry ground, Noah and his family first built an altar and sacrificed thereon in token of their preservation. Then we are told, "Noah began to be an husbandman, and he planted a vineyard: and he drank of the wine, and was drunken." Vine culture and fermentation of the grape are skilled processes, so it seems logical to conclude that, although this is the first biblical reference to vineyards and wine, viticulture was a flourishing art long before the Flood. The Flood was retribution for man's incessant evil conduct, and drunkenness was presumably an accompanying factor to the widespread degeneracy of the lusty and "mighty men which were of old, men of renown" (*Genesis* 6/4).

This ancient wine must have been a heady drink, for in the nineteenth chapter of *Genesis* we read of Lot's being so intoxicated that he had no recollection of events during two succeeding nights, which under the circumstances was just as well. Lot was a temporary resident in Sodom; *Deuteronomy* (32/32) tells of the vintage of the doomed city: "Their vine is of the vine of Sodom, and of the fields of Gomorrah; their grapes are grapes of gall, their clusters are bitter: their wine is the poison of dragons." A more temperate and dignified use of wine is related in *Genesis* (14/18), where the regal high priest Melchizedek offered Abram bread and wine. In the forty-ninth chapter of *Genesis* we find Jacob blessing his sons and symbolically prophesying the destiny of the tribes who will bear the names of his children. Judah is characterized in part thusly: "Binding his foal unto the vine, and his ass's colt unto the choice vine; he washed his garments in wine, and his clothes in the blood of grapes: his eyes shall be red with wine." Judah was famed for the quality of its vintage, and two of the place-names associated in the Scripture with choice grapes, Eshcol and En-gedi, lay within

[86]

its bounds. It was from Eshcol that the spies brought to Moses and the sceptical Israelites a cluster of grapes so heavy that one man could not carry it. Other districts noted for their vineyards, Submah, Heshbon, and Elealeh, lay on the other side of the Jordan valley, east of Judah.

Jacob's declaration that the people of Judah would wash their clothes in wine is not as extravagant as it appears. A passage from *Isaiah* (63/1-3) gives a clue: "Who is this that cometh from Edom, with dyed garments from Bozrah? . . . Wherefore art thou red in thine apparel, and thy garments like him that treadeth in the winefat? I have trodden the winepress alone; and of the people there was none with me: for I will tread them in mine anger, and trample them in my fury; and their blood shall be sprinkled upon my garments, and I will stain all my raiment." The thousands of plump ripe grapes bursting open under the rhythmic tread of the wine pressers must have saturated their scanty garments with juice, to be wrung dry, as in washing, at the end of the day.

Isaiah grumbled at his solitary task, for pressing of the vintage was one of the red letter days of the farmer's year, a communal effort where neighbor joined neighbor and excitement ran high. Different vineyards ripened successively, dependent on variety, climate, aspect and pruning technique used, and from September to November the merry shouts of the wine pressers rang out, fortified by heady draughts of new wine. "He shall give a shout, as they that tread the grapes," says *Jeremiah* (25/30) and again, (48/33): "Joy and glad ness is taken from the plentiful field. . . . and I have caused wine to fail from the winepresses: none shall tread with shouting; their shouting shall be no shouting.' *Isaiah* (16/10) similarly laments: "In the vineyards there shall be no singing, neither shall there be shouting: the treaders shall tread out no wine in their presses; I have made their vintage shouting to cease." Isaiah wrote just after the forced deportation of the northern tribes of Israel, as the shadow of Assyrian power clouded Judah, and one detects a nostalgic yearn ing for the good old days when he had tramped the winepress and sung with the best of the merry groups: "The new wine mourneth, the vine languisheth, all the merry-hearted do sigh. The mirth of tabrets ceaseth, the noise of them that rejoice endeth, the joy of the harp ceaseth. They shall not drink wine with a song" (*Isaiah* 24/7-9).

[87]

Large vineyards had wine presses built in, hewn out of rock and lined with mortar. Small growers worked cooperatively in a communal press. *Joel* (3/13) refers to two receptacles, one for the fruit and the other for the expressed juice, and archaeological research has uncovered similar specimens. Joel here uses a word, translated "fats" in English, to describe the container into which the wine flowed, and the casual reader may be excused for considering fat a synonym for the juice of the grape. However, the correct translation is "vat," a hollow vessel, and not "fat," an oily substance. *Haggai* (2/16) speaks of the "pressfat," while *Mark* (12/1) uses the phrase "digged a place for the winefat." In *Antony and Cleopatra*, Act 2, Scene 7, Shakespeare has the same medieval term:

> Come, thou monarch of the vine
> Plumpy Bacchus, with pink eyne,
> In thy fats our cares be drowned,
> With thy grapes our hairs be crowned.

While the poor peasant and his family did their own harvesting, the larger vineyards used itinerant labor, just as commercial fruit growers do today in America and elsewhere. *Jeremiah* (49/9) and *Obadiah* (-5) tell of the coming of the grape gatherers, while with more detail *Jeremiah* (6/9) describes how "they shall thoroughly glean the remnant of Israel as a vine: turn back thine hand as a grape gatherer into the baskets."

The vintage season with its rejoicing and joviality was incorporated into the religious festival of the Feast of Tabernacles, perhaps to tone down excesses and channel emotion into praise for Jehovah, giver of all good. Unfortunately the neighboring pagan tribes and the remnants of the original Canaanites were also good viticulturists, and their harvest thanksgiving festivals to Baal and Astarte were accompanied by authorized licentious orgies and promiscuity, condemned and deplored by the chaste Hebrew priests and prophets. Much of the fulminations against the idolatrous practices of the sensual Israelites may be laid to their opportune yielding to the lusts of the flesh with the neighboring Baalites' womenfolk, rather than to any credence in the superior powers of Baal over Jehovah as a deity, although no doubt the heathen priests did their best to

[88]

win Jewish converts. The old native deity always carried a certain amount of influence, as the seventeenth chapter of 2 *Kings* teaches, and as the Assyrian settlers in Samaria discovered when they took over the vineyards and farms of the deported northern Israelites. "And so it was at the beginning of their dwelling there, that they feared not the Lord: therefore the Lord sent lions among them, which slew some of them. Wherefore they spake to the king of Assyria, saying, The nations which thou hast removed, and placed in the cities of Samaria, know not the manner of the God of the land: therefore he hath sent lions among them, and, behold, they slay them, because they know not the manner of the God of the land. Then the king of Assyria commanded, saying, Carry thither one of the priests whom ye brought from thence; and let them go and dwell there, and let him teach them the manner of the God of the land. Then one of the priests whom they had carried away from Samaria came and dwelt in Bethel, and taught them how they should fear the Lord . . . . . So they feared the Lord, and served their own gods."

The vine flourished in Egypt, but on higher ground than the banks of the Nile, with their periodic inundations. In *Genesis* (40/11) is a reference to the drinking of grape juice, as distinct from wine. *Deuteronomy* (32/14) tells of drinking "the pure blood of the grape." Everything pertaining to the vine was prohibited to the Nazarite sect: "When either man or woman shall separate themselves to vow a vow of a Nazarite, to separate themselves unto the Lord: he shall separate himself from wine and strong drink, and shall drink no vinegar of wine, or vinegar of strong drink, neither shall he drink any liquor of grapes, nor eat moist grapes, or dried. All the days of his separation shall he eat nothing that is made of the vine tree from the kernels even to the husk" (*Numbers* 6/2-4). The vow included other abstentions, and could be of limited duration or a lifetime obligation. Samuel, Saul and John the Baptist were members of this ascetic group.

The interest of the gardener is intrigued by the brief account of King Uzziah in the twenty-sixth chapter of 2 *Chronicles*, but unfortunately we can only speculate on the implication of the 10th verse: "He built towers in the desert, and digged many wells: for he had much cattle, both in the low country, and in the plains:

[89]

husbandmen also, and vine dressers in the mountains, and in Carmel: for he loved husbandry." This ruler was a mighty warrior as well as a good farmer, and successfully subdued his turbulent neighbors. Apparently he lacked the literary talents which Solomon used to such advantage in telling us of his gardens and vineyards. Uzziah's biographer gives considerable detail to his warlike prowess and inventions, but only one verse to his agricultural activities. His active mind and wide interests deserve a better write-up than the Bible accords him.

Rich as is the Old Testament in the fragrance of the grape blossom and the heady fumes of red wine, it is Jesus who glorifies the vine, and in the process furnishes much viticultural detail. "I am the true vine, and my father is the husbandman. Every branch in me that beareth not fruit he taketh away: and every branch that beareth fruit, he purgeth it, that it may bring forth more fruit . . . . As the branch cannot bear fruit of itself, except it abide in the vine, no more can ye, except ye abide in me. I am the vine, ye are the branches: He that abideth in me, and I in him, the same bringeth forth much fruit: for without me ye can do nothing. If a man abide not in me, he is cast forth as a branch, and is withered; and men gather them, and cast them into the fire, and they are burned" (*John* 15/1-6). It is only in St. John's Gospel that Jesus symbolizes his ministry by a vine and its cultivation. The other three gospels feature parallel versions of the parable of the vineyard and the wicked husbandmen. Jesus' teaching was marked with association of ideas, usually tied to the most familiar examples of everyday rural practice and current events; the prevalence of absentee ownership and the existence of a class of mercenary professional husbandmen or farm managers may be deduced from this latter allegory.

Another parable from which we infer the employment of seasonal casual labor is found in the first part of the 20th chapter of *Matthew*. Here a vineyard owner hires unemployed farmhands "early in the morning." Only men actively seeking work would be available at the dawn hour. Presumably it is the vintage season. After collective bargaining, a daily rate of a penny (Greek denarius, approx. 17 cents) is agreed upon. Later during the day additional series of laborers are hired for vineyard work, but these are surplus employees with weakened bargaining power and are in no position to argue over wages, so they are glad to sell their services for whatever their employer thinks them worth. Not unnaturally the difference in the hourly rate, disclosed at paytime, is resented by the men who have put in a full day's work; Jesus' rejoinder indicates the prevailing sentiment of pre-union days. "Is it not lawful for me to do what I will with mine own?" The Moffat edition of the New Testament, written in modern English, brings the argument right up to date: "My man, I am not wronging you. Did you not agree with me for a shilling? Take what belongs to you and be off. I choose to give this last man the same as you. Can I not do as I please with what belongs to me? Have you a grudge because I am generous?" It is from this parable that we get the phrase, "the eleventh hour." From it, too, Churchill drew a line famous in one of his early war speeches: " (we) which have borne the burden and heat of the day."

The peasant grape grower, whose holding was too small and finances inadequate to hire labor, is also featured in a vine parable in the 21st chapter of *Matthew*. The peasant's two sons were asked by their father to help in the vineyard. One promised he would, but failed to show up, while the other, who objected originally, changed his mind and went to work on the grapes. Jesus' hostile audience agreed that the repentant objector was the better man, and the Master drove home the lesson to the discomfited priests.

Jesus partook of wine on occasion, and the Pharisees of the day held it against Him. "And the Lord said . . . . John the Baptist came neither eating bread nor drinking wine; and ye say, He hath a devil. The Son of man is come eating and drinking; and ye say Behold a gluttonous man, and a wine bibber, a friend of publicans and sinners! But wisdom is justified of all her children" (*Luke* 7/33-35).

"This beginning of miracles did Jesus in Cana of Galilee, and manifested forth his glory; and his disciples believed on him." So *John* (2/11) concludes the account of the turning of water into wine at the marriage feast, the first demonstration of the Divine power of Jesus. Three short years later, with the shadow of the Cross darkening His mission, He celebrated the ancient rite of the Passover at the last free meeting of His disciples. Having sipped the wine, He passed the cup: "Drink ye all of it; for this is my blood of

[91]

the new testament, which is shed for many for the remission of sins. But I say unto you, I will not drink henceforth of this fruit of the vine, until that day when I drink it new with you in my Father's kingdom" (*Matthew* 26/27-29). As He hung on the Cross in the agony of the crucifixion, one of the more compassionate of the attendant soldiers offered Him wine mixed with myrrh, to deaden the pain, but Jesus refused it.

The 9th chapter of *Joshua* recounts a wily and successful stratagem whereby the men of Gibeon, one of the Canaanite cities marked for destruction by the advancing Israelites, retained life at the expense of liberty. Part of their faked evidence was "wine bottles, old, and rent, and bound up." Wine bottles reappear in the more familiar passages of the New Testament; "No man putteth new wine into old bottles: else the new wine doth burst the bottles, and the wine is spilled, and the bottles will be marred: but new wine must be put into new bottles" (*Mark* 2/22). In the Revised Version "bottles" is rendered as "skins," which the containers actually were. The fermentation and chemical action of new wine required a receptacle which would resist splitting and cracking, with consequent loss of the contents. Old wine imposed no stress on the containers beyond its own weight and volume, so old wine skins were suitable. That even new skin bottles were not immune against careless wine making is shown in the down to earth words of *Job* (32/19): "Behold, my belly is as wine which hath no vent; it is ready to burst like new bottles."

Wine bottles were usually made of goat skin, although that of oxen was used when large capacity was desired. The goat, or other animal, was cased, by having the head and the lower parts of the legs cut off, and the skin peeled back from the flesh, thus leaving the hide intact except for the neck and leg cuts. The skin was then cured and rendered soft and pliable. Male goats were used for the purpose while skins of kids furnished a conveniently smaller size for the use of travellers.

New wine was the drink of the common people, abundant and cheap and heady. Evidently daytime drinking was socially unacceptable, for Paul says, (1 *Thessalonians* 5/7): "They that be drunken are drunken in the night." And in *Acts* (2/13, 15), when the apostles are accused of being full of new wine, Peter denies the charge,

[92]

pointing out, "For these are not drunken, as ye suppose, seeing it is but the third hour of the day" (*i.e.,* three hours after sunrise).

The last verse of the 5th chapter of *Luke* suggests Jesus was a connoisseur of vintage wine: "No man also having drunk old wine straightway desireth new: for he saith, The old is better." In the miracle of the marriage feast the Master transformed water into very choice wine, superior to that which had already been consumed, to the surprise of the host who followed the custom, not unknown in this day, of serving mature beverages to the respected and temperate guests who partook in moderation, and then bringing out cheaper and rawer alcohol for those with little discrimination and large capacity.

In the Old Testament we find the expression, "wines on the lees." *Isaiah* (25/6) praises the generosity of God who will provide his people "a feast of wines on the lees, of fat things full of marrow, of wines on the lees well refined." *Jeremiah* (48/11), evidently a vintner as well as a prophet, compares the placidity of Moab to old wine, carefully mellowed in a cool cellar: "Moab hath been at ease from his youth, and he hath settled on his lees, and hath not been emptied from vessel to vessel, neither hath he gone into captivity: therefore his taste remained in him, and his scent is not changed." Even the expression "neither hath he gone into captivity" in this verse is apposite, if we recollect the German invasions of France and the damage done to vintage wine by the occupying armies; here and there in isolated non-strategic regions the old traditional rites of aging of wine were carried on without interference. Lees were the sediment which settled on the bottom of containers of maturing wine. If the decanting from one wineskin to another was carelessly done, some of the acrid dregs were disturbed and flowed with the wine, rendering it inferior. Our expression, "the dregs to the wicked," refers to the bitter lees of wine, and is taken from *Psalms* (75/8): "For in the hand of the Lord there is a cup, and the wine is red; it is full of mixture; and he poureth out of the same: but the dregs thereof, all the wicked of the earth shall wring them out, and drink them."

CHAPTER 9

Flowers

SPRING CARPETS the hills and valleys of Palestine with myriads of wild flowers. From the steaming heat of the lower Jordan valley and the salt-laden air of the Dead Sea shores, upwards through the terraced hillsides and cool mountain glens, lushly painting the fertile plains and shyly dotting the mountain reaches of Lebanon, finally to disappear beneath the snow line, hundreds and hundreds of varieties proclaim nature's annual awakening. A British botanist recognized half a thousand species common in his native soil, while almost as many again have been identified as being unknown beyond Bible lands.

This verdant costume, this bloom of color, has brought joy to the soul of man each springtime, in all lands. Solomon voiced the vernal tribute which every poet feels in his heart at nature's resurrection.

Yet spring was fleeting, and early summer heat and rainless skies parched and shrivelled the tender little blooms, and the shepherds and husbandmen of Judah and Galilee felt the melancholy which mankind knows at the passing of youth and beauty and innocence. The ancient Hebrew, like the Scot, had a somber strain in his rugged character. The most heart-stirring Scottish music and poems are tied to laments and dirges. *The Flowers of the Forest*, Scotland's poignant coronach for her dead heroes, is unutterably sad music, yet it stirs deep wells of hope and faith as well as sorrow and heartbreak. We find similar life within death in some floral passages of the Bible.

Nahum, in his first chapter, mourns the languishing of the flower of the forest of Lebanon, yet in the last verse hope rises anew: "Behold upon the mountains the feet of him that bringeth good tidings, that publisheth peace!" The *Psalmist* (103/15) sees man's brief span as the ephemeral life of the flower: "As for man, his days are as grass: as a flower of the field, so he flourisheth. For the wind passeth over it, and it is gone; and the place thereof shall know it

[94]

no more." *Isaiah* (40/6-8) voices a similar strain: "The voice said, Cry. And he said, What shall I cry? All flesh is grass, and all the goodliness thereof is as the flower of the field: the grass withereth, the flower fadeth: because the spirit of the Lord bloweth upon it." Eight hundred years later another devout naturalist, Peter, wrote almost identical words (1 *Peter* 1/24). Many pages of history filled the space separating these two men, yet each responded alike to nature's brave brief flourish. The Apostle *James* (1/11) warns the wealthy man who trusts in his riches, "because as the flower of the grass he shall pass away. For the sun is no sooner risen with a burning heat, but it withereth the grass, and the flower thereof falleth, and the grace of the fashion of it perisheth: so also shall the rich man fade away in his ways."

Yet, in spite of the profusion of flowers which greeted the Children of Israel each springtime, the Bible pages are almost empty of floral texts. If we discount references to blossoms of trees such as the almond, pomegranate, vine and fig, and confine our research to flowers of the garden and field category, we find but three: the rose, the camphire and the lily. They are so named in the Authorized Version: in the Revised Version the rose becomes, alternatively, the autumn crocus; the camphire is called hennaflowers, but the lily remains the lily. Biblical botanists, however, are not content with this classification, and the inquiring reader can find, in Bible literature, numerous speculations on the identity of these flowers.

Only the lilies blossom in the New Testament. In *Matthew* (6/28-30) Jesus pays a tribute to nature's handiwork displayed in a simple wild flower, which it is unlikely that anyone will ever equal. Standing on a hilltop, surrounded by a multitude who thronged the grass-covered, flower-studded slopes below Him, the Master bent down and plucked a beautiful wild flower in its full bloom of vivid colors. A tiny flower would have been indiscernible to many of His audience, so it was probably long stemmed and full bodied. We may take our choice of any of the flowers suggested for this reference by botanical investigators, anemone, asphodel, field daisy, marta gon, tulip, gladiolus, iris—and, of course, the ordinary white lily. "Consider the lilies of the field," said Jesus. He may have held several wild flowers in His hand. Some commentators hold that lily was a generic name applied to wild field flowers in general, just as we speak of

[95]

grass and lump clover, alfalfa, timothy and a dozen other varieties under the common name. "Consider the lilies of the field, how they grow; they toil not, neither do they spin: and yet I say unto you, That even Solomon in all his glory was not arrayed like one of these. Wherefore, if God so clothe the grass of the field, which to-day is, and tomorrow is cast into the oven, shall he not much more clothe you, O ye of little faith?"

If we meditate on these verses, and study their implication, the idea may unfold that the Master was an expert botanist, thoroughly familiar with plant structure and processes. He did not say, "Consider the lilies" but "Consider the lilies, how they grow." Then, shifting His gaze to sweep His audience of working men and women, He went on "They toil not, neither do they spin" and He probably paused to let the contrast sink in. And then, with an emphasis and assurance ringing with authority and knowledge, "And yet I say unto you." This is a stronger assertion than Jesus' more frequent "Verily, verily, I say unto you." Solomon was the most resplendent and magnificent figure in Jewish history, and the Master deliberately contrasted what His rather drab audience considered the acme of regal splendor with a familiar wildflower, and then stamped the lily as surpassing Solomon's greatest glory.

Solomon, too, had his lilies, intimately symbolized and identified with the great lover. "I am the rose of Sharon, and the lily of the valleys. As the lily among thorns, so is my love among the daughters" (*Song of Solomon* 2/1-2). Solomon's lilies are subject to as much botanical speculation as those of Jesus, but there is general agreement that the lily of the valleys is not *Convallaria majalis* with its drooping little bells. The *Song of Solomon* gives us several clues, following the one above mentioned. The expression "feeding among the lilies" occurs three times (2/16, 4/5, 6/3), the middle one referring to roes or gazelles, the others to the loved one. The inference seems to be that these lilies grew in lush pastures.

A variation on the feeding theme is found in the same Book (6/2): "My beloved is gone down into his garden, to the beds of spices, to feed in the gardens, and to gather lilies." This appears to be the lone Biblical mention of the picking of flowers for their aesthetic value, and even this meaning is conjectural, for the plant may have been edible, or yielded fragrant oil or perfume. This latter assumption gets support from another passage (5/13): "His lips like lilies, dropping sweet smelling myrrh." A Persian variety of lily secretes a liquid comparable to myrrh. In the Orient the bulbs of the tiger lily are considered an edible delicacy, and in parts of Russia the martagon lily is eaten. Thus, once more, we can only guess the identity of a Bible plant, and its significance to men and women of old. Yet the lily, whatever species of flower it was, symbolized Israel's true being and finer qualities. "I will be as the dew unto Israel: he shall grow as the lily," promised Jehovah, through his servant *Hosea* (14/5).

The implication of the opening verses of the 2nd chapter of *Solomon's Song* seems to be that the rose of Sharon, and the lily of the valleys, were beautiful wildflowers which here and there brightened a landscape otherwise choked with thorns and briers. The plain of Sharon was remarkably fertile, although sandy stretches and rocky hillocks broke up the cultivated acres, and there the rose of Sharon may have bloomed amongst wilder vegetation. The rose of the Scriptures is even harder to classify than is the lily. On both occasions when it is mentioned the reference is allegorical. *Isaiah* (35/1) in a countryman's lyric of enthusiasm proclaims, "The wilderness and the solitary place shall be glad for them; and the desert shall rejoice and blossom as the rose. It shall blossom abundantly."

The same Hebrew word designates the rose of Isaiah and that of Solomon, which in the Revised Version is given the alternative name of autumn crocus. There is reason for believing that the rose bush which we know and admire budded in yearly beauty in Old Palestine; certainly the rose was cultivated in the most ancient times in the Levant and adjacent countries for the exquisite and precious attar of roses expressed from its petals. Various Bible botanists advance the validity of claims for rose honors by the tulip, the narcissus, the oleander and the autumn crocus, or meadow saffron as it is sometimes called. This last is based on a breakdown of the Hebrew name, *habazzeleth* or *chabatstseleth,* which translates into English as "acrid bulb." This flower was common throughout Bible lands and yielded extracts valuable for medicinal and culinary purposes.

If our research did not go beyond the Authorized Version of the Bible, we would be inclined to classify camphire as a shrub or a tree. Solomon rhapsodizes, "My beloved is unto me as a cluster of camphire in the vineyards of En-gedi" (*Song of Solomon* 1/14); and again (4/13), "Thy plants are an orchard of pomegranates, with pleasant fruits; camphire, with spikenard." In both these passages a marginal note against "camphire" gives the alternative "cypress." The Revised Version does not use the word camphire but substitutes henna flowers, and henna, respectively, with a marginal note *Hebrew: Copher*, against the first mentioned. The Hebrew *Copher* or *Kopher* becomes *Al Khanna* in Arabic, *Khenna* in Egyptian and *Henna* in Persian, which last name has come into English usage In England the plant is called *Egyptian privet*, while the West Indies have adopted it as *Jamaica mignonette*. Its botanical name is *Lawsonia inermis*. Delicate four-petalled white flowers bloom fragrantly on this slim shrub; the clustered flowers are set off from lance-shaped leaves.

Henna is one of the oldest of cosmetics. The dried leaves were powdered and then made into a paste which was used to dye the skin, and enhance the beauty of the hands and feet, and particularly the nails. An Egyptian woman who permitted her nails to be seen without henna stain was considered as immodest as one who exhibited her body. Traces of henna dye have been observed on the nails of mummies. "King Solomon loved many strange women, together with the daughter of Pharaoh." We may surmise that henna was imported for the beauty salon of this foreign princess, who was exalted above Solomon's other wives by having a magnificent palace built for her. Not only fashionable women used henna, but the beards and hair of men, and even the manes and tails of horses were dyed with this orange-red stain. Mohammed is reputed to have henna-dyed his beard and the fashion spread to other famous Moslems.

It is rather remarkable that the Bible is so sparse in mention of flowering plants, considering that the most sacred religious decorations of the Jewish religion, the ephod, the golden candlesticks of the altar, the great temple of Solomon with its elaborate sacred furnishings and ornaments, were embellished with carved and woven lilies, pomegranates, almond blossoms and open flowers not otherwise identified. Of all religions, the ancient Jewish was most mandatory in its prohibition of anything faintly pertaining to idolatry. One

[98]

of the ten commandments delivered by Moses on Mt. Sinai starts, "Thou shalt not make unto thee any graven image, or any likeness of any thing that is in heaven above, or that is in the earth beneath, or that is in the water under the earth" (*Exodus* 20/4).

The Mosaic Law not only laid down and codified religious observance and ritual, but regulated much of the social, political and economic life and customs of Israel. The inclusion of flower representations on sacrosanct objects pertaining to worship, some specifically enumerated and formally arranged as on an architect's blueprint, must have stemmed from a much more esoteric source than artistic design. We recall the lotus of Egypt, which ornaments so many records of the Pharaohs. In the mystery religions of Tibet, in China and India and Assyria the mystic lotus represented, to the initiate, the soul of man rising in ethereal beauty from its earth-rooted mortal shell, as the white petals of the lotus rose from the mud-silted waters; the ignorant admired or revered the outward representation, and nothing more. The Egyptian lotus was a water-lily, *Nymphaea lotus,* as was the sacred lotus of India, *Nelumbium nelumbo.* The lily of Israel may have been a water one. In Hebrew it is called *shoshan, shoshannah,* and *shushan.* The latter name appears in Esther's romance in "Shushan the palace." The same peculiar phrase occurs in the first verse of *Nehemiah;* perhaps we should think of it as " the lily palace." One of the few women named in the history of Jesus was "Susanna .. which ministered unto him" (*Luke* 8/3). As the etymology indicates, her English name would be Lily.

Vegetables

WERE IT not for the sullen anger and discontent of the half-starved, manna-cloyed Israelites, tantalized by memories of the abundant meat, tangy vegetables, and luscious fruit of Egypt, our brief list of Bible vegetables would be diminished by nearly half. As it is, the catalogue is scant enough.

The eleventh chapter of *Numbers* is a turbulent one. The Chosen People are crabbed and morose and would unhesitatingly trade their divine heritage with the Promised Land thrown in for a good square meal. Moses begs Jehovah to strike him dead if He cannot give him respite from the constant bickerings of his charges, while the Lord displays a peculiarly human exasperation and vindictiveness and an "I'll fix them" spirit.

Here is a condensation of the scene. "And when the people complained, it displeased the Lord . . . and his anger was kindled; and the fire of the Lord burnt among them, and consumed them that were in the uttermost parts of the camp. . . . And the mixt multitude that was among them fell a lusting: and the children of Israel also wept again, and said, Who shall give us flesh to eat? We remember the fish, which we did eat in Egypt freely; the cucumbers, and the melons, and the leeks, and the onions, and the garlick: but now our soul is dried away: there is nothing at all, beside this manna, before our eyes . . . and the taste of it was as the taste of fresh oil . . . . Then Moses heard the people weep throughout their families, every man in the door of his tent: and the anger of the Lord was kindled greatly; Moses also was displeased. And Moses said unto the Lord, Wherefore hast thou afflicted thy servant . . . . that thou layest the burden of all this people upon me? Have I conceived all this people? have I begotten them, that thou shouldst say unto me, Carry them in thy bosom, as a nursing father beareth the sucking child . . . . Whence should I have flesh to give unto all this people? for they weep unto me, saying, Give us flesh, that we may eat. I am not able to bear all this people alone, because it is too heavy for me . . . . kill me, I pray thee, out of hand . . . . and let me not see my wretchedness. And the Lord said unto Moses . . . . say thou unto the people, Sanctify yourselves against tomorrow, and ye shall eat flesh: for ye have wept in the ears of the Lord, saying, Who shall give us flesh to eat? for it was well with us in Egypt: therefore the Lord will give you flesh, and ye shall eat. Ye shall not eat one day, nor two days, nor five days, neither ten days, nor twenty days; but even a whole month, until it come out at your nostrils, and it be loathsome unto you." When poor Moses, whose spirits were too crushed to visualize miracles, showed scepticism, Jehovah gave him a sarcastic rejoinder, "Is the Lord's hand waxed short? thou shalt see now whether my word shall come to pass unto thee or not." Then came huge flocks of quail, covering the ground for miles around the desert encampment.

Vegetables have little place in the domestic economy of nomads, for man too requires roots in order to cultivate the soil and raise crops. The patriarchs were shepherds and herdsmen, leading their flocks to fresh pastures as the old got cropped up; their milch animals gave them butter and cheese and milk, while kids and calves provided constant fresh meat. When they trekked across desert wastes to greener fields, they required food which was small in bulk and not subject to deterioration from climatic conditions, so they carried dried fruits, raisins and dates and figs, and grain. For these they traded their livestock, their fleece and their wool, in city markets. The hunting of game furnished variety for the pot.

Early biblical man, Adam, and Cain, and Noah, were cultivators of the soil rather than shepherds, but they left no record of any vegetables they grew. It is in the story of the cattle-minded patriarchs that the first mention of vegetables appears. The 29th verse of the 25th chapter of *Genesis* tells us quaintly, "And Jacob sod pottage." In modern words, Jacob cooked soup. Or, it might be equally correct to say, Jacob boiled cereal. The words "pottage," "porridge" and "potage" are variants of the same root. From the last verse of the chapter we learn that the pottage was made of lentiles, and was served with bread. "Jacob gave Esau bread and pottage of lentiles, and he did eat and drink, and rose up, and went his way. Thus Esau despised his birthright." The pottage was thin, for Esau drank it, and the 30th verse tells us it was red.

Lentiles, or lentils, are the seed of the plant known as *Lens esculenta,* one of the vetch family. Their early appearance in the Bible is not accidental, for lentils are believed to have been one of man's first cultivated crops, specimens dating back to the Bronze Age having been found in the Lake dwellings of Switzerland. The optical term, lens, owes its name to the resemblance of the ground glass to the lentil bean; the lentil seed is a miniature double convex lens, the two halves occupying a little pod half an inch or so in length. The flowers are pale blue, the leaves compounded of alternate leaf-lets. The lentil plant has an ancient reputation as a milk stimulant for dairy cattle, so a stand of it growing wild would have influenced a nomad band to stop over for pasture, while the lentil beans provided a dietary change for the herdsmen.

We next read of lentils in 2 *Samuel* (17/28), where David and his fighting men were presented with much needed food, "wheat, and barley, and flour, and parched corn, and beans, and lentiles, and parched pulse." Later, in chapter 23/11, one of David's captains defeated the Philistines at a site identified only by "where was a piece of ground full of lentiles." Lentils make their last Biblical appearance in *Ezekiel* (4/9), where they form one of the ingredients of an ancient variety of austerity loaf, a particularly sustaining type of bread, symbolically ordained for use during famine or siege. "Take thou also unto thee wheat, and barley, and beans, and lentiles, and millet, and fitches, and put them in one vessel, and make thee bread thereof." Lentils were, and are, one of the staple foods of the poor in the countries bordering the eastern Mediterranean; there, messes of red pottage are still brewed, seasoned with olive oil and garlic.

There is no further mention of beans beyond the two verses quoted in the preceding paragraph, and research encounters an almost complete absence of data regarding their culture and use in Palestine. Kidney beans and horse beans were varieties grown in Syria.

It was not until the Sojourn in Egypt that the Hebrews acquired a taste for, and had the opportunity to grow or conveniently purchase, fresh vegetables. Every market gardener knows the value of rich black delta soil, and the ancient Egyptians made the fullest use of the bounty of the Nile flats. The land of Goshen, headquarters of the Israelites, lay in the lower Delta. The staple diet of the Egyptian lower classes was vegetables and fish, both being abundant and cheap. Modern Japanese laborers eat likewise, for the same economic reasons. Naturally the bonded Hebrews would get their full share, if only to sustain their physique and energy in the heavy manual labor they sweated under.

Egyptian onions were noted for their large size and fine flavor, being milder and less pungent than our varieties. Leeks, similar to those we know, were also grown in Egypt, but it is doubtful if the Hebrew word translated leeks in *Numbers* (11/5) is an accurate rendering. The same word occurs about twenty times and is elsewhere interpreted grass, herb, and hay. Some authorities consider that the term salad greens would be a more descriptive translation. Egyptians greatly esteemed a plant called *fenugrec* or *fenugreek,* (lit. "Greek hay") and enormous quantities were consumed, usually purchased in bundles in the marketplace, but sometimes eaten as it grew on the ground, in the manner of cattle grazing. It has been suggested that the Bible leek was *fenugrec.* The tenth precious stone in the foundation of the wall of the heavenly Jerusalem (*Revelation* 21/20) was chrysoprasus, a Greek word whose literal meaning is "golden leek." The jewel has a pale leekgreen tinge.

The botanical family *Cucurbitaceae* claims a number of Old Testament edible plants, which Bible botanists agree belong to this extensive order. When it comes to identifying the species, translated as cucumbers, gourds, knops, and melons, we find, as usual, contending claims by different authorities.

In *Numbers* (11/5), where memories of melons and cucumbers aroused nostalgic desire, the relative Hebrew words are distinctly different. The concordance agrees that melons are melons, but suggests that while cucumbers may still be cucumbers, they also may be water-melons or gourds. In *Isaiah* (1/8) where the only other mention of cucumbers occurs, the original term bears no resemblance to that used in *Numbers,* and the concordance tags it as "a place of water melon." Water-melon does not appear in the English Bible text, and melon makes its sole appearance in *Numbers.* When we start to track the gourd down, we naturally think of Jonah's famous shade vine, "which came up in a night, and perished in a night" (*Jonah* 4/10); a marginal reference offers *Palma Christi* instead of gourd, a plant which has no relation to the gourd family.

[103]

However, the Bible has a botanical gourd, a wild variety, and the 4th chapter of 2 *Kings* spins a human interest story around it.

"Elisha came again to Gilgal: and there was a dearth in the land; and the sons of the prophets were sitting before him; and he said unto his servant, Set on the great pot, and seethe pottage for the sons of the prophets. And one went out into the field to gather herbs, and found a wild vine, and gathered thereof wild gourds his lap full, and came and shred them into the pot of pottage: for they knew them not. So they poured out for the men to eat. And it came to pass, as they were eating of the pottage, that they cried out, and said, O thou man of God, there is death in the pot. And they could not eat thereof. But he said, Then bring meal. And he cast it into the pot; and he said, Pour out for the people, that they may eat. And there was no harm in the pot."

A casual reading of this passage gives the impression that the pottage was poisonous, and that the poison was neutralized by a minor miracle of Elisha, the throwing in of a handful of meal being a symbolic gesture. On second reading, however, we observe that Elisha does not necessarily accept the complaint, "There is death in the pot," as evidence that the contents were poisonous. The pottage may merely have been very bitter, or acrid, or nauseating. There is no mention that any of the partakers became ill, only that they could not eat of it. The addition of meal may have served as a catalytic agent, or may have reduced the strong flavor of the wild gourds to that of a pungent but eatable seasoning.

The vine was an unusual species in that part of the country, for its fruit was unrecognized by the company. Some authorities consider that this wild gourd was the bitter apple or *colocynth,* related to the water melon and having cucumber-type foliage. The pulp is intensely bitter, and the fruit yields a quick-acting purgative drug. Another school of thought advances the opinion that the Hebrew word implies a "bursting apart," and suggests the squirting cucumber, which ejects its seeds and liquid contents by spasmodic contraction of its walls when the mature fruit is detached from its stem. It furnishes one of the strongest purgatives known and causes acute griping. Whether Elisha's remedy was miraculous or merely anti-cathartic, it was succeeded by a spiritual demonstration of the same nature as the better known example of Jesus' feeding of the multitude with a few loaves and fishes; Elisha's mental control of material supply is related in the last three verses of the chapter.

In 1 *Kings* (6/18, 7/24) we read that the inside of Solomon's temple was carved with knops and open flowers. The Revised Version gives a marginal alternative reference to gourds, in place of knops, and the Hebrew word here used somewhat resembles the term for wild gourds. The concordance offers gourds and cucumbers as the meaning. This old Anglo-Saxon word knop also occurs frequently in the 25th and 37th chapters of *Exodus,* where it translates a different Hebrew word than the temple knops; here knops are ornaments on the golden candlesticks.

Whatever variety were the melons, cucumbers and gourds of the Old Testament, we know that species similar to our domestic ones grew plentifully in Egypt, and presumably in Palestine. That they were a valuable and extensively cultivated crop is implicit in *Isaiah* (1/8), "left as a cottage in a vineyard, as a lodge in a garden of cucumbers." They rated a watchtower, with a resident guardian in the growing season to tend the vines and protect them against predatory man and beast.

Besides cultivated vegetables, the Bible mentions, usually in rather obscure fashion, certain wild plants and roots which were used as food by the poor, in time of famine, or by travellers forced to live on the countryside. The story of the prodigal son is one of the best known of Jesus' parables and the simile is often met in contemporary literature. *Luke* (15/16) tells us "and he would fain have filled his belly with the husks that the swine did eat." The Greek word rendered husks literally signifies "little horns," and for once there is agreement among naturalists that the pods of the carob tree constituted this particular hog feed which tempted the famished spendthrift. The carob, or locust tree *(Ceratonia siliqua),* is common in Palestine and other countries of the eastern Mediterranean. The pods are slightly curved (hence the "little horn" significance), about three inches long and hard to the touch. If the ripe pod is shaken, the seed may be heard rattling inside. The pods are edible, having a rather insipid, sweet taste, and are eaten by the poor as well as fed to swine and cattle. In Sicily wine and syrup are derived from them. The carob is also known as "St. John's Bread," but this name appears to have been applied erroneously, the locust tree having been associated

[105]

with the locusts which the Baptist ate sweetened with wild honey (*Matthew* 3/4). John's locusts were grasshoppers, an Eastern delicacy.

In the 30th chapter of *Job*, the old aristocratic cattle baron bitterly flays the proletariat of the time, and in the process we learn something of the foods eaten by the lowest classes. "But now they that are younger (lit: of fewer dogs) than I have me in derision, whose fathers I would have disdained to have set with the dogs of my flock.... for want and famine they were solitary.... who cut up mallows by the bushes, and juniper roots for their meat." In the Revised Version "salt-wort" replaces "mallows," and "broom" supplants "juniper."

Mallows or salt-wort may have been sea purslane, *Atriplex halimus,* a thornless sort of bramble growing near the sea, thriving on salty soil. The young leaves of this plant, resembling lettuce in texture and olive in shape, were gathered and eaten by the poor. The mallow was usually found, along with other plants, in hedges. The roots of the broom are bitter, and as far as we can judge would be eaten from dire necessity rather than choice.

No doubt many other wild plants furnished food to the poor of the Bible lands, as they do to-day, but the Scriptures give us no further information. Desire appears under as many guises in the original language as it does in human experience, but the Revised Version transmutes one into an edible plant. *Ecclesiastes* (12/5), warning that old age never comes alone, observes "desire shall fail." Later translators, including the Revising Committee and the experts of the concordance, suggest "the caper-berry shall fail." This allusion is even more obscure than that of the flourishing of the almond tree in the same passage. The caper is a rock-loving trailing shrub whose berries are unimportant in modern times, but whose unopened flower buds are preserved in vinegar and used for culinary purposes.

CHAPTER 11

Field Crops

IN THE Authorized Version of the Bible the word "corn" is used as a generic term for various types of cereal grain, and the American reader is apt to mentally transfer one of the main features of the Midwest agricultural scene to the fields of Canaan and Egypt. American corn is, of course, native to this continent and was unknown to the pre-Columbus Old World. The word "corn" comes from the Anglo-Saxon, and originally meant any small hard particle, not only a seed but also a grain of sand, salt, etc. "Kernel" comes from the same root. Gradually the meaning narrowed to cereal seeds such as wheat, oats, barley, and rye, although even yet the wider meaning is preserved in words such as peppercorn. In his poem *John Barleycorn,* Burns symbolizes malt spirits with this prototype. The significance of corn became even more specialized with the passage of time, and it was applied to the principal cereal crops of a country. Thus, the Englishman designates his main cereal crop of wheat as corn, while over the border in Scotland the prevalent oats and barley are so called. In the United States the early settlers applied the word to the staple crop of the native Indians, with the prefix Indian, which latterly fell into disuse. The term "Indian corn" still persists in Britain, along with the alternative "maize."

To the men who translated the King James Version of the Bible in the early years of the 17th century, corn meant grain, both collectively and individually. The latter is evident in *John* (12/24): "Except a corn of wheat fall into the ground and die." In the Revised Version of this passage, grain is substituted for corn. The Authorized and Revised Versions render *Mark* (4/28) almost identically, "first the blade, then the ear, after that the full corn in the ear." The Moffat version differs: "the blade first, the ear of corn next, and then the grain full in the ear."

Corn provided an easy generalization for the Bible translators, but in the original tongue there is no such unanimity. The Old Testament gives seven distinct words which in the English translation are sometimes called corn but are in other passages varied into mixed produce, wheat, barn, threshing-floor, field, stalk, victuals, grown-up and son, to mention but a few of these alternates. The New Testament Greek words appear as corn in some texts, with variants elsewhere. When we investigate classified varieties such as ground corn, parched corn, beaten corn, standing corn, old corn, ears of corn and so on, we run into a very involved etymology, which we will not investigate further, except to mention that the word *shibboleth,* which in English denotes a password, in Hebrew meant "ears of corn," or "stream."

Long before the Children of Israel marched into Canaan, that ancient land was famous for its corn. When the dying Isaac gave his blessing to the unscrupulous Jacob, he said "God give thee . . . plenty of corn and wine" (*Genesis* 27/28). Similarly did Moses, warned his end was near, bless his followers, "Israel shall dwell in safety alone: the fountain of Jacob shall be upon a land of corn and wine" (*Deuteronomy* 33/28). Moses' successor Joshua led the Hebrews across the Jordan and into the Promised Land, "and they did eat of the old corn of the land; . . . neither had the children of Israel manna any more; but they did eat of the fruit of the land of Canaan that year" (*Joshua* 5/11-12). The word "fruit" here should not be taken literally, as it implies, and is so used elsewhere as, increase, gain, and revenue.

Palestine under Hebrew rule continued to be a grain-producing country. Solomon sent Hiram king of Tyre two hundred thousand bushels of wheat and a like amount of barley annually (2 *Chronicles* 2/10). King Uzziah was a great husbandman, but his successor Jotham must have neglected the corn fields, for among the reparations he exacted from the defeated Transjordan tribe of Ammonites were one hundred thousand bushels of wheat and barley respectively, payable annually for three years (2 *Chronicles* 27/5).

The twenty-seventh chapter of *Ezekiel* is the trade index and commercial record of the great Phoenician city of Tyre, and here amongst the luxurious treasures and everyday necessities bartered in the bazaars, we find evidence of the wheat belt of Palestine. "Judah, and the land of Israel, they were thy merchants: they traded in thy market wheat of Minnith, and Pannag, and honey and oil, and balm." Minnith, meaning "distribution," was a town about twenty-five miles east of Jericho. Pannag remains unidentified, the weight of opinion considering it to have been a spice. The village of Pannag lay on the road from Damascus to Baalbeck.

Amos was not only a prophet of God; he was an ardent economic reformer, disgusted with merchants' greed and sharp practices. In his condemnation of these mercenary customs we find further evidence of the importance of grain in Palestine trade, and a voice from the past echoes in modern times. "Hear this, O ye that swallow up the needy, even to make the poor of the land to fail, saying, When will the new moon be gone, that we may sell corn, and the sabbath, that we may set forth wheat, making the ephah small, and the shekel great, and falsifying the balances by deceit? That we may buy the poor for silver, and the needy for a pair of shoes; yea, and sell the refuse of the wheat?" (*Amos* 8/4).

Jacob's statement of fact, "There is corn in Egypt," has developed into a proverb in its passage down the centuries; the story of his son Joseph is in essence the story of Egypt's corn. As Jacob grew in years the hard life of a nomad lost some of its appeal, and we see him settling on a bit of land, and, by inference, growing a little grain. *Genesis* (33/18-19) tells us "Jacob came to Shalem, a city of Shechem, which is in the land of Canaan . . . and he bought a parcel of a field, where he had spread his tent, . . . for an hundred pieces of money" (Heb.: lambs). Family feuding with neighbors made his departure advisable, but in the first verse of the 37th chapter we find him still dwelling in Canaan. Besides raising cattle he evidently grew corn, for a few verses later in the chapter his somewhat precocious and tattle-tale son Joseph dreamt that the family was harvesting grain. Years later, Joseph stepped overnight from rags to riches, because Pharaoh was impressed with his captive's interpretation of the ruler's dream of corn and cattle.

The belief in cyclic progression affecting the lives and interests of man is older than the pyramids. Modern science has an institute devoted to this research. There is general agreement that meteorological records indicate cyclic recurrences of abnormal and subnormal temperature, precipitation, and other atmospheric phenomena. Trappers and fishermen plan expansion and contraction of their activities in accordance with expectations of these fluctuations, and gardeners are familiar with the recurring periodic increase and gradual disappearance of the tent caterpillar in a predictable cycle.

[109]

Famine may be the end result of man's inhumanity to man following upon the destruction of war, a scorched earth policy, or siege. When
nature reduces her edible yield it is usually a consequence of severe
drought, or, more seldom, excessive and unseasonable rain. Frost too,
takes its toll, but it is precipitation which normally determines the
abundance or scantiness of the customary cereal crops, the staff of life
of man and animal. In the Bible lands hordes of locusts and grasshoppers created as much destruction of grain fields as the most abnormal
weather. Locust swarms have a seventeen year cycle.

The pleasant land of Canaan suffered from periodic famine, and
the three great fathers of the Jewish race had first-hand experience of
hard times during their sojourn there. Abram went to Egypt, where
the crops were still good, and Isaac in his turn forsook the barren fields
of Palestine and headed south, but was advised by God to go no further
than the neighboring territory of the Philistines. These two famines
were localized, perhaps caused by insufficient rain. Egyptian famine,
while having its predisposing cause in reduced rain or snowfall on the
mountain watersheds feeding the Upper Nile, had its observable results
because the annual Nile inundations failed, and this disaster was often
accompanied by hot dry winds from the deserts of the south and east.
In Pharaoh's dream the seven lean ears of corn were "withered, thin,
and blasted with the east wind" (*Genesis* 41/23). The great famine of
Jacob's era was widespread: "The famine was over all the face of the
earth: . . . and the famine waxed sore in the land of Egypt. And all
countries came into Egypt to Joseph to buy corn; because that the famine was so sore in all lands" (41/56-57).

It is a common human failing to take good things for granted, but
to complain bitterly and clutter up the pages of history with the croak-
ings of hard times and shortages. Thus, the account of the seven abundant years of Egypt is confined to three verses (41/47-49). "And in the
seven plenteous years, the earth brought forth by handfuls. And he
gathered up all the food of the seven years, which were in the land of
Egypt, and laid up the food in the cities: the food of the field, which
was round about every city, laid he up in the same. And Joseph gathered corn as the sand of the sea, very much, until he left numbering;
for it was without number." The tale of the seven years of famine is
expanded into half a dozen chapters, with the human interest background playing up the ever popular theme, "local boy makes good."

Grains of Egyptian wheat have been recovered from excavations and mummy cases, but there is no evidence to support the yarns that these ancient seeds have been germinated in modern times. One variety of wheat grown in Egypt, *Triticum compositum,* had several ears growing on one stalk, and appears to have been the species of Pharaoh's dream.

The cereal grains of the Bible include barley, wheat, rye, millet, spelt, fitches and pulse. Oats are not mentioned. The Hebrew word for "barley" also signifies "long hair," or "bristling," while the Greek one implies "pointed" or "piercing," the association depicting the bearded ears of the plant. Barley was an important crop in Palestine, ranking next to wheat in volume, but having lower market value, and it was used as animal feed as well as for making bread. This subordination to wheat in public regard is implicit in the distinction between the meat offering (*Leviticus* 2/1) which employed fine (wheat) flour, and the offering for a woman suspected of adultery (*Numbers* 5/15) which specified barley meal. A corresponding connection with the latter may be read in *Hosea* (3/1-2). In 2 *Kings* (7/1), barley is quoted at half the price of wheat flour, while by the time of John (*Revelation* 6/6) it had depreciated to one-third the relative value.

There are a number of references to barley bread in the Old Testament, but the best known occurs in the Gospels, where (*John* 6/9-13) five loaves of barley bread and two small fishes were transformed into abundant food for the multitude. Barley, with its hardy characteristics, was extensively grown in the more elevated regions of Palestine, and was the poor man's staff of life more than the rich man's sceptre of sustenance. Solomon fed it to his horses and dromedaries, and this chore was no light task, for the potentate had forty thousand stalls of horses for his chariots (1 *Kings* 4/26-28).

Barley was harvested from March to May, depending on the climate and the location of the farm. It invariably preceded wheat harvest, sometimes one merged into the other while on other occasions they were a month apart. As a consequence to the Egyptian plague of hail (*Exodus* 9/31-32), "The flax and the barley was smitten; for the barley was in the ear, and the flax was bolled. But the wheat and the rie were not smitten for they were not grown up."

In this account of hail damage, rie, or rye, is first mentioned, and the word occurs for a second and last time in the informative agricultural section with which the 28th chapter of *Isaiah* concludes, where rie is given a marginal alternative, spelt. The Revised Version deletes rie and substitutes spelt in both these passages. In some editions of the Authorized Version the word fitches in *Ezekiel* (4/9) has a marginal equivalent rie, in other editions spelt is used, while the Revised Version gives spelt in the main text with no side note. Whichever we choose to call this grain, fitches or spelt or rie, it retained the same name, *kussemeth*, in Hebrew. The word fitches in *Isaiah* (28/25, 27) is a doubtful translation of a quite different original word meaning black cummin. Fitches is a corruption of the word vetches, and is a member of that family. Informed opinion leans to the view that spelt is a more accurate definition than rye. *Triticum spelta* or spelt is a variety of wheat, an important crop of Central Europe, and is sometimes known as German wheat. It has a smooth bald ear.

Wheat was the principal cereal grain of Palestine both in volume and in value, and in the good old times prior to population density and progressive urbanization it was an important export crop. By Roman times it had become an import. It may be assumed in many instances that the word corn refers specifically to wheat, although definite proof is lacking. Its first mention is in *Genesis* (30/14): "Reuben went in the days of wheat harvest, and found mandrakes." The scene is believed to have lain in upper Mesopotamia, although some commentators suggest Syria. Wheat was of course one of the staple Egyptian crops and varieties grown in Bible times are still harvested. In the 15th chapter of *Judges* is a lusty tale, culminating in the destruction of the wheat harvest of Samson's *bête noire*, the Philistines. On returning to visit his attractive Philistine wife, Samson discovered that the man whom he had considered a friend had supplanted him, so, embittered at the duplicity of the Philistines whom he had entertained, he "caught three hundred foxes, and took firebrands, and turned tail to tail, and put a firebrand in the midst between two tails. And when he had set the brands on fire, he let them go into the standing corn of the Philistines, and burnt up both the shocks, and also the standing corn, with the vineyards and olives." The opening verse of the chapter reports that this happened at the time of wheat harvest, so the shocks were probably barley, the standing corn wheat.

There are many other references to the time of wheat harvest, one of which clearly casts Jehovah in the role of Lord of the Harvest, a title which the prophets of Baal claimed for their god, and correspondences to which may be found in the attributes of divinities of all ancient religions and mythologies. "Now therefore stand and see this great thing, which the Lord will do before your eyes. Is it not wheat harvest to day? I will call unto the Lord, and he shall send thunder and rain; that ye may perceive and see that your wickedness is great . . . so Samuel called unto the Lord; and the Lord sent thunder and rain that day: and all the people greatly feared the Lord and Samuel" (1 *Samuel* 12/16-17).

Evidence of a sea-borne trade in wheat may be found in the 27th chapter of *Acts,* which tells of Paul's voyage to Rome, in the course of which a ship carrying the apostle became wrecked. The vessel was registered in the Egyptian port of Alexandria, but it was at Myra (on the south coast of what is now Turkey) that Paul boarded the doomed craft. When four anchors barely held the ship off the lee shore, the seamen "lightened the ship, and cast out the wheat into the sea" (27/38).

The literature of the Old Testament uses wheat to typify the very best food, God's rich recompense to the righteous. Moses' Song, in the 32nd chapter of *Deuteronomy,* speaks of "fat of kidneys of wheat." *Psalms* (147/14) proclaims, "He (the Lord) maketh peace in thy borders, and filleth thee with the finest of the wheat," and a similar promise concludes the 81st *Psalm.* Failure of the wheat crop or the appearance of thorns and weeds in place of grain is used several times to symbolize the punishment of evil.

In his agricultural parables Jesus uses no other grain than wheat. Corn, when it is mentioned, is employed in the singular, denoting an individual kernel. Benevolent wheat is contrasted with harmful tares, and the comparison transferred to the righteous versus the wicked. John the Baptist uses wheat and chaff in a corresponding sense. In the 15th chapter of 1 *Corinthians,* Paul builds one of the clearest and most powerful analogies ever employed to help mankind understand the mystery of death and resurrection, on the phenomena of grain germination. "But some man will say, How are the dead raised up? and with what body do they come? Thou fool, that which thou sowest is not quickened, except it die: and that which thou sowest, thou sowest not that body that shall be, but bare grain, it may chance of wheat, or of some other grain: but God giveth it a body as it hath pleased him,

[113]

and to every seed his own body . . . It is sown in corruption; it is raised in incorruption . . . it is sown in weakness; it is raised in power . . . O death, where is thy sting?" Wheat ends its biblical span in *Revelation* (18/13) where it is listed, along with fine flour, amongst the doomed treasures of Babylon.

Millet appears only once, in the famine bread recipe of *Ezekiel* (4/9). The Hebrew word is derived from an Arabic root signifying "smoky," and the ripe grains are a dark smoke color. The growing plant is used for animal fodder, and the mature grains for bread making and pottage, but the result is unpalatable to foreigners. Millet is a prolific producer, the stalks resembling those of wheat or rye.

Mention of pulse is confined to two verses in *Daniel* (1/12, 16), and from the context it was obviously the most austere of fare. Marginal alternatives in the Authorized and Revised Versions offer vegetables and herbs respectively. The word may mean "leguminous plants," such as peas and beans.

In 2 *Samuel* (17/28) we find parched corn and parched pulse. It will be observed that corn and pulse are in italics, which indicates that the word is not given in the original manuscript, but that the context indicates an implied, but omitted, word. Conflicting syntax, grammar and idiom render literal translation from almost any language into another impracticable at times, and the sense of the context sometimes suggests interpolation. In English the adjective is used occasionally as a noun, as in rye for rye whiskey, Valencias for Valencia oranges, and Java or Mocha for coffee. Thousands of italicized words augment the English versions of the Bible.

Sharing importance with the growing of grain was the raising of flax, and its subsequent manufacture into cloth. We associate flax with linen, and so did the people of old. Linen flax has been found in the ancient Lake dwellings of Switzerland, and royal mummies from the land of Pharaoh still retain their linen winding sheets; in some instances, the mortal remains of Egyptian children have been found wrapped and preserved in cotton.

In the count of natural wealth and agricultural fertility of the Promised Land which Moses and Aaron dangled before the sceptical and recalcitrant Israelites like a carrot before a donkey, the flax of Canaan was not mentioned, although the original Egyptian garments of the expedition must have been pretty threadbare, and desert nights get bitterly cold. That Canaan flax antedated the arrival of the tribes of Israel is evident in the second chapter of *Joshua*. Here, too, we observe the repetition of ancient history in modern times. There is espionage and counter-espionage, with a courtezan turned traitor, perhaps in revenge for her social ostracism, perhaps only in reluctant collaboration to save the lives of her beloved family. From her clients' tales and the first-hand reports of travellers who visited her boudoir, Rahab assessed better than most of the citizens of Jericho the strength of the approaching Hebrew invasion. With feminine intuition she discerned the nationality of the spies, and as competent intelligence agents have to be versatile and accomplished, the young harlot probably took a liking to her inquisitive guests. When the local Gestapo learnt of the strangers' undue interest in Jericho's defenses, they came to arrest them. Rahab made her choice. "And the woman took the two men, and hid them, and said thus, There came men unto me, but I wist not whence they were: and it came to pass about the time of shutting of the gate, when it was dark, that the men went out: whither the men went I wot not: pursue after them quickly; for ye shall overtake them. But she had brought them up to the roof of the house, and hid them with the stalks of flax, which she had laid in order upon the roof. . . . Then she let them down by a cord through the window: for her house was upon the town wall, and she dwelt upon the wall."

Four chapters later we read how the massive walls of Jericho fell down flat at the coordinated mass shout of the Israelites, but evidently the foundations beneath Rahab's residence remained intact, for at Joshua's orders the spies entered her house and conducted to safety the entire family of this early fifth columnist. The flax stalks under which the spies hid were undergoing their first process of drying. This was followed by peeling of the stems, retting and separation of the fibres, and the hackling of the fine from the coarse threads.

King Solomon lauds the virtuous wife, "She seeketh wool, and flax, and worketh willingly with her hands. . . . she layeth her hands to the spindle, and her hands hold the distaff . . . she maketh herself coverings of tapestry . . . she maketh fine linen, and selleth it; and delivereth girdles unto the merchant" (*Proverbs* 31/13, 19, 22, 24). If the much married monarch applied these precepts to the management of his thousand-girl harem, the output must have made a sizeable contribution to the linen and garment trades.

[115]

Isaiah (19/9) speaks of "they that work in fine flax, and they that weave networks." A marginal note calls "networks" "white works," while the Revised Version substitutes combed flax, white cloth, and cotton respectively.

There are scores of references to linen in the Bible, listed under several unrelated Hebrew and Greek words, but most lie outside the scope of this book. The few examples following indicate the antiquity and importance of linen, and by implication the extent and value of flax cultivation.

Linen is first mentioned in *Genesis* (41/42), where Pharaoh arrayed Joseph "in vestures of fine linen." Marginal alternatives give silk in the Authorized, and cotton in the Revised Versions. Evidently the booty which the Israelites took from Egypt included a good supply of high grade linen, for shortly after the Exodus we read (*Exodus* 39/ 27-29): "And they made coats of fine linen of woven work for Aaron, and for his sons. And a mitre of fine linen, and goodly bonnets of fine linen, and linen breeches of fine twined linen, and a girdle of fine twined linen, and blue, and purple, and scarlet, of needlework." In the time of Solomon, Egyptian linen evidently was considered superior to the local variety, and in parallel passages (1 *Kings* 10/28; 2 *Chronicles* 1/16) we find state monopoly and price fixing. "And Solomon had horses brought out of Egypt, and linen yarn: the king's merchants received the linen yarn at a price." A follow-up of this import-restricted linen yarn may be found in the Revised Version of *Proverbs* (7/16) where the courtezan tempts the callow youth: "I have spread my couch with carpets of tapestry, with striped cloths of the yarn of Egypt." The Authorized Version renders the latter phrase "fine linen of Egypt." In a remarkable feminine fashion review towards the end of the third chapter of *Isaiah*, fine linen takes the expensive role of our modern silk and satin (or should it be nylon?). Rich owners of private yachts and galleys on the Phoenician coast were marine customers: "Fine linen with broidered work from Egypt was that which thou spreadest forth to be thy sail" (*Ezekiel* 27/7).

In the New Testament all four Gospels recount that the body of the crucified Lord was wrapped in linen. That linen was valuable and expensive is indicated in *Luke* (16/19-20): "There was a certain rich man, which was clothed in purple and fine linen, and fared sumptuously every day: and there was a certain beggar named Lazarus . . ."

[116]

In *Revelation,* (19/8) linen is accorded its supreme tribute. To the mystical bride, the Lamb's wife, "was granted that she should be arrayed in fine linen, clean and white; for the fine linen is the righteousness of saints." This sacred garb receives confirmation in *Revelation* (15/6): "angels . . . clothed in pure and white linen."

Rather obscure parallel passages occur in *Isaiah* (42/3) and *Matthew* (12/20). "A bruised reed shall he not break, and the smoking flax shall he not quench." Marginal substitution renders ". . . and the dimly burning flax shall he not quench it." We turn to *Isaiah* (43/17) for a clue: ". . . they are quenched as tow." Tow here translates the same Hebrew word given in the previous chapter as flax. Research reveals that this Hebrew word also meant the wick of a lamp, and the Revised Version gives this marginal alternative. The word "wick" does not occur in the Bible text except in this note.

CHAPTER 12

"While the Earth Remaineth"

THE FARMER'S YEAR

IN THE last verse of the eighth chapter of *Genesis,* God promises that "While the earth remaineth, seedtime and harvest, and cold and heat, and summer and winter....shall not cease." As we read this verse, we usually consider it a series of opposites or counter-balances, rather than an enumeration of the agricultural seasons of Palestine, but the latter meaning is equally correct.

Ancient Egypt divided the year into three seasons, the inundation, the growth, and the harvest. Israel, experiencing entirely different climatic rhythm, recognized six seasons. Seedtime was the period from early October until early December. The first rains preceded it, softening the hard baked earth. Sunny skies gradually became interspersed with clouds and overcast, and nights grew chillier. The deciduous trees shed their leaves in November, and the snowline on Mt. Hermon crept lower. The second week of December ushered in winter, and the highlanders banked their fires: "Now the king sat in the winterhouse in the ninth month (December-January) and there was a fire on the hearth burning before him" (*Jeremiah* 36/22).

Snow covered the higher reaches, but was a fleeting wonder on the low plains. Brooks and gullies filled up, and water was no longer rationed and hoarded. Roads became virtually impassable: "Pray ye that your flight be not in the winter" (*Mark* 13/18).

Thunder storms and hail squalls stampeded the cattle. February saw winter change into the so-called cold season. Green began to return to the fields and to the bare trees. Nights and early mornings were still cold, but noonday sun warmed the earth and man. The almond tree burst into bloom in February, in favored locations still earlier, and soon other fruit trees decked themselves in color. Rain tapered off but thunder storms increased. As March merged into April came the copious and tepid latter rains, collected and stored by those whose wells ran dry in summer. Barley was ripening fast and wheat was heading.

The April days which the North American gardener devotes to spading and seeding his plot, the Palestine countryman spent sharpening his sickle and grinding his scythe for grain harvest. No wonder the peasant of the Holy Land rejoiced as he offered up his virgin sheaf of ripe barley under the full moon of April, and sang with Solomon, "For lo, the winter is past, the rain is over and gone . . . Arise, my love, my fair one, and come away . . . for sweet is thy voice, and thy countenance is comely." Spring in Palestine not only brought sunshine and flowers, as it does elsewhere, but it also brought a harvest of nature's bounty. The official harvest season lasted fifty days, from the Passover in April to the Feast of Ingathering, or Pentecost, in June. In practice, these limits were approximate only. When crops were good, it was a busy, high-spirited time. "They joy before thee according to the joy in harvest, and as men rejoice when they divide the spoil" (*Isaiah* 9/3).

Harvest was succeeded by the season of heat, lasting until August. A few late wheat crops, planted in January, were reaped in July, and about this time the early vintage grapes were gathered and pressed. Keeping plants watered, and himself cool, took up much of the husbandman's time. As the heat increased, sleeping on rooftops became the style. The soil became impacted and parched as the last vestiges of subsoil moisture evaporated; whirling dust eddies stifled the nostrils of man and beast. *Job* (38/38) describes it as the time "when the dust groweth into hardness, and the clods cleave fast together."

Summer, from August to October, was fruit time. Late September nights offered a welcome coolness and a rare shower of rain to break nearly half-a-year's drought, but the little rain that fell vanished into the arid ground. Heavy dews had more superficial effect and a carpet of green bravely struggled forth. As the last grapes were being gathered in October, and thanksgiving was being offered in the Feast of Tabernacles, the first plowmen were breaking up the soil for seeding. The fecundity of Palestine was stressed by Jehovah (*Leviticus* 26/5): "And your threshing shall reach unto the vintage, and the vintage shall reach unto the sowing time." In similar vein *Amos* (9/13) predicted the return of good times: "Behold, the days come, saith the Lord, that the plowman shall overtake the reaper, and the treader of grapes him that soweth seed."

Cultivation of the soil was a primitive process. We read of plowing and harrowing, but scraping and scratching would be more accurate terms. Farm implements usually were wooden, light and inefficient. The moldboard plow is a comparatively recent invention, an invention unknown to or unused by myriads of good farmers who continue to till the soil with contraptions which the patriarchs would recognize.

On the banks of the Nile, seed often was sown without previous soil preparation, merely scattered onto the muddy delta silt as the river receded, and tramped in by the feet of cattle. Solomon's advice (*Ecclesiastes* 11/1), "Cast thy bread upon the waters: for thou shalt find it after many days," may refer to this practice, as may the passage from *Isaiah* (32/20), "Blessed are ye that sow beside all waters, that send forth thither the feet of the ox and the ass."

The first Bible reference to soil cultivation antedates Adam: "The Lord God made the earth and the heavens. . .and every plant of the field before it was in the earth, and every herb of the field before it grew: for the Lord God had not caused it to rain upon the earth, and there was not a man to till the ground. But there went up a mist from the earth, and watered the whole face of the ground" (*Genesis* 2/4-6). The unknown recorder of this second account of Creation was obviously garden-minded, for the inference is unmistakable that the main reason for the creation of man was to provide a means of keeping the soil in good tilth: "and the Lord God took the man, and put him into the garden of Eden to dress it and to keep it" (*Genesis* 2/15).

The English words "till" and "dress," used in the foregoing references, together with the later-appearing words "plow" and "ear," are variants of a single Hebrew word, which also appears under other English forms such as "work" and "labor." It is used in this latter sense in the 4th commandment, "Six days shalt thou labor." Evidently it had a generic meaning in Hebrew, similar to our verbs "to cultivate" or "to farm," used in their widest sense. The same word occurs in the expulsion sentence of Adam, "The Lord God sent him forth from the garden of Eden, to till the ground from whence he was taken" (*Genesis* 3/23). Cain was a tiller of the ground and part of his curse was, "When thou tillest the ground, it shall not henceforth yield unto thee her strength" (*Genesis* 4/12).

Nowhere is there any mention of the implements of tillage, nor of the techniques of cultivation in pre-deluge times, and the patriarchal era is equally blank. *Genesis* (26/12) tells us, "And Isaac sowed in that land, and received in the same year an hundredfold: and the Lord blessed him." By inference, this represented an unusually heavy return, and suggests an advanced knowledge of soil requirements. Although corroborative detail is missing, there is little reason to doubt that the patriarchs were versed in skilled agricultural practices. Abram spent the first seventy-five years of his life in Ur of the Chaldees, a Mesopotamian town.

Sumerian records, dating back to 3500 B. C., depict wooden plows, some oxen-drawn and some man-hauled. The Accadians superseded the Sumerians in this area, and their agricultural records, still preserved, advised plowing, raking, and manuring in the preparation of a seedbed. The tenth verse of the tenth chapter of *Genesis* tells of Babel and Accad, cities which gave their name to Babylonia and Accadia. Abram, brought up in this advanced civilization, must have been familiar with the requirements of good agriculture. Isaac's wife, Rebekah, came from the same Mesopotamian district, while Jacob spent twenty years with relatives there. Egyptian records, contemporary with the farming tablets of Accadia and early Babylonia, are blank insofar as agriculture is concerned. Perhaps the reason why Abram was welcomed in Egypt (*Genesis* 12/16) was because of his skilled plant lore, as well as for his pretty wife. Joseph, Jacob's favorite son, may have absorbed grain-growing techniques from his father, and put them to good use in Egypt when the opportunity presented itself.

Whatever agricultural implements the patriarchs used, they must have had good digging tools, for we have many accounts of wells being dug; the 26th chapter of *Genesis* tells of several, and any man who has plowed a field and dug a well will usually choose the former as the lighter task. A piece of circumstantial evidence suggesting early plowing is in *Genesis* (27/40): "Thou shalt break his yoke from off thy neck." Oxen were yoked, singly or in pairs, to the plough. We find the first plow in *Deuteronomy* (22/10): "Thou shalt not plow with an ox and an ass together." The second appearance, in *Judges* (14/18), is presented in a rather slangy expression of Samson's, "If ye had not ploughed with my heifer," the meaning being "If you had not brought pressure to bear on my wife."

One of the more important peace term restrictions imposed on Germany and Japan by the victorious Allies, was the reduction of steel-making to a fraction of its former output in the vanquished nations.

[121]

No steel works, no war potential, was the convincing logic. More than three thousand years ago the Philistines drew the fighting teeth of Israel in similar fashion, and from the account in 1 *Samuel* (13/19-22) we learn indirectly of many of the agricultural implements of the Hebrews. "Now there was no smith found throughout all the land of Israel; for the Philistines said, Lest the Hebrews make them swords or spears: but all the Israelites went down to the Philistines, to sharpen every man his share, and his coulter, and his ax, and his mattock. Yet they had a file for the mattocks, and for the coulters, and for the forks, and for the axes, and to sharpen the goads. So it came to pass in the day of battle, that there was neither sword nor spear found in the hand of any of the people." The file reference is doubtful, and some translators consider that that sentence should read "when the edges of the mattocks. . .and of the axes were blunt." The Revised Version has this marginal alternative.

As we so often find, the translation from the Hebrew is loose. The English words "coulter," "share," "fork," and the doubtful "file," occur only in this passage. The original word for coulter is rendered plowshare in three texts, *Isaiah* (2/4), *Joel* (3/10) and *Micah* (4/3), which report the beating of swords into ploughshares and vice versa. These reconversion measures, usually regarded more as a figure of speech than as a statement of fact, rather confirm the enforced scarcity of iron and iron-workers in Hebrew territory. Mattock and share are almost identical in the original language, and each word uses a common plural. The etymology of fork implies a three pronged instrument.

Mattock occurs in two other passages besides 1 *Samuel,* each of the three native words being different. The mattock of the last verse of the 7th chapter of *Isaiah* is unmistakably a digging tool: "And on all hills that shall be digged with the mattock, there shall not come thither the fear of briers and thorns." The remaining mattock is a very dubious translation; it is used in connection with the destruction of idols by King Josiah (2 *Chronicles* 34/6). The Authorized Version gives a marginal alternative "mauls," while the Revised Version uses "ruins" in the text, with a marginal "axes." In other texts the Authorized Version, with fine impartiality, labels Josiah's mattock ax, dagger, knife, sword and tool. Its use in the last sense evidently denotes a mason's chisel, or hammer, or both: "If thou wilt make me an altar of stone, thou shalt not build it of hewn stone: for if thou lift up thy tool upon it, thou hast polluted it" (*Exodus* 20/25).

There is no doubt but that the early Hebrews were well versed in the smelting and forging of iron and other ores, and that their agricultural tools were metal shod where wear was greatest. Some authorities consider that Cain, Eve's firstborn, was so-named as the Hebrew equivalent of smith; his lineal descendent, Tubal-cain, was "an instructor of every artificer in brass and iron" (*Genesis* 4/22). The mineral wealth of Canaan was depicted by Jehovah (*Deuteronomy* 8/9): "A land whose stones are iron, and out of whose hills thou mayest dig brass." Iron deposits were mined in northern Palestine, south-east of the Dead Sea in Edom, and in the land of the Hittites. Damascus still retains the reputation for fine swords which it has held for thousands of years.

Isaiah (44/12) tells of the forging of metal images: "The smith with the tongs both worketh in the coals, and fashioneth it with hammers, and worketh it with the strength of his arms," and elaborates further (54/16), "I have created the smith that bloweth the coals in the fire, and that bringeth forth an instrument for his work." When the Jews were taken captive to Babylon by Nebuchadnezzar, among the prisoners were "craftsmen and smiths, a thousand" (2 *Kings* 24/16). 1 *Chronicles* (4/14) speaks of the inhabitants of "the valley of Charashim; for they were craftsmen." Charash is the Hebrew word for various types of skilled workers, including smiths, artificers, such as wrought, engravers, etc., and it is also associated with plows and plowing. Nowadays we use the maker's name as the descriptive noun for many manufactured articles, including farm tractors, and the ancient Hebrews may have done the same.

The harrow is another farm implement we read of in Scripture, where in the original tongue it appears in two different forms. The first occurs in parallel passages in 2 *Samuel* (12/31) and 1 *Chronicles* (20/3), and tells how David put the children of Ammon to death "under saws, and under harrows of iron, and under axes of iron." More interesting to the farmer is the harrow of *Job* (39/9-12). If instead of the fabulous unicorn of the Authorized Version we substitute the more prosaic wild-ox of the Revised translation, the passage gains in meaning. "Will the unicorn be willing to serve thee, or abide by thy crib? Canst thou bind the unicorn with his band in the furrow? or will he harrow the valleys after thee? Wilt thou trust him, because his strength

[123]

is great? or wilt thou leave thy labor to him? Wilt thou believe him, that he will bring home thy seed, and gather it unto thy barn?" The expression "Will he harrow the valleys after thee?" indicates that the ox dragging the harrow was led by the farmer; the particular Hebrew word designating valleys in this text, was the one usually applied to fertile bottomlands.

The word translated "harrow" in this last text, is rendered "breaking up clods" in two other places, both of which are rich in agricultural meaning. *Hosea* (10/10-12) relates: "The people shall be gathered against them, when they shall bind themselves in their two furrows. And Ephraim is as an heifer that is taught, and loveth to tread out the corn; but I passed over upon her fair neck; I will make Ephraim to ride; Judah shall plow, and Jacob shall break his clods. Sow to yourselves in righteousness, reap in mercy; break up your fallow ground."

If we analyze these verses, the opening sentence suggests the use of a two-furrow plow, and the (unquoted) context signifies that danger will threaten when Israel is fully occupied, with its hands full, and so, handicapped in defending itself. It should be noted that both Authorized and Revised Versions regard the translation as doubtful. The Ephraim references will be discussed later in the chapter. The Judah-Jacob text is self-explanatory, whether we use "break his clods" or "harrow." In the final sentence the same Hebrew word is repeated in "break up" and in "fallow ground." We use a corresponding idiom in English when we say "farm your farm," "plant your plant,' the verb doubling as a noun. This usage also occurs in the original text of *Jeremiah* (4/3): "Break up your fallow ground, and sow not among thorns."

The concluding verses of the 28th chapter of *Isaiah* present the Bible passages richest in agricultural information. Here again the Hebrew term for "break the clods" is the same as designates the "harrow" of Job. "Give ye ear, and hear my voice; hearken, and hear my speech. Doth the plowman plow all day to sow? doth he open and break the clods of his ground? When he hath made plain the face thereof, doth he not cast abroad the fitches, and scatter the cummin, and cast in the principal wheat and the appointed barley and the rie in their place? For his God doth instruct him to discretion, and doth teach him. For the fitches are not threshed with a threshing instrument, neither is a cart wheel turned about upon the cummin; but the fitches are beaten out with a staff, and the cummin with a rod. Bread corn is bruised; because he will not ever be threshing it, nor break it with the wheel of his cart, nor bruise it with his horsemen. This also cometh forth from the Lord of Hosts, which is wonderful in counsel, and excellent in working."

The Revised Version rendering of this passage gives a clearer idea of Isaiah's meaning. For example "Doth the plowman plow continually to sow? Doth he continually open and break the clods of his ground? . . . and put in the wheat in rows, and the barley in the appointed place, and the spelt in the border thereof? . . . Bread corn is ground; for he will not ever be threshing it; and though the wheel of his cart and his horses scatter it, he doth not grind it." The etymology of the original suggests that the fitches (vetches: black cummin: *nigella sativa*) were broadcast in handfuls, while the cummin was lightly sprinkled with the fingertips.

Even when steel-shod, the ancient plow was a light and relatively inefficient implement. In friable soil it opened an adequate furrow but in hard stony soil or sod it bounced along the surface. The plowman had to bear heavily on the plow to keep the share at the desired depth, and this was a full time effort. Bearing this in mind, we recognize the import of Jesus' saying: "No man, having put his hand to the plough, and looking back, is fit for the kingdom of God" (*Luke* 9/62). *Jeremiah* (14/4) recognized the hopelessness of trying to plow sunbaked fields: "Because the ground is chapt, for there was no rain in the earth, the plowmen were ashamed, they covered their heads." David, on the other hand, praised God for the beneficent rains which softened the earth for plowing and sowing. Substituting the more poetical marginal alternatives for the main text, we read (*Psalms* 65/9-10): "Thou visitest the earth and waterest, after thou hadst made it to desire rain; thou greatly enrichest it with the river of God, which is full of water; thou preparest them corn, when thou hast so provided for it. Thou waterest the ridges thereof abundantly; thou causest rain to descend into the furrows thereof; thou makest it soft with showers." In *Psalms* (129/3) this joy of the farmer turns into a lament: "The plowers plowed upon my back: they made long their furrows." *Job* (31/38.40) avowing his record as a landowner, exclaims, "If my land cry against me, or that the furrows likewise thereof complain. . .let thistles grow instead of

[125]

wheat, and cockle instead of barley." *Hosea* (10/4), also weed-conscious, observes, "Judgment springeth up as hemlock in the furrows of the field."

Six different Hebrew words are translated furrow; sometimes ridge, or bed, or cutting is used for an English equivalent. The same original word rendered furrows in *Ezekiel* (17/7, 10): "This vine did bend her roots towards him . . . that he might water it by the furrows of her plantation . . . when the east wind toucheth it . . . it shall wither in the furrows where it grew," is changed to beds in *Song of Solomon* (5/13): "His cheeks are as a bed of spices," and (6/2), "My beloved is gone down into his garden, to the beds of spices." In less romantic mood, Solomon warns (*Proverbs* 20/4) the weather-shy farmer, "The sluggard will not plow by reason of the cold (margin: winter); therefore shall he beg in harvest, and have nothing." October-November were the plowing months in Palestine and the man who procrastinated ran into winter weather.

The status of plowmen appears to have deteriorated with urbanization and the development of commerce in the Holy Land. In 1 *Kings* (19/19) we find Elisha "plowing with twelve yoke of oxen before him, and he with the twelfth." We infer that the eleven other teams were handled by his servants, under his supervision. When Elijah summoned him, he burned his bridges behind him, or, more accurately, he burned his plow. "He . . . took a yoke of oxen, and slew them, and boiled their flesh with the instruments of the oxen, and gave unto the people, and they did eat. Then he arose, and went after Elijah." This gesture was not unique, for 2 *Samuel* (24/22) tells us, "Araunah said unto David . . . here be oxen for burnt sacrifice, and threshing instruments and other instruments of the oxen for wood." Evidently fuel was scarce, or plows were of little value and easily improvised; on the other hand it may have been a dramatic gesture, the owner deliberately sacrificing valuable farm implements in honor of the occasion.

Isaiah, whose writings reveal a great store of farm knowledge, evidently considered plowing to be menial work, for he says (61/5-6): "The sons of the alien shall be your plowmen and your vinedressers. But ye shall . . . . eat the riches of the Gentiles, and in their glory shall ye boast yourselves." In the times of Jesus, the plowman doubled as cook and houseboy after his field chores were ended, and got little thanks for it. "But which of you, having a servant plowing or feeding cattle, will say unto him by and by, when he is come from the field, Go and sit down to meat? And will not rather say unto him, Make ready wherewith I may sup, and gird thyself, and serve me, till I have eaten and drunken; and afterwards thou shalt eat and drink? Doth he thank that servant because he did the things that were commanded him? I trow not" (*Luke* 17/7-9).

The Hebrew word denoting such cultivating duties as tilling, earing and dressing is also used for servant, bondage and manual labor in general, thus seeming to indicate that such work was menial. In 2 *Kings* (10/19-23) this same word identifies both the servants and the worshippers of Baal, and inasmuch as Baal was a nature God and was adored in groves and in gardens, it is likely that these so-called servants and worshippers were actually gardeners and cultivators in the service of the temple grounds, rather than lay devotees.

With one exception, the various Hebrew words translated "dig" have little agricultural significance. They refer to the digging of wells, pits, graves, and through the earthen walls of houses. The exception is an interesting one, occurring twice in *Isaiah*. The unprofitable vineyard is cursed (5/6); "it shall not be pruned, nor digged; but there shall come up briers and thorns." The converse appears in (7/25): "And on all hills that shall be digged with the mattock, there shall not come thither the fear of briers and thorns." The Revised Version changes "digged" into "hoed" in the first quotation but follows the Authorized text in the latter passage. This word for digged is found once more in the original, in an entirely different sense. In 1 *Chronicles* (12/33) we read: "Of Zebulun, such as went forth to battle. expert in war, with all instruments of war, fifty thousand, which could keep rank." The concluding words, "keep rank," have the same Hebrew original as "digged" or "hoed" in *Isaiah*. This meaning of order and form and discipline suggests much more skilled horticultural attention than digging; a more suitable term might be cultivated, in its embracing sense of good husbandry practices. The eradication of briars and thorns is explicit, but more may be read into the text. In the New Testament we find the word dig used once in its gardening sense, where the vineyard keeper begs the owner to spare the barren fig tree for another year "till I shall dig about it, and dung it" (*Luke* 13/8).

Standard equipment for the Palestine farmer was a yoke of oxen. These strong plodding beasts dragged his plow and his harrow and hauled his creaking wheat-laden cart to the threshing floor, where, in a changed role, they helped thresh the golden sheaves. Several Hebrew words are translated yoke; one indicates the shaped wooden block which rested on the necks of the team; another signifies the bands or straps with which the yoke was attached to the plowbar or shafts; while a third denotes the curved bar or staff which rested on the shoulders. Yoke is also used as a synonym for harness, for team, and also for the amount of land a yoke of oxen could plow in a day. The yoke was heavy or light according to the tractability of the animal and the ideas of the farmer, and the word is used symbolically in many passages. "Take my yoke upon you, and learn of me . . . for my yoke is easy, and my burden is light" (*Matthew* 11/29-30). In the parable of the great supper, one guest asked to be excused saying, "I have bought five yoke of oxen, and I go to prove them" (*Luke* 14/19). The Israelites applied the yoke term to any team of work animals, but this is obscured in the English translation, which uses the word two in the following examples "two asses saddled" (*Judges* 19/10), and "two mules' burden" (2 *Kings* 5/17).

The goad of the Old Testament, one of the farm tools taken to Philistine blacksmiths to be sharpened, is featured as a death-dealing weapon in *Judges* (3/31): "Shamgar . . . slew of the Philistines six hundred men with an ox goad." Three different Hebrew words appear in English as goad. The same implement shows up in the New Testament, under another name: "Saul, Saul . . . it is hard for thee to kick against the pricks" (*Acts* 9/4-5). The goad was a dual-purpose contrivance, being a tapered rod eight feet or more in length, so balanced that the plowman guiding his plow could prod the laggard ox with the sharp tip. The handle of the goad terminated in a chisel-shaped piece of iron, used for cutting roots and clearing the plowshare of adhering earth and debris. A goad, steel shod at both ends, could be more dangerous than a spear in the hands of a man accustomed to its use.

When a suitable seedbed had been prepared, the seed was sown according to the passage from *Isaiah* (28/25) quoted in this chapter. There is little in the Bible to indicate that the seed was systematically covered with earth. After it had been broadcast the usual procedure was to drive cattle over the field, their hoofs pressing the seed into the ground and their droppings supplying a top dressing of manure. It is

[128]

this practice which *Isaiah* refers to: "Blessed are ye that sow . . . that send forth thither the feet of the ox and the ass" (32/20), and in another place (30/23-24): "Then shall he give the rain of thy seed, that thou shalt sow the ground withal . . . the oxen likewise and the young asses that ear the ground shall eat clean provender." The Hebrew word translated "ear" in this verse means "to serve" or "work," differing from the ear in 1 *Samuel* (8/12), where it is synonymous with plow.

Another *Isaiah* quotation, part of which has been already reviewed, confirms what to us is an unusual method of seeding (7/25): "On all hills that shall be digged with the mattock, there shall not come thither the fear of briers and thorns: but it shall be for the sending forth of oxen, and for the treading of lesser cattle." Superficially, this might indicate the cultivation of hillsides to eradicate thorns so that cattle could pasture without injury. Actually there was ample common land with natural vegetation, which cattle cropped, and there is scant evidence that fields were cultivated and sown to grass, so this last reference may be assumed to indicate the tramping in of seed by the feet of animals.

Jesus' famous parable of the sower, related in the first three Gospels, gives no hint that seed was covered with soil. This is the version in *Matthew* (13/3-8): "A sower went forth to sow; and when he sowed some seeds fell by the wayside, and the fowls came and devoured them up: some fell upon stony places, where they had not much earth; and forthwith they sprung up, because they had no deepness of earth: and when the sun was up, they were scorched; and because they had no root, they withered away. And some fell among thorns; and the thorns sprung up, and choked them: but others fell into good ground, and brought forth fruit, some an hundredfold, some sixtyfold, some thirtyfold." The phrase "into good ground" seems to imply penetration of the soil, but the Greek etymology indicates that "on" or "upon" is more accurate, and in the versions of *Mark* (4/8) and *Luke* (8/8) the phrase used is "on good ground." Yet, why should birds eat the seed which fell by the wayside, and pass up the seed on the fertile earth? On the other hand, nature raises a bumper crop of weeds and wild plants each year from seed which germinates on the surface of the soil.

In the Apocryphal *Book of Jubilees*, written in the 2nd century B. C. by a fundamentalist Pharisee, there is an interesting account of a seed-sowing device, which Abram gets credit for introducing. Corroboration of the antiquity of this invention is furnished by a Babylonian seal of the 14th century B. C., which depicts an oxen-drawn plow, the plowshare having a hollow tube attached, into which an attendant is feeding grain, the seed trickling into the furrow. "Abram taught those who made implements for oxen, the artificers in wood, and they made a vessel above the ground, facing the frame of the plow, in order to put the seed therein, and the seed fell down therefrom upon the share of the plow and was hidden in the earth, and they no longer feared the ravens." Abram probably introduced this improvement into Canaan when he arrived from Ur of the Chaldees. The Chaldees were Babylonians.

Bible farming jumps from seedtime to harvest with no mention of weeding, or cultivating, or mulching. Only Solomon suggested that good husbandmen kept weeds down (*Proverbs* 24/30-31). Sometimes late sown crops failed: "The seed is rotten under their clods" (*Joel* 1/17), due to unseasonable drought; "I have witholden the rain from you, when there were yet three months to the harvest" (*Amos* 4/7). In a passage in *Ecclesiastes* (11/6) the Preacher advises the farmer to diversify the time of sowing: "In the morning sow thy seed, and in the evening withhold not thine hand: for thou knowest not whether shall prosper, either this or that, or whether they both shall be alike good." This verse is open to more than one implication, the meaning of morning and evening being the disputed point. Some take the strictly literal sense, while others consider that the advice refers to sowing at the beginning and end of the grain-planting season, approximately November and January. The word "morning" also has the less specific meaning of "early," and is so translated elsewhere. Planting in the waxing and waning of the moon has also been suggested.

Seedtime was a season of hard work in deteriorating weather, and it evoked little enthusiasm. Harvest with its warm sunny days, its productive returns, and its joyous festivals was eagerly anticipated and welcomed. *Psalms* (126/5-6) tells us: "They that sow in tears shall reap in joy. He that goeth forth and weepeth, bearing precious seed (margin: seed-basket) shall doubtless come again with rejoicing, bringing his sheaves with him."

Barley was the first spring crop harvested, and wheat followed. In the book of *Ruth*, the second chapter describes the reaping and the third tells of the winnowing. We find a gang of reapers, probably

[130]

hired help, supervised by an overseer, a trusted servant of Boaz. Work started early, and when the owner arrived from nearby Bethlehem later in the forenoon good progress had been made, and the privileged gleaners were gathering their little hoard. Boaz greeted his men traditionally, "The Lord be with you," and they gave the customary response, "The Lord bless thee." Three hundred years later, *Psalms* (129/8) deplored the lapse of the old salutation: "Neither do they which go by say, The blessing of the Lord be upon you; we bless you in the name of the Lord."

Boaz spotted the attractive young widow amongst the local gleaners and questioned the foreman about her; discovering she was a relative by marriage, and was well spoken of for her kindness to her mother-in-law, he assured her that her presence was very welcome and offered her the courtesy of unlimited gleaning. He invited her to partake of the midday meal, a democratic affair: "At mealtime come thou hither, and eat of the bread, and dip thy morsel in the vinegar. And she sat beside the reapers: and he reached her parched corn, and she did eat, and was sufficed, and left." Ruth continued to glean daily in Boaz's fields "unto the end of barley harvest and of wheat harvest." Bethlehem, outside which Ruth gleaned her corn, must have been noted for its crops for the name means "house of bread." Harvest was late there, for the elevation was high. The reapers had probably completed their work in the heavy-bearing fields of the coastal plains a couple of weeks previously, and earlier than that had started the season in the low Jordan valley, near Jericho. The book of *Ruth* is a romance and the harvesting details are incidental. We must seek elsewhere for information of the technique and the implements used.

The only reaping instrument the Bible mentions is the sickle, which appears under two Hebrew names. Egyptian art depicts a sickle not very different from our modern type, and *Deuteronomy* (16/9), which tells of events after the Exodus, speaks of its use: "Such time as thou beginnest to put the sickle to the corn." Probably the Israelites took the tools they had used in Egypt along with them. The other Hebrew sickle may have been a Babylonian model, judging by the context in *Jeremiah* (50/16): "Cut off the sower from Babylon, and him that handleth the sickle in the time of harvest." There is a marginal note "scythe" against "sickle" in this verse.

Job (24/24) tells us that the stalks were not cut close to the

[131]

ground, but at a convenient height, a little below the ears: "cut off as the tops of the ears of corn." An interesting sidelight is found in the etymology of the Hebrew word for "reaper," the literal meaning being "shortener." The reaper grasped a handful of corn stalks with his left hand, just below the ears, and sheared the stalks a little lower down with the sickle in his right hand. The severed handful was dropped and the process continued. The binder followed the reaper, picking up the short-stemmed stalks and cradling them between his arm and his chest until a sheaf was assembled. It was this sequence which is referred to in *Psalms* (129/7): "The mower filleth not his hand; nor he that bindeth sheaves his bosom." *Jeremiah* (9/22) mentions the practice: "The carcasses of men shall fall as dung upon the open field, and as the handful after the harvestman, and none shall gather them."

When Joseph related his dream to his brothers (*Genesis* 37/7), the scene lay in the harvest field: "Behold, we were binding sheaves in the field, and, lo, my sheaf arose, and also stood upright; and, behold, your sheaves stood round about, and made obeisance to my sheaf." Sometimes the grain crop was harvested by pulling up the stalks by the roots. "And the whole valley . . . and all the fields . . . shall not be plucked up, nor thrown down any more for ever" (*Jeremiah* 31/40). In a chapter predicting a crop failure, *Isaiah* (17/5) says: "It shall be as when the harvestman gathereth the corn, and reapeth the ears with his arm; and it shall be as he that gathereth ears in the valley of Rephaim." Here the inference is that the stand of grain is so thin that plucking the stalks by hand is the easiest method of reaping. The meaning of the reference to the valley of Rephaim is buried in the folklore of the period, but elsewhere in Isaiah *rephaim* is translated as "the dead," and "the deceased."

The careful farmer not only bound his sheaves; he methodically picked out the weeds, and tied them in separate bundles. Asia has never been time-conscious in the hectic way of the Western world, and cheerful or resigned attention to a pattern of infinite detail is the way of life. "In the time of harvest I will say to the reapers, Gather ye together first the tares, and bind them in bundles to burn them: but gather the wheat into my barn" (*Matthew* 13/30).

Sometimes the sheaves were stacked, but more commonly they were taken directly to the barn or threshing floor. The references to stacks or shocks of corn are confined to early biblical history, from the 16th to the 12th century B. C. *Exodus* (22/6) warns against the danger of fire burning "the stacks of corn, or the standing corn." In *Judges* (15/5) Samson avenges himself on his enemies by an arson device and flames broke out in "the standing corn of the Philistines, and burnt up both the shocks and also the standing corn." Eliphaz encouraged his despondent friend with a homely simile, "Thou shalt come to thy grave in a full age, like as a shock of corn cometh in (Hebrew: ascendeth) in his season (*Job* 5/26).

While the Bible mentions carts and wagons several times, only in one passage do we find them carrying sheaves to the threshing floor. "I am pressed under you, as a cart is pressed that is full of sheaves," complained *Amos* (2/13). Yet carts must have been used for this purpose, and *Nehemiah* (13/15) denounces Sabbath-breaking, "bringing in sheaves, and lading asses," probably envisaging this use, as well as the lading of the panniers of the asses.

When we come to threshing, we find the Hebrew vocabulary richer than the English equivalent, while the balance is reversed in the case of threshing-floor; here one Hebrew word multiplies into English as "barn," "barnfloor," "corn," "corn floor," "floor," "threshing floor," "threshing place" and even "void place." We normally associate a floor with a covered building, but the threshing floors of the Bible lands had no roofs or walls. They were located on relatively high ground, open to the prevailing winds, and consisted of a level plot, fifty feet or upwards in diameter, the earth being trodden and packed down hard, like the surface of a road. If a suitable rocky surface was available, it was particularly prized.

As the terrain of many farmers would be unfitted for this purpose, communal threshing floors may have been shared, or a fee paid for the use of a privately owned one. Several biblical characters are identified by their ownership of a threshing floor, the first being found in *Genesis* (50/10-11). When Jacob died in Egypt, he was accorded a state funeral, and the cortege, "a very great company, came to the threshing floor of Atad, which is beyond Jordan . . . and when the inhabitants of the land, the Canaanites, saw the mourning in the floor of Atad, they said, This is a grievous mourning to the Egyptians."

The location of a threshing floor on a level piece of high ground made the site competitive with the high places of Scripture, reservations dedicated to altars and groves, where the worship of Jehovah or

[133]

Baal was solemnized. The wind-up of grain harvest was celebrated by the Feast of Pentecost, lasting but one day, and it was but natural to observe the festival at the threshing floor where the crowd was assembled; in some instances threshing floors and high places became linked together, the sanctity of the consecrated ground protecting the heaps of valuable grain against pilferage and looting. Solomon's temple was built on the site of a threshing floor, which God instructed David to purchase. The story is told in 2 *Samuel* (24) and with slight variations in 1 *Chronicles* (21) and 2 *Chronicles* (3/1).

David had numbered the Israelites, contrary to the Lord's orders, and the nation was suffering the penalty of pestilence and destruction. Jerusalem had been partially destroyed, when God relented, "and said to the angel that destroyed, It is enough, stay now thine hand. And the angel of the Lord stood by the threshing floor of Ornan the Jebusite. Then the angel . . .commanded . . . that David should . . . set up an altar unto the Lord in the threshing floor of Ornan the Jebusite . . . Now Ornan was threshing wheat . . . Then David said to Ornan Grant me the place of this threshing floor, that I may build an altar therein unto the Lord: thou shalt grant it me for the full price . . . And Ornan said unto David, Take it to thee, and let my lord the king do that which is good in his eyes; lo, I give thee the oxen also for burnt offerings, and the threshing instruments for wood, and the wheat for the meat offering; I give it all. And king David said to Ornan, Nay; but I will verily buy it for the full price . . . So David gave to Ornan for the place six hundred shekels of gold by weight. And David built there an altar unto the Lord."

Thus the site of the temple cost David $10,000 at Fort Knox prices, although 2 *Samuel* (24/24) reports that the transaction was effected for a nominal fifty shekels of silver, about $25. David commenced preparations for the erection of the great temple, and his son completed the work. "Then Solomon began to build the house of the Lord at Jerusalem . . . in the place that David had prepared in the threshing floor of Ornan the Jebusite."

The open air character of a threshing site is evident in *Judges* (6/37): "Behold, I will put a fleece of wool in the floor; and if the dew be on the fleece only, and it be dry upon all the earth beside, then shall I know that thou wilt save Israel." *Job* (39/12) queries whether the unicorn "will bring home thy seed, and gather it into thy

barn." The Revised Version replaces the latter phrase with the more accurate translation "gather the corn of thy threshing floor."

Hosea (9/1-2) indicates that loose women frequented the threshing floors. "Rejoice not, O Israel, for joy, as other people: for thou hast
gone a whoring from thy God, thou hast loved a reward upon every
cornfloor. The floor and the winepress shall not feed them." The word
"reward" here is elsewhere translated "hire," and the original is always
associated with prostitution. Festivity and drinking accompanied the
windup of threshing, and of sheep shearing, so the setting was provided
for immorality. Ruth's unconventional visit to Boaz may have been to
discover if his intentions were honorable. The opening of the third
chapter of *Ruth* reveals Naomi's matchmaking plans for her daughter-
in-law. "Behold, he winnoweth barley to night in the threshing floor.
Wash thyself therefore, and anoint thee, and put thy raiment upon
thee, and get thee down to the floor. But make not thyself known unto
the man, until he shall have done eating and drinking . . . And when
Boaz had eaten and drunk, and his heart was merry, he went to lie
down at the end of the heap of corn: and she came softly, and uncovered his feet, (Hebrew: lifted up the clothes that were on his feet) and
laid her down." When Boaz awoke later, she identified herself: "I am
Ruth thine handmaid; spread therefore thy skirt over thine handmaid; for thou art a near kinsman." Evidently bundling was an ancient
custom. Boaz assured her, "Fear not . . . all the city of my people doth
know that thou art a virtuous woman . . . And she lay at his feet until
the morning: and she rose up before one could know another." Fearing
scandal, Boaz warned the threshers: "Let it not be known that a woman
came into the floor." Ruth was veiled, so Boaz asked her to take her
veil and hold it while he poured in six measures of barley as a gift.

Threshing was accomplished in various ways, depending on the
type of plant and seed, and on the ultimate use of the product obtained. Accordingly, different implements and techniques were employed and it is necessary to go to the Hebrew terms for a better understanding of the processes involved. As we analyze the passage in *Isaiah*
(28/27), primitive threshing methods become clearer. "For the fitches
are not threshed with a threshing instrument, neither is a cart wheel
turned about upon the cummin; but the fitches are beaten out with a
staff, and the cummin with a rod." The word "threshed" here is the
same as that used in 1 *Chronicles* (21/20): "Ornan was threshing

wheat." It appears as "tear" (with a marginal "thresh") in connection with the crudest sort of threshing implement, in *Judges* (8/7): "I will tear your flesh with the thorns of the wilderness, and with briers."

"Tread out" is yet another rendering: "Ephraim is as an heifer that is taught, and loveth to tread out the corn" (*Hosea* 10/11). *Micah* (4/13) employs it in its generic sense: "Arise and thresh, O daughter of Zion: for I will make thine horn iron, and I will make thy hoofs brass: and thou shalt beat in pieces many people." (It is permissible to substitute "hill" for "horn" in this passage, a variation the translators use elsewhere, iron hill suggesting an elevated threshing space with a particularly hard floor.) *Amos* (1/3) uses it in combination with the same threshing instrument of the Isaiah passage under examination, "They have threshed Gilead with threshing instruments of iron." This particular threshing instrument of Isaiah and Amos appears for the third, and last time, in the Hebrew version of *Job* (41/30), the English translation of which reads, "He spreadeth sharp pointed things upon the mire." The Revised Version changes this to "He spreadeth as it were a threshing wain upon the mire." This threshing machine consisted of a flat heavy board, to the underside of which were affixed short, sharp iron spikes. The board was dragged by a heifer or ox and it acted something like a comb, tearing the husks and breaking up the straw, or it might be compared to a harrow, the Hebrew name of which, *charits*, resembles the *charuts* which designates this threshing board.

Fitches and cummin, because of their delicate seeds and relatively small production compared to barley and wheat, were threshed by hand flailing. While the flail is of remote antiquity, the word is not used in our English translation. Both rod and staff translate several different Hebrew words, and the context in which Isaiah's harvesting rod and staff appear suggests types of flails. This particular staff occurs frequently elsewhere in the term "staff of bread," the breaking of which was synonymous with poverty and disaster. Both rod and staff are associated with shaking and beating in several Bible passages. Small amounts of barley and wheat were sometimes beaten out in this individual manner. Ruth, finishing her first day in Boaz' harvest field, "beat out that she had gleaned: and it was about a ephah of barley" (*Ruth* 2/17). An interesting confirmation of this hand-beating process is found in *Judges* (6/11), where the English word "thresh" translates the Hebrew term elsewhere rendered "beat." "Gideon threshed wheat by the winepress, to hide it from the Midianites." Had Gideon taken his wheat to the threshing floor, in the normal manner, the occupying Midian forces would have confiscated it, in whole or in part. In *Deuteronomy* (24/20) we find this word "beat" used in another variety of farming task, "When thou beatest thine olive tree."

Getting back to our examination of the 28th chapter of Isaiah, we note two references to the use of a cart wheel in threshing: "neither is a cart wheel turned about upon the cummin," and, "break it with the wheel of his cart." Two Hebrew words denote these wheels, one having the broader meaning of a "rolling thing." Indeed, this latter term is its translation in *Isaiah* (17/13): "The nations . . . shall be chased as the chaff of the mountains before the wind, and like a rolling thing before the whirlwind." The same sense is found in *Psalms* (83/13): "O my God, make them like a wheel; as the stubble before the wind." *Ecclesiastes* (12/6) speaks of "the wheel broken at the cistern." A cistern wheel, as any countryman knows, is a broad cylinder or roller round which the well rope is wound and unwound, rather than a narrow wheel or pulley.

In both passages connected with threshing, the singular "wheel" is used, rather than the plural "wheels," so the cart referred to may have rested on a roller rather than on disc or spoke wheels. A threshing instrument, consisting of multiple rollers set in a frame, was used by the Hebrews, and is still employed in primitive agricultural communities in the Near East. The Hebrew name of this machine was *morag*, and the name still persists, corrupted to *noreg* in Egypt. The contemporary model usually has three parallel rollers, armed with metal discs, and the framework supports a seat for the driver. It is a *morag* which *Isaiah* (41/15) refers to: "Behold, I will make thee a new sharp threshing instrument having teeth." The word "teeth" here is unrelated in the original to the common words for teeth, and the concordance defines the term as "possessor of edges," which would describe agricultural discs. The threshing instrument which David bought of Ornan the Jebusite was the *morag* type.

In a passage in *Jeremiah* (51/33), the word translated "thresh" means "to tread down," and is so employed in many references to the treading of the winepress, and of olives. "The daughter of Babylon is like a threshing floor, it is time to thresh her; yet a little while, and the time of her harvest shall come." The Revised Version combines the

[137]

first sentence thusly, "The daughter of Babylon is like a threshing floor at the time when it is trodden."

Two more Hebrew words complete the threshing vocabulary; each occurs once only. *Isaiah* (21/10) exclaims, "O my threshing, and the corn of my floor." Here the end product rather than the process is indicated. *Daniel* (2/35), interpreting Nebuchadnezzar's dream of the great image with feet of clay which crumbled and disappeared "like the chaff of the summer threshing floors," uses a Babylonian (Aramaic) expression for threshing floors.

This simile of chaff being blown away by gusts of wind impressed several scriptural authors. The wicked, says *Job* (21/18), "are as stubble before the wind, and as chaff that the storm carrieth away." *Psalms* (1/4) reiterates this: "The ungodly . . . are like the chaff which the wind driveth away." Linked to the sudden gusts and whirls which spun through the Judean valleys, it provided one of Isaiah's favorite figures of speech: "chased as the chaff of the mountains before the wind . . as chaff that passeth away; yea, it shall be at an instant suddenly ... the whirlwind shall take them away as stubble" (17/13, 29/5, 40/24). *Hosea* (13/3) draws a word picture of ephemeral nature: "They shall be as the morning cloud, and as the early dew that passeth away, as the chaff that is driven with the whirlwind out of the floor, and as the smoke out of the chimney."

In two places in *Isaiah,* chaff is the translation of a word which designates dry grass or hay, rather than grain husks: "As the fire devoureth the stubble, and the flame consumeth the chaff" (5/24); and "Ye shall conceive chaff, ye shall bring forth stubble: your breath, as fire, shall devour you" (33/11). The Hebrew word rendered "stubble" refers to the refuse of the threshing floor as well as to that part of the stalk remaining attached to the roots after reaping. *Job* (13/25) plaintively asks: "Wilt thou break a leaf driven to and fro? and wilt thou pursue the dry stubble?"

Winnowing followed threshing, and while the word "winnow" appears only twice in English, the Hebrew original occurs much more frequently, being translated elsewhere as "fan," "scatter," "spread," "strew," etc. A shovel and a fan were the winnowing implements. We find them both in *Isaiah* (30/24): ". . . clean provender, which hath been winnowed with the shovel and with the fan"; further on, (41/15-16), the Prophet elaborates: "Thou shalt thresh the mountains and beat them small, and shalt make the hills as chaff. Thou shalt fan them, and the wind shall carry them away, and the whirlwind shall scatter them." *Jeremiah* (51/1-2) speaks of both fanners and fans: "I will raise up against Babylon . . . a destroying wind: and will send unto Babylon fanners, that shall fan her, and shall empty her land." And in another place (15/7) he says, "I will fan them with a fan in the gates of the land." To understand this latter allusion, we turn to 1 *Kings* (22/10) (also 2 *Chronicles* 18/9): "And the king of Israel and Jehosophat the king of Judah sat each on his throne, having put on their robes, in a void place in the entrance of the gate of Samaria; and all the prophets prophesied before them." The Hebrew word for "void place" is the same as for "threshing floor," as marginal references confirm in both Authorized and Revised Versions.

John the Baptist, referring to Christ's mission, uses the winnowing process in a strong passage, whose import is usually glossed over: "Whose fan is in his hand, and he will thoroughly purge his floor, and gather his wheat into the garner; but he will burn up the chaff with unquenchable fire" (*Matthew* 3/12). We have little information on the shovel and the fan. The shovel is believed to have been a light multi-pronged fork which tossed the corn mixture into the air, where gravity and the prevailing breeze winnowed it; the fan culled the husks from the grain and may have been a broad-bladed, light wooden shovel. Winnowing was strenuous work, so evening and night were favored for the task, the heat of the prevailing east wind being then tempered. "A dry wind of the high places in the wilderness . . . not to fan, nor to cleanse" (*Jeremiah* 4/11). Boaz followed the custom: "Behold, he winnoweth barley to night in the threshing floor" (*Ruth* 3/2).

Winnowing completed, the grain was sifted. "I will sift the house of Israel among all nations, like as corn is sifted in a sieve, yet shall not the least grain fall upon the earth" (*Amos* 9/9).

A marginal alternative gives "stone" against "grain," and this is obviously the correct meaning. The purpose of the sieve was to retain the grit and pebbles while permitting the grain to fall through. In *Luke* (22/31), Jesus says, "Simon, Simon, behold, Satan hath desired to have you, that he may sift you as wheat."

The final process was the removal of the clean grain to the barns and storehouses, and the Bible is vague about this transfer. Storage places are well documented, however. While "barn" is employed in one

[139]

instance as a synonym for "threshing-floor," it is generally used to designate a collection and storage bin for grain, and it is in this latter sense that *Haggai* (2/19) inquires, "Is the seed yet in the barn?" John the Baptist spoke of wheat being gathered into the garner, and *Joel* (1/17) describing times of acute famine, says, "The garners are laid desolate, the barns are broken down; for the corn is withered." Garner is an old word for granary. Several Hebrew words denote different types of grain storage spaces, some being rendered storehouse in English. "Hezekiah had . . . storehouses also for the increase of corn" (2 *Chronicles* 32/27-28). A passage in *Jeremiah* (41/8) may imply that grain was stored in protected pits, or caves. Here we read that Ishmael, one of the royal family of Judah, slew a number of Jews who had returned from Babylon in the service of the collaborationist governor of Judah. Ten men offered ransom, and were spared: "Slay us not; for we have treasures in the field, of wheat, and of barley, and of oil, and of honey." Evidently these caches were so well camouflaged that only the owners could find them.

From the granary, the grain was sold to the householders in small amounts, and was ground into meal or flour daily, or as required. Every home had its mill, and the domestic music of the spinning upper grindstone, crunching grain into grits against the nether stone, was a friendly household note, welcomed as a token of God's generous supply to man, and equally lamented when hard times silenced the millstones. With this concept, *Ecclesiastes* (12/3-4) takes on new meaning: "The grinders cease, because they are few . . . when the sound of the grinding is low." The marginal version gives a clearer picture, "the grinders fail, because they grind little." Sufficient grain had to be fed steadily to permit the upper mill to revolve freely. Too little allowed the bearing surfaces of the stones to touch and the resultant friction stopped the mill, or at best reduced the steady hum of the well-fed mill to a lower and more spasmodic note. Grinding was the first task of the day, in winter being performed by candle-light, and the low roar of a score of grindstones was a dawn alarm clock. "I will take from them the voice of mirth, and the voice of gladness . . . the sounds of the millstones, and the light of the candle. And this whole land shall be a desolation" (*Jeremiah* 25/10). In the doom of Babylon (*Revelation* 18/22) the millstones are silenced "and the sound of a millstone shall be heard no more at all in thee."

[140]

While primitive rubbing stones were used in early times, the more efficient domestic mill was standard equipment in most households, being considered indispensable: "No man shall take the nether or the upper millstone to pledge: for he taketh a man's life to pledge" (*Deuteronomy* 24/6). Desperate situations require desperate sacrifices, and an unnamed Amazon in *Judges* (9/53) did not hesitate: "A certain woman cast a piece of a millstone upon Abimelech's head, and all to break his skull," says the Authorized Version somewhat quaintly, and the suggestion is that a broken piece of a millstone was used. The Revised Version is more precise: "A certain woman cast an upper millstone upon Abimilech's head and brake his scull."

A mill consisted of two circular stones, each eighteen to twenty-four inches in diameter and a few inches thick. The upper surface of the nether stone was slightly convex, fitting into the concave depression in the base of the upper one. The lower stone was proverbially hard: "His heart is as firm as a stone; yea, as hard as a piece of the nether millstone" (*Job* 41/24). The center of the upper stone was hollowed out and served as a funnel into which grain was fed; an upright handle was affixed near the rim. Two women normally ran the mill, usually an older and a younger one, frequently mother and daughter. Jesus mentions this (*Matthew* 24/41): "Two women shall be grinding at the mill; the one shall be taken, and the other left."

When enemies swept down on a settlement in a dawn raid, they raced off with the younger women across their saddles. The women faced each other, seated on the ground; each grasped the handle and commenced rotating the rider or upper stone, feeding grain into the funnel with the disengaged hand. Grinding was hard monotonous work, despised by the aristocracy. "Come down, and sit in the dust, O virgin daughter of Babylon, sit on the ground: there is no throne, O daughter of the Chaldeans: for thou shalt no more be called tender and delicate. Take the millstones, and grind meal: uncover thy locks, make bare the leg" (*Isaiah* 47/1-2). This was probably the most degrading task Isaiah could conceive of for a gentlewoman. *Exodus* (11/5) lends emphasis to this conclusion: "From the first born of Pharaoh that sitteth upon his throne, even unto the firstborn of the maidservant that is behind the mill," while *Judges* (16/21) relates that Samson "did grind in the prison house."

Another grinding appliance was the pestle and mortar, in an

[141]

Egyptian model of which the Israelites pounded their manna *(Numbers* 11/8). Under a different Hebrew title it appears for a second and last time in *Proverbs* (27/22): "Though thou shouldest bray a fool in a mortar among wheat with a pestle, yet will not his foolishness depart from him."

CHAPTER 13

Perfumes, Spices, and Ointments

THE EARLIEST distillers of perfume were the flowers. When man first rubbed a fragrant leaf between his fingers, the sweet essential oil which moistened his skin was the primordial ointment. The spice-laden tropic breeze wafted the news of Nature's pungent aromas to her newest guest.

Like so many of the customs which the West has adopted, the art of perfumery and the culture of sweet smelling lotions and ointments came from the East. That it was one of the most ancient and precise of arts is evident in Jehovah's instructions to Moses, setting forth the ingredients of the holy anointing oil and of the sacred incense, and further stipulating that these sanctified compounds be prepared according to the art of the apothecary. The English word "apothecary" is derived from a Greek one of similar sound, and in its modern sense signifies a druggist or medical chemist. The old Hebrew word designated a distiller of perfume and blender of spices and ointments, and the Revised Version recognizes this by substituting "perfumer" for the "apothecary" of the King James Bible. The associated words, "confection," "confectionary," and "compound," should be understood as pertaining to the processes and results of the perfumer's art rather than in their modern meaning.

Certain ordinances of the Mosaic Law reflect the influence of the older traditions, customs, and observances of Egypt, and this is but natural, for Egypt, no matter how oppressively she treated the Israelites prior to their revolt, was and had been for centuries the only home that the Hebrew nation knew. When a nonconforming section of the populace is brutally treated by a new regime which has overthrown the preceding friendly and tolerant government, the fleeing or expelled minority usually concentrate their animosity and their propaganda on the recent conquerors, while they continue to cherish and observe the old customs and traditions of their homeland. Thus the White Russians who fled from Bolshevik terror set up their own Orthodox churches and brewed their tea in samovars, thinking and talking nostalgically of Mother Russia while execrating the Soviet government.

In the case of the Israelites, the political influence and prestige of Joseph, and the warm welcome the early settlers received, together with the pleasant and productive life of the Nile valley, tended to fan a patriotic ardor for their adopted land in the colonists of Goshen. Moses, brought up as an Egyptian prince, was accustomed to the culture and advanced civilization of the royal court. Like many of the leading reformers of history, he was a patrician who espoused the cause of the oppressed. His life interest was to emancipate his kinsmen from slavery and to protect their right to free monotheistic worship. There is little in his teachings to indicate that he regarded the civilization or secular customs of Egypt as decadent or degenerate.

From the most ancient tombs of Egypt, antedating Abraham by thousands of years, flasks and containers of perfumes, ointments, and spices have been recovered, and some still yielded a faint trace of the original scent. The breast of the Sphinx carries an inlaid tablet depicting a Pharaoh, of a dynasty contemporary with the Israelite settlement, offering incense and sacred oil. By that time the priests had become the official perfumers, and the formulas were a guarded secret; thus it is not surprising to find the aromatic art of Egypt reappearing under the aegis of the Hebrew priesthood, as it does in the 30th chapter of *Exodus*. "Moreover the Lord spake unto Moses, saying, Take thou also unto thee principal spices, of pure myrrh five hundred shekels, and of sweet cinnamon half so much, even two hundred and fifty shekels, of sweet calamus two hundred and fifty shekels, and of cassia five hundred shekels, after the shekel of the sanctuary, and of olive oil an hin: and thou shalt make it an oil of holy ointment, an ointment compounded after the art of the apothecary." In modern terms, about fifty pounds of dry spices were mixed in a gallon and a half of oil. The reference to the shekel of the sanctuary was to the standard legal weight, available for comparison in the sanctuary, a forerunner of the Bureau of Standards.

Further on in the chapter we find the prescription for the sacred perfume: "Take unto thee sweet spices, stacte, and onycha, and galbanum; these sweet spices with pure frankincense: of each shall there be a like weight: and thou shalt make it a perfume, a confection after the art of the apothecary, tempered together, pure and holy." A marginal note, and the text of the Revised Version, gives "salted" for "tempered," and the injunction in *Leviticus* (2/13) emphasizing the use of salt in sacred offerings lends credence to this interpretation. Both the ointment and the perfume were sacred, and their manufacture or use other than for the specified religious purposes was prohibited under penalty of excommunication.

More than three centuries later we still find that "some of the sons of the priests made the ointment of the spices" (1 *Chronicles* 9/30), but that it was no longer an exclusive privilege of the hierarchy is evident from 1 *Samuel* (8/13); there the displeased old man warns the king-struck Israelites that the monarch they crave "will take your daughters to be confectionaries (perfume-makers), and to be cooks, and to be bakers." We read next of the perfumer's art in 2 *Chronicles* (16/14), in connection with the ceremonial burial of Asa, king of Judah: "And they buried him in his own sepulchres, which he had made for himself in the city of David, and laid him in the bed which was filled with sweet odors and divers kinds of spices prepared by the apothecaries' art: and they made a very great burning for him."

Embalming was not a customary Jewish practice, although Jacob and Joseph were embalmed after their death in Egypt. However, the practice of using sweet spices and ointments in the funeral rites was common, while the burnings spoken of may have been of fragrant wood, perhaps augmented by incense cones. Thus *Jeremiah* (34/5) tells King Zedekiah: "Thou shalt die in peace: and with the burnings of thy fathers, the former kings which were before thee, so shall they burn odors for thee." The word "odors" is an italicized interpolation and is not used in the Revised Version. Some commentators believe that the bodies were cremated, as in the case of Saul and his sons (1 *Samuel* 31/12), and consider that sweet-scented preparations were used to mitigate the smell of burning flesh. In a ghoulish passage, *Ezekiel* (24/10) refers to this funereal deodorant: "Heap on wood, kindle the fire, consume the flesh, and spice it well, and let the bones be burned." The word "spice" in this quotation is the same as that used for "apothecary" in Exodus. The Gospel of *John* (19/39-40) gives a straightforward account of the use of funeral ointments and spices: "And there came also Nicodemus . . . and brought a mixture of myrrh and aloes, about an hundred pound weight. Then took they the body of Jesus, and wound it in linen clothes with the spices, as the manner

[145]

of the Jews is to bury." The version of *Luke* (23/56-24/1) declares that some female Galilean converts prepared spices and ointments for the body of the crucified Master.

As we might expect, the writings of Solomon pay tribute to the scented garden and its offerings. *Proverbs* (27/9) declares: "Ointment and perfume rejoice the heart." In the *Song of Solomon*, the references, both direct and veiled, to perfume, spices and sweet odors are very numerous, and only a few will be quoted. The third verse of the first chapter proclaims the intoxicating influence of perfume: "Because of the savor of thy good ointments thy name is as ointment poured forth, therefore do the virgins love thee." We get a glimpse of the commercial background in (3/6): "Who is this that cometh out of the wilderness like pillars of smoke, perfumed with myrrh and frankincense, with all powders of the merchant." The Hebrew word here translated "merchant" appears as "spice merchant" in the account of Solomon's riches given in 1 *Kings* (10/15). "Pillars of smoke" could be translated "smoking palm trees," and the allusion is perhaps to the heat eddies shimmering on the desert horizon from the still concealed tops of the palm trees, indicating to the experienced traveller the presence of an unsighted oasis. A veritable catalog of blended spices and balm laden breezes adorns the concluding verses of the fourth chapter: "Camphire, with spikenard, spikenard and saffron; calamus and cinnamon, with all trees of frankincense; myrrh and aloes, with all the chief spices. . . . Awake, O north wind; and come, thou south; blow upon my garden, that the spices thereof may flow out."

The temptress whom Solomon warns against in the seventh chapter of *Proverbs* knew the aphrodisiac allure of some perfumes: "I have perfumed my bed with myrrh, aloes and cinnamon. Come, let us take our fill of love until the morning: let us solace ourselves with loves." Rebuking the idolatry of the Israelites, and their regard for sensory rather than spiritual values, *Isaiah* (57/9) says: "And thou wentest to the king with ointment, and didst increase thy perfumes . . . and didst debase thyself even unto hell."

The trade in aromatics was extensive and of great value. The first Bible record is in *Genesis* (37/25): "Behold, a company of Ishmeelites came from Gilead with their camels bearing spicery and balm and myrrh, going to carry it down to Egypt." These Ishmeelites, or Midianites as they are called later in the chapter, were wealthy Bedouin traders, ancestors of the Arab race. Gilead, whence the caravan had originated, was as famous for its balm as Vermont is for maple sugar. "Is there no balm in Gilead? Is there no physician there?" cried *Jeremiah* (8/22) in words which have become proverbial. So prized were the spices and aromatic oils of the Canaan region that Jacob considered them a suitable and acceptable gift to offer the mighty governor of Egypt (*Genesis* 43/11).

The Palestine plant growers who specialized in the extraction and distillation of choice perfumes and the processing of essential oils and spices were proud of their reputation. It was not until the momentous visit of the queen of Sheba that they realized the meagreness of their stocks and varieties; the 10th chapter of 1 *Kings* tells the tale: "And when the queen of Sheba heard of the fame of Solomon . . . she came to Jerusalem with a very great train, with camels that bare spices . . . and she gave the king . . . of spices very great store, and precious stones: there came no more such abundance of spices as those which the queen of Sheba gave to King Solomon." Not only the queen of Sheba but "all the earth sought to Solomon . . . and they brought every man his present, vessels of silver, and vessels of gold, and garments, and armor, and spices, horses, and mules, a rate year by year." The high regard in which spices were held is implicit here. Three centuries later they were still royal treasure, guarded along with gold and silver and jewels.

2 *Kings* (20/13) tells how the Judean monarch proudly displayed his wealth to the visiting Prince of Babylon and his entourage: "And Hezekiah . . . shewed them all the house of his precious things (Hebrew: spicery), the silver, and the gold, and the spices, and all the precious ointment, and all the house of his armor, and all that was found in his treasuries." Isaiah took a pessimistic view of this royal show-off to foreign cupidity, and foretold that all the king's possessions would eventually wind up in Babylon, but the philosophic Hezekiah shrugged it off with an *After me the deluge* attitude. Here again we observe the important place held by spices and ointments in the royal treasury.

When we revisit our merchandise mart, the twenty-seventh chapter of *Ezekiel,* we are not disappointed in our expectation that the products of the perfumer would be found holding a prominent place in Vanity Fair. The famous balm of Canaan's valleys is featured in the

[147]

17th verse. Two verses later we read: "Dan also and Javan going to and fro occupied in thy fairs; bright iron, cassia, and calamus, were in thy markets." The Revised Version gives a quite different rendering of the first half of the verse, "Vedan and Javan traded with yarn for thy wares," while a marginal note against "with yarn" reads according to some ancient versions "from Uzal." Practically all commentators rule out the Israelite Dan. Vedan and Javan are believed to have been in southern Arabia, Vedan perhaps being what is now the seaport of Aden. Javan is thought to have been the port of ancient Uzal, the modern Sanaa, capital city of the Yemen.

This was the land of the old Minaeans and Sabaeans, known to Greece and Rome for its great spice trade, and holding the monopoly of frankincense. Pliny tells that three thousand families controlled the manufacture of incense. Some authorities consider that the queen of Sheba was the queen of Saba, and the 22nd verse of the chapter relates: "The merchants of Sheba and Raamah, they were thy merchants: they occupied in thy fairs with chief of all spices, and with all precious stones, and gold." The wealth of India and beyond was transported by shipping to ports at the southern end of the Red Sea, including Sabaean harbors, thence by camel caravan to Egypt, Canaan, and Syria. Regular traders on this route brought the queen of Sheba tales of the exploits and wisdom of Solomon, and her journey north was along a conventional and much travelled highway.

Isaiah (60/6) gives further confirmation of the spicery and natural wealth of Sheba. "All they from Sheba shall come: they shall bring gold and incense: and they shall show forth the praises of the Lord." Isaiah's prophecy is repeated in *Psalms* (72/10-11): "The kings of Sheba and Seba shall offer gifts. Yea, all kings shall fall down before him." Do these passages foretell the Christmas tale of the New Testament? "Behold, there came wise men from the east to Jerusalem, saying, where is he that is born King of the Jews? for we have seen his star in the east, and are come to worship him . . . and when they were come into the house, they saw the young child . . . and fell down, and worshipped him: and when they had opened their treasures, they presented unto him gifts; gold, and frankincense, and myrrh" (*Matthew* 2/1-2, 11). Here we have the products of Sheba rather than the geographically eastern Babylon. The Hebrews used only the four cardinal points of the compass, and Arabia was considered a country of the east.

[148]

As we read these sacred passages, with mingled emotions and impressions, exotic names jostle common kitchen spices, romance and religion become interwoven; oldtime treasures of kings and mystical rites of the holy priesthood seem to be a departed glory. Has the Revelator's curse on Babylon come to pass? "And the merchants of the earth shall weep and mourn over her; for no man buyeth their merchandise any more: . . . cinnamon, and odors, and ointments, and frankincense . . . thou shalt find them no more at all (*Revelation* 18/11,13).

Most of these aromatic substances which the ancients prized are still with us; some still retain high value and sacred usage, others are industrialized and commercialized. Frankincense has a legendary ring, a word that seems to belong in an ancient spice bazaar. Yet it is compounded from two Old French words, meaning "free incense' or "pure incense." The roots from which the English words "incense" and "perfume" derive are almost identical, but in the process of time perfume has greatly broadened its meaning while incense has narrowed until now it is almost synonymous with frankincense. The sweet odor of its burning still ascends in Greek and Roman Catholic churches, just as it did from the portable altars of desert tents, from the more elaborate temple of Jerusalem and the competing high places of Baal, and from the holy places of Egypt and India and Greece. Its Hebrew name, *lebonah*, resembles the Greek *libanos*, both signifying "white"; as the Lebanon Range or White Mountains the foreign words are more familiar to English speaking people. A modern name for frankincense, olibanum, reveals the same root.

In its original form frankincense is a resin derived from certain species of trees of the *genus Boswellia, order burseraceae*, resembling the sumach. An incision is made in the tree and the bark peeled back. The primary exudation is allowed to harden, then the incision is deepened and the gum is tapped into a receptacle. The collecting season lasts throughout the summer and early autumn. While the color of the gum is amberish, a white powdery deposit appears on the surface of the drops when they are rubbed together or jostled, and as most of the rosin is marked by this white dust by the time it reaches the user, the *lebonah* name was no doubt considered descriptive. Frankincense ignites readily and burns with a clear white flame, yielding a pleasant odor.

Numerous references to frankincense are found in the Mosaic

law, particularly in *Leviticus*. Frankincense formed part of many offerings and sacrifices, but its use was prohibited in the sin and the jealousy offerings. A thousand years later Nehemiah reinstituted in Jerusalem ceremonial sacrifices incorporating frankincense. While biblical mention appears to confine its use to aromatic purposes, the ancient world from Greece to China regarded it highly for its medicinal properties.

Lebonah appears in the English Bible as both "frankincense" and "incense," but another distinct word is also translated "incense" and this latter covers a wide variety of odors, from that of perfume to the incense of rams, quoted in *Psalms* (66/15).

Myrrh is another famous scriptural perfume and lotion which means little to modern readers. With frankincense, it was one of the precious gifts offered the infant Jesus by the Magi. It is possible that a deep symbolic meaning was connected with these presents, far outweighing their intrinsic value. Myrrh appears in the Bible under two Hebrew names, one being *mor*, a variant of the Arabic *murr*. The other word, *lot*, is confined to *Genesis*, where it appears as part of the cargo of the Ishmaelite spice caravan, and as one of the gifts sent by Jacob to Egypt. This early variety was *ladanum*, no relation of laudanum which is obtained from the opium poppy. This ladanum-myrrh is derived from a shrub of the cistus family, known as the oak rose or rock rose, and common in Mediterranean countries. The shrub is "whipped" with a lash having thongs, the resin adhering to the latter, from which it is scraped off with a knife blade or similar tool. Sometimes a loosely strung bow is used to collect the ladanum, the bow-cord being woven with wool to which the gum sticks in the friction process. Ladanum is sweet-scented and has medicinal as well as aromatic properties.

The myrrh mentioned in later biblical passages was imported from the warmer lands of Arabia and Africa. The myrrh tree of modern times is a descendant of the original, botanically classified as *Balsamodendron myrrha* of the *order Terebinthaceae*. Myrrh is also obtained from trees of the species *commiphora* of the family *Burseraceae*, and this resin is sometimes termed *bdellium*. Bdellium appears in the Bible, in *Genesis* (2/12) and *Numbers* (11/7), but the experts play the animal-mineral-or-vegetable game over its identification. Its comparison to manna in the second quotation seems to favor the vegetable claim.

[150]

The Bible story of myrrh presents itself on many diverse stages. We follow it from the desert encampment of the high priesthood of Israel to the royal palace of Persia. Still flaunting regal glory, it appears in the mystical court of heaven, in a Psalm entitled A Song of Loves. In the word pictures of Solomon it rises from the perfumed bed of a prostitute to haunt another Song of Loves, the redolent *Song of Songs*. Myrrh opens the divine story of Jesus with joy, and closes it in anguished tragedy on the cross.

Pure myrrh was the first ingredient of the holy ointment prescribed by God to Moses. The next few references are all on the distaff side. In the women's quarters of the Lily Palace of Xerxes, hopeful and ambitious maidens groomed themselves to capture the Emperor's fancy and the vacant crown of his Queen. First, however, came the lengthy prescribed ritual of purification, probably laid down in the "law of the Medes and Persians, which altereth not." No beauty contestant would be received by the monarch until "after that she had been twelve months, according to the manner of the women, (for so were the days of their purification accomplished, to wit, six months with oil of myrrh, and six months with sweet odors, and with other things for the purifying of the women)" (*Esther* 2/12). This purification of the women appears to have been an entirely different rite from the Israelite purification of females, and apparently was a prelude to concubinage and marriage.

The 45th *Psalm* is symbolical, but its symbolism is evidently based in part on a procedure related to that at the Persian court of King Ahasuerus. A similar pattern, wound round the king's preference for the most beautiful maiden, is found in several of the verses in the *Song of Solomon*. In all the passages the girls are heavily perfumed with myrrh to allure the senses of the monarch: "All thy garments smell of myrrh, and aloes, and cassia, out of the ivory palaces, whereby they have made thee glad" (*Psalms* 45/8). At the other end of the social scale, the harlot scents her bed with myrrh, aloes and cinnamon (*Proverbs* 7/17), virtually the same bouquet as the king's favorite, for cassia was a cheaper substitute for cinnamon. Oriental perfumes usually seem heavy and cloying to our senses.

Myrrh is mentioned eight times in the *Song of Solomon*, and the various contexts show the familiarity of the writer with myrrh in its different forms, a familiarity which is as foreign to us as the substance

[151]

itself. "A bundle of myrrh is my well-beloved unto me; he shall lie all night betwixt my breasts" (1/13), is the first rhapsody, perhaps indicating that a little sachet of myrrh hung from a necklace. "Who is this that cometh . . . perfumed with myrrh and frankincense" (3/6) is the next reference, followed by: "I will get me to the mountain of myrrh, and to the hill of frankincense" (4/6), an illusion apparently connected with the preceding verse. (4/14) speaks of myrrh and aloes and all the chief spices of a scented garden. The fifth chapter opens with the collecting of myrrh: "I am come into my garden, my sister, my spouse: I have gathered my myrrh with my spice," while the fifth verse tells of the anointing with the rich fragrant unguent: "I rose up to open to my beloved: and my hands dropped with myrrh, and my fingers with sweet smelling myrrh." Finally, in the thirteenth verse Solomon tells, not of gilding the lily but of perfuming it: "His lips like lilies, dropping sweet smelling myrrh."

In the New Testament, myrrh is presented to the infant Jesus, lying in his manger cradle. Dying on the Cross, His brief mission ended, He is offered an anodyne: "And they gave him to drink wine mingled with myrrh: but he received it not" (*Mark* 15/23). Finally, the tortured body of the Master is tenderly anointed with myrrh by Nicodemus. Thus myrrh, that vibrant word, reverberates through the Bible, ministering impartially to the things of the spirit and of the flesh.

Cinnamon and cassia have fallen from their high estate, and from being the delight of kings and court beauties, and enjoying the sanctity of the holy temple, have come to rest on democratic kitchen shelves. Every housewife knows cinnamon but few have used cassia, yet they are closely related and the cheaper and coarser cassia is sometimes substituted for cinnamon. In some Mediterranean countries the more pungent cassia is preferred to cinnamon. Both are composed of the bark of treees of the order *Lauracea,* the cinnamon being peeled from *Cinnamomum zeylanicum,* with *Cinnamomum cassia* yielding cassia. Nowadays most cassia comes from China, while Ceylon is the cinnamon Isle, and probably the Holy Land supply came from the same two countries. The spices come in the dry bark form, or pulverized into powder. A fragrant aromatic oil may be expressed from the bark, and possibly this was the medium used for the holy anointing oil of Moses and the perfume of Solomon. Cassia, calamus and myrrh are linked together in several Bible passages.

[152]

Aloes are bracketed with myrrh in the four scriptural texts to which they are limited; in *Psalms* (45/8) and *Proverbs* (7/17) the blend is a feminine perfume; *Song of Solomon* (4/14) speaks of "myrrh and aloes, with all the chief spices," while *John* (19/39) describes their use as a burial ointment. Aloes was a very precious resin obtained from the heart wood of *Aquilaria ovata* and *Aquilaria agallocha,* natives of southern Asia. The aloe tree (lign-aloe) is discussed in the chapter on trees of the field and forest.

Spikenard, *nerd* in Hebrew and *nardos* in Greek, was another very precious perfume and ointment. In parallel, but slightly differing passages from *Mark* (14/3) and *John* (12/3), we read of Mary anointing the Master with spikenard ointment. Mark tells of "an alabaster box of ointment of spikenard (margin: pure nard or liquid nard) very precious; and she brake the box, and poured it on his head." This breaking of the box is an idiomatic translation and means breaking the seal or stopper rather than the container. The John text mentions a pound of spikenard, and gives the same valuation as Mark, three hundred pence. The penny was the Greek denarius, equivalent to about seventeen cents, so the ointment was worth $50 in modern coinage. However, a penny was then the average payment for a day's labor, so, transferred to our inflated currency Mary's tribute represented at least $1500, not out of line with postwar prices of good French perfume.

Old Testament mention of spikenard is confined to the *Song of Solomon.* The first allusion is (1/12): "While the king sitteth at his table, my spikenard sendeth forth the smell thereof." If this passage is read in combination with the other references (4/13-14) "Thy plants are an orchard . . . camphire with spikenard, spikenard and saffron . . . " we may speculate that the odor of spikenard and other plants was wafted from the palace gardens or conservatory into the king's chamber, or accept the usual idea that the beloved's garments and body were perfumed. Spikenard ointment is derived from the root stocks (spikes) of a plant of the valerian family, *Nardostachys jatamansi,* still cultivated in the highland valleys lying between India and Tibet. In biblical times Indian spikenard was imported into Palestine through Arabia. From the roots of another member of the valerian group, *Valeriana officinalis,* a volatile oil is extracted. "Turner's Herbal," written in the 16th century, tells us that dried valerian roots were used to scent clothing and linen delicately, just as we use a pot-pourri

[153]

sachet. By modern standards the odor is offensive to the human scent, but it still fascinates cats who rub themselves and roll all over the plant. The American spikenard is unrelated to the valerian family, being of the *aralia* or *ginseng* group; the British variety is *Inula squarrosa*.

Camphire, mentioned in *Song of Solomon* (1/14) and (4/13), is described in the flower chapter, under its alternate name, henna flower.

The attempt to identify calamus leads us in a merry-go-round. The Hebrew word used on the few occasions that calamus appears in the English Bible, serves also the following miscellaneous assortment of translations; balance, bone, branch, cane, reed, staff and spearman. The reed rendering occurs twenty-eight times, branch twenty-four and calamus but thrice. In the New Testament the Greek word *kalamos* is translated eleven times as reed, once as pen.

From the context it is obvious that calamus was no common reed grass. Sweet calamus formed part of the holy anointing oil of *Exodus* (30/23). The same native word appears as sweet cane in two allusions to sacrifices: "Thou hast bought me no sweet cane with money" (*Isaiah* 43/24), and in *Jeremiah* (6/20), "To what purpose cometh there to me incense from Sheba, and the sweet cane from a far country?" Its exotic nature is further documented by its inclusion in the chapter on Tyrian merchandise (*Ezekiel* 27/19), which suggests its southern Arabian source, either directly or as a transfer point from ship to camel. Solomon includes it among the plants of his spice garden. Some Bible botanists identify calamus as *Andropogon aromaticus,* alternatively called *Calamus odoratus,* of which the choicest varieties were grown in India and southern Arabia, and an inferior grade in Egypt and Canaan. Roots, stems and leaves all yielded a fragrant essence when crushed.

The ingredients of the holy anointing oil—myrrh, cinnamon, calamus, cassia and olive oil—were well known and much used aromatics throughout the Scriptures. Yet three of the four components of the sacred perfume, *stacte, onycha* and *galbanum,* have no further record in the Bible. The injunctions forbidding profane use of this perfume are even more stringent than the restrictions governing the anointing oil. The latter is spoken of as holy, the perfume most holy. Yet there is no taboo against the use of individual constituents; it is only the specific formulae which are consecrated. Why did these perfumes disappear from Holy Writ, associated and sanctified as they were with some of the most solemn and sacred ceremonies of Jewish religion? The ingredients were specified just a few months after the Israelites had left Egypt, while they still possessed ample stocks of Egyptian merchandise. Perhaps some of the components were scarce or even unprocurable in Canaan. A clue suggesting a different explanation may be found in *Isaiah* (1/13): "Incense is an abomination unto me." The Hebrew word here translated "incense" is elsewhere rendered "perfume." The religious observances of many of the major and minor prophets differed as sharply from those of Moses and Aaron as those of the Puritans did from the Roman Catholic liturgy. Incense or perfume was too closely associated in their mind with idol worship and sensual excess to tolerate its ecclesiastical use, and it probably fell under a ban. Frankincense, the fourth ingredient of the Mosaic perfume, apparently outlived the interdict.

Stacte in its Hebrew form means "drops," and is so used to indicate rain drops in a passage in *Job* (36/27). In Greek *stacte* designates the purest myrrh, natural exudations of the tree without breaking the bark or tapping, and in this state appearing as globular drops. *Stacte* may be the gum of the *Styrax officinalis* or storax tree, the *Populus alba* or white poplar, or the *Balsamodendron kataf* or *amyria,* an Arabic species. Each of these has its advocates, the storax probably drawing the majority support.

The perfume of *onycha* may be either of animal or vegetable origin. Some research opinion identifies it with the musky odor emitted by a shell of the mussel family, *Murex ramosus,* when the shell is heated. This shellfish is found in Red Sea and Indian waters. Other students consider *onycha* to have been the gum yielded by the *storax benzoin,* an Asiatic tree which still furnishes a perfume base to commerce.

Galbanum has persisted down to modern times, and is a resinous product of *Ferula galbaniflue,* a tree native to Iran. Some biblical botanists also identify it as an exudation of *Opoidia galbanifera,* also common in Persia, while others give the name to the gum of *Bubon galbanum,* which flourishes in Syria and Arabia. *Galbanum* reaches us in irregular shaped masses interspersed with symmetrical drops, varies in color from light brown to greenish-yellow, and has a rather unpleasant

[155]

musky odor. When mixed with other perfumes, it was credited with husbanding the diffusion of their scent over a long period of time. Medicinally, *galbanum* was prescribed by Hippocrates and Pliny; nowadays it is used as an antispasmodic.

CHAPTER 14

Reeds and Rushes

CHILD LIFE was cheap in the ancient world, and rulers such as Pharaoh in the Old and Herod in the New Testament sometimes decreed whole-sale slaughter of infants for political reasons. Naturally many parents sought means to circumvent this brutality, and the story of Moses opens with one such successful stratagem.

"Pharaoh charged all his people, saying, Every son that is born ye shall cast into the river, and every daughter ye shall save alive. And there went a man of the house of Levi, and took to wife a daughter of Levi. And the woman conceived, and bare a son: and when she saw him that he was a goodly child, she hid him three months. And when she could no longer hide him, she took for him an ark of bulrushes, and daubed it with slime and with pitch, and put the child therein; and she laid it in the flags by the river's brink" (*Exodus* 1/22-2/3).

In the Revised Version, we find marginal alternatives of "papy-rus" for "bulrushes," and "bitumen" for "slime." The Hebrew word translated "ark" is a marine term, the same as that designating Noah's famous vessel, and is not related to the ark of the covenant, which was a chest. The romantic story of Moses' floating cradle, and his timely discovery and adoption by Pharaoh's daughter, is known to all Bible readers. Less familiar is the nautical reference in the first two verses of the 18th chapter of *Isaiah*: "Woe to the land shadowing with wings, which is beyond the rivers of Ethiopia: that sendeth ambassadors by the sea, even in vessels of bulrushes upon the waters, saying, Go, ye swift messengers . . ." Non-biblical writers such as Pliny, Theophrastus and Plutarch confirm the use of bulrushes, or more properly papyrus reeds, in the construction of small marine craft. Light and maneuverable, their utility might be compared to that of the birchbark canoes of the Indians.

In Bible times the papyrus reeds of the Nile were famous, and Assyrian records designate the plant as the reed of Egypt, and even use it to symbolize that country, just as we speak of the American eagle and the Russian bear. In 2 *Kings* (18/19-21) Sennacherib's envoy warns Hezekiah: "Thus saith the great king, the king of Assyria . . . now on whom dost thou trust, that thou rebellest against me? Now, behold, thou trustest upon the staff of this bruised reed, even upon Egypt, on which if a man lean, it will go into his hand and pierce it: so is Pharaoh king of Egypt unto all that trust on him." A parallel passage occurs in *Isaiah* (36/6).

Boat construction was but one of the uses of papyrus, and not even the most important. On a smaller scale, the plant rivalled the date palm in its service to man. In whatever debt that civilization owes to popular knowledge of reading and writing, and it is a great debt, must be recognized the pioneer contribution of papyrus. Our modern word "paper" is a linguistic derivative of papyrus, which furnished the earliest durable, portable and convenient writing surface. Papyrus rolls are depicted in ancient Egyptian sculpture, and actual documents written on papyrus are preserved in modern museums. Papyrus reeds no longer grow in Egypt, but are still found in the higher stretches of the Blue Nile, where it flows through Abyssinia (Ethiopia).

Papyrus paper was prepared by cutting the reeds into thin longitudinal slices, which were then trimmed and laid side by side to the required width, and overlaid by short transverse strips. It is not known whether an adhesive was used, but the sheets were soaked in Nile water until they blended together. They were then pounded and smoothed, and sun-dried. The better varieties were further rubbed to the required degree of thinness and even texture. Depending on the length of the manuscript, additional sheets were appended lengthwise to the bottom of the preceding ones, and attached with paste. When completed, the long document was rolled up loosely, the best quality papyrus forming the outer part of the roll, thus protecting inferior inner sheets.

The papyrus reed flourished in the Nile shallows, at wading depths. The main root of the mature plant was a thick horizontal stem stretching from twelve to twenty feet, and shooting out shorter vertical roots which anchored in the mud and silt. The jointless triangular stalks, six to twelve feet long, tapered up to a narrow tip, crowned by a remarkable large tufted head. The roots were used for handles and utensils as well as for fuel. The pliant stems were woven into baskets, mats, sails, ropes and sandals. The pith was eaten, both raw and

[158]

cooked, and so was the aqueous part of the stem. This dual role as writing paper and food is believed to underlie the biblical references to eating of books, and of words, such as occur in the closing verses of the 2nd and the opening verses of the 3rd chapter of *Ezekiel*: ". . . son of man . . . eat that I give thee. And when I looked, behold, an hand was sent unto me; and, lo, a roll of a book was therein; and he spread it before me; and it was written within and without (on both sides) . . . Moreover he said unto me, Son of man, eat that thou findest; eat this roll, and go speak unto the house of Israel. So I opened my mouth, and he caused me to eat that roll . . . then did I eat it; and it was in my mouth as honey for sweetness." Other relevant passages may be found in *Jeremiah* (15/16) and *Revelation* (10/8-10).

Isaiah (58/5) refers to a bulrush in a passage criticizing the hypocrisy of formal fasting without inward penitence: "Is it to bow down the head like a bulrush?" Although the Hebrew word here used differs from the other bulrush references, an associated type appears to be indicated. The long pliant stem of the papyrus reed with its large panicle bent and swayed even in a light breeze.

We are told that Moses' mother laid the ark of bulrushes "in the flags by the river's brink" and that when Pharaoh's daughter saw the ark "among the flags, she sent her maid to fetch it." *Isaiah* titled his 19th chapter "The burden of Egypt." In the 6th and 7th verses we read "They shall turn the rivers far away: and the brooks of defence (moats?) shall be emptied and dried up: the reeds and flags shall wither. The paper reeds by the brooks, by the mouth of the brooks, and everything sown by the brooks, shall wither." While some authorities attempt to define the genus of these flags, most consider that the word designates general aquatic weedy growth as found by the banks of rivers and marshes, and this latter view is strengthened by the Hebrew use of this word to designate what we call the Red Sea; they knew it as the Weedy, or Flaggy, Sea. A different native word is translated "flag" in *Job* (8/11-12): "Can the rush grow up without mire? can the flag grow without water? Whilst it is yet in his greenness, and not cut down, it withereth before any other herb." This word for "flag" is of Egyptian origin, and is also found in the account of Pharaoh's dream (*Genesis* 41/2, 18), where the Authorized Version translates it "meadow," and the Revised "reedgrass." The Egyptian original was used to designate in a general way coarse marsh grass and reeds.

Both Hebrew words rendered "bulrush" in the preceding paragraphs are in other Bible passages termed "rush," one instance being that just quoted (*Job* 8). Its damp habitat is confirmed in *Isaiah* (35/ 7): "And the parched ground shall become a pool, and the thirsty land springs of water: in the habitations of dragons, where each lay, shall be grass with reeds and rushes." This rush is the papyrus one associated with Moses' cradle. The other, employed in Isaiah's parable of fasting, is also mentioned by this prophet in a comparison of extremes. "Therefore the Lord will cut off from Israel head and tail, branch and rush, in one day" (*Isaiah* 9/14). A similar metaphor may be found in *Isaiah* (19/15). The idiom is thought to contrast the ceremonial palm branch with the lowly rush trodden underfoot.

Like the rush, the reed also has two Hebrew names, one of which is more commonly translated "pool" or "pond." Its sole appearance as "reed" is in *Jeremiah* (51/32): "The passages are stopped, and the reeds they have burned with fire." Perhaps this Hebrew word was used in the same sense as we use swamp or marsh, to include both the water and the vegetation growing therein.

In the chapter on perfumes it was noted that calamus, cane, and reed were three of several English variants used to translate one Hebrew word. The "reed" rendering is common, usually employed in its botanical sense or to symbolize frailty, but in many passages in *Ezekiel* a reed is used as a measuring rod: "There was a man . . . with a line of flax in his hand, and a measuring reed, and he stood in the gate . . . And behold a wall on the outside of the house round about, and in the man's hand a measuring reed of six cubits long by the cubit and an hand breadth: so he measured the breadth of the building, one reed; and the height, one reed" (*Ezekiel* 40/3, 5). This reed was nearly eleven feet long. *Revelation* (11/1; 21/15-16) also tells of a measuring reed, and the same Greek word is used and uniformly translated "reed" throughout the New Testament except in one instance, where it is interpreted pen: "I had many things to write, but I will not with ink and pen write unto thee" (3 *John* 13). A species of the calamus reed was used for making ancient pens, and probably other varieties were also adapted. The earlier writing reeds had the ends frayed, and were brushes rather than sharp implements, and to this day many Asiatic alphabets are written with a fine brush rather than with a pen. Later, reeds were pointed and split, somewhat similar to our pen nibs, and scribes employed a special knife for this purpose, as we learn in *Jeremiah* (36/23), "He cut it with the penknife." Thus our debt to the humble reed is twofold, for it provided both paper and pen with which to preserve the records of antiquity.

CHAPTER 15

Weeds

MAN'S PRIMAL sin, in the most literal sense of the Bible, was disobedience to God's command, and this disobedience was manifested in eating of the fruit of the tree of knowledge of good and evil. Immense study, many volumes and much oratory have built religious and philosophical creeds and dogmas around this transgression. Reduced to its simplest terms, it appears that original man was not conscious of any moral or practical differentiation dividing phenomena, actions, or motives, into good and bad, right and wrong, helpful and harmful. To the pure, all things were pure.

The first chapter of *Genesis* affirms the equitable and benevolent nature of Creation: "And God said, let the earth bring forth grass, the herb yielding seed, and the fruit tree yielding fruit after his kind, whose seed is in itself, upon the earth: and it was so. And the earth brought forth grass, and herb yielding seed after his kind, and the tree yielding fruit, whose seed was in itself, after his kind: and God saw that it was good . . . God created man in his own image .. . and God blessed them, and God said unto them . . . I have given you every herb bearing seed, which is upon the face of all the earth, and every tree, in the which is the fruit of a tree yielding seed; to you it shall be for meat. And to every beast of the earth, and to every fowl of the air, and to every thing that creepeth upon the earth, wherein there is life, I have given every green herb for meat: and it was so. And God saw everything that he had made, and, behold, it was very good."

Here is no justification to assume that some plants were beneficial for man and beast, while others were harmful or useless. All were good.

There are no separate and distinct botanical orders of weeds. Every weed is related to a cultivated plant, an unabashed and embarrassing relative who thrives lustily in slum soil across the tracks. Parsley and carrots are kin of waterhemlock and cowbane. Spinach and pigweed, peas and wild tares, peppermint and stinging nettle, sunflower and sow thistle, all claim family ties.

It has been said that weeds are plants whose virtues have not been discovered, or which grow where they are not wanted. Sometimes Cinderella meets the Fairy Prince; milkweed and Russian dandelion attained wartime respectability and even international importance as sources of rubber. It is unquestionable that medical and household properties inherent in many weeds were known to and utilized by ancient people, as well as by our forefathers, and it is only the advent of synthetic commercial chemistry and the corner drug store which has crowded them out in modern civilized lands.

Nature's interest is in maintaining and restoring the fertility of the earth, too often impoverished and ravished by man. As nature heals wounds and abrasions in her own inimitable way, even though the process of suppuration and formation of new scar tissue may offend our over-delicate senses, so she restores to harmony and fecundity the devastated soil, sometimes with a dressing of what man chooses to term noisome and stinking weeds. Perhaps they intend to offend the nose and scratch the skin of their prejudiced lord and master, in order to survive to carry out their appointed tasks. Thorns are nature's "Keep Off" sign, and a thicket of briers may protect and conceal a bank of rich humus.

The weeds of the Bible lands, as far as we can judge from Holy Writ, were predominantly of the thorns and thistles, briers and brambles type, rather than the small spikeless varieties which harass the gardener. The anathema which accompanied Adam's expulsion from the garden of Eden (*Genesis* 3/17, 18)—"Cursed is the ground for thy sake . . . thorns also and thistles shall it bring forth to thee"—may not be as vindictive as it sounds, for the Hebrew word translated "curse" has a number of other meanings, two appropriate alternatives being "heath" and "make bare." In any case, the Flood terminated the power of this original penalty, for *Genesis* (8/21) finds Jehovah promising, "I will not again curse the ground any more for man's sake."

The word weed occurs only once in the Bible text, and the reference is to seaweed. In Jonah's prayer, invoked from the belly of the great fish which swallowed him, he testifies: "The waters compassed me about . . . the depth closed me round about, the weeds were wrapped about my head" (*Jonah* 2/5). A marginal alternative in *Job* (31/40) gives "noisome weeds" for the "cockle" of the text. Elsewhere specific words are used, the Old Testament list comprising thorns, thistles, briers, brambles, cockles and nettles. The New Testament adds tares, but omits nettles and cockles.

When we refer to the original text, we find, as we might expect by now, that one English word does collective duty for several distinct Hebrew terms. For example, the word given in English as "thorn" has eleven Hebrew stems, only two of which appear to be related. Furthermore, the English translation is not consistent, for three of the native expressions rendered thorn are elsewhere changed to brier, bramble and thistle.

As we scrutinize the Bible weeds under their Palestine names, we find it convenient to divide them into two groups. The first, mentioned many times throughout the Scriptures, comprises thorns, briars and brambles; the latter section, cockle, thistles, nettles and tares, contains plants confined to few passages, and will be examined first.

Cockle makes its solitary appearance in *Job* (31/40), where the ruined rancher concludes an impassioned declaration of his integrity by avowing that if he speak not the truth, "let thistles grow instead of wheat, cockle instead of barley. The words of Job are ended." As mentioned three paragraphs back, "noisome weeds" is the marginal variation for "cockle." The Hebrew word signifies "shameful" or "noisome," and that appears to be the only clue. We may surmise that the weed was one which had an affinity for barley crops, and that its appearance in quantity marked the field of a careless and slothful farmer. On the other hand, it may have been a particularly obnoxious weed. There seems to be no evidence either for or against it being a cockle species, such as Purple Cockle or Cow Cockle, both common in grain fields and particularly objectionable because of the adulteration of the threshed grain by the ill-flavored and sometimes poisonous seeds of the cockle.

The English word "nettle" is used to designate two Hebrew terms. One of these signifies "pricking" or "burning," and apparently this led the translators towards the stinging nettle. In one of the passages where the word occurs, (*Job* 30/7), the text suggests that the weeds were quite tall, shady, and harmless to the touch, which would seem to rule out nettles. Job is referring to the dregs of the populace who subsisted on wild roots and goes on: "Among the bushes they brayed; under the nettles they were gathered together." The Revised Version gives a marginal rendering of the latter phrase "under the wild vetches they stretch themselves." Solomon introduces this particular nettle in *Proverbs* (24/

31) to describe a broken-down farm, "all grown over with thorns, and nettles had covered the face thereof." This nettle makes its last appearance in a gloomy passage from *Zephaniah* (2/9): "even the breeding of nettles, and saltpits, and a perpetual desolation." The association of saltpits with nettles may help identification, for certain weeds, such as "Russian thistle" and "shepherd's purse" thrive in a salty soil.

The second Hebrew word listed as "nettle" is uniformly translated in both Versions, with no marginal option. It closely resembles one of the words denoting thorns, and on the two occasions it is used the text is associated with desolation and ruin: "And thorns shall come up in her palaces, nettles and brambles in the fortresses thereof; it shall be an habitation of dragons, and a court for owls" (*Isaiah* 34/13), and "the pleasant places for their silver, nettles shall possess them: thorns shall be in their tabernacles" (*Hosea* 9/6).

As in the case of the nettle, two distinct Hebrew words are construed as "thistle." One of these is elsewhere rendered "thorn," "bramble" and "thicket," and in the Revised Version of 2 *Chronicles* (33/11) it becomes "chains," with a marginal alternative "hooks." The other native word for thistle occurs twice only, each time in conjunction with the same species of the thorn family. These particular thistles and thorns share the dubious honor of the first mentioned biblical weeds, threatened by God as He expelled the unfortunate Adam (*Genesis* 3/18). *Hosea* (10/8) uses the same couplet in denouncing the idolatrous worship at Aven (Bethel): "The thorn and the thistle shall come up on their altars." The derivation of this word suggests luxuriant growth, and thistles flourish and attain great size in Palestine.

In the New Testament the Greek word translated "thistles" in *Matthew* (7/16)—"Do men gather grapes of thorns, or figs of thistles?" —is changed to "briers" in *Hebrews* (6/7-8). "For the earth which drinketh in the rain that cometh oft upon it, and bringeth forth herbs meet for them by whom it is dressed, receiveth blessing from God: but that which beareth thorns and briers is rejected, and is nigh unto cursing; whose end is to be burned." The Revised Version uses "thistles" instead of "briers" in this latter text. The Greek name for thistle implies a three barbed plant, and we may surmise that the species under discussion had this characteristic.

Tares are the only weeds whose mention is confined to the New Testament. In the 13th chapter of *Matthew* the parable of the tares and

[165]

the wheat is set forth, and woven into the tale is sufficient corroborating evidence to justify us in assuming that a species of darnel was the growth referred to. "The kingdom of heaven is likened unto a man which sowed good seed in his field: but while men slept, his enemy came and sowed tares among the wheat, and went his way. But when the blade was sprung up, and brought forth fruit, then appeared the tares also . . . the servants of the householder came and said unto him . . . Wilt thou that we go and gather them up? But he said, Nay; lest while ye gather up the tares ye root up also the wheat with them. Let both grow together until the harvest: and in the time of harvest I will say to the reapers, Gather ye together first the tares, and bind them in bundles to burn them: but gather the wheat into my barn."

It was not until "the blade was sprung up, and brought forth fruit" that the crop revealed the presence of weeds. Some species of darnel in their early stages so closely resemble growing wheat that only close observation can detect the difference, but as soon as the blade sprouts and grain appears, the distinction is unmistakable. At this advanced stage any attempt to eradicate the darnel by pulling it up naturally would cause great damage to the wheat.

We now come to the major weed family of the Scriptures, barbed varieties of bushes referred to in English as thorns, briers or brambles. The Hebrew designations are much more diverse, and sixteen different words in the original tongue are condensed into the three mentioned in the Authorized Version.

Such a diversity of thorny species is not surprising, for we need only think of the numerous kinds of prickly bushes which grow wild in our own countryside and damage the skin and clothing of the unwary trespasser. The Holy Land had, and has, a particularly lush crop of armored plants, and travellers tell that certain infested regions are virtually impassable to the pedestrian on account of the spiked undergrowth. This barrier feature was utilized by farmers and husbandmen to protect their fields and vineyards against thieves and trespassers, both two and four-footed. Hardy fast-growing thorns offered a cheap and convenient hedge for an orchard or cultivated plot, the bushes providing the densest obstruction during the growing and harvesting seasons of the enclosed crops, by virtue of their own parallel development.

Two symbolical passages compare the ungodly to a hedge of thorns. Solomon observes, "The way of the slothful man is as an hedge of thorns: but the way of the righteous is made plain" (Hebrew: is raised up as a highway) (*Proverbs* 15/19). Deploring wickedness in high places, *Micah* (7/4) declares, "The best of them is as a brier: the most upright is sharper than a thorn hedge." It is this same Hebrew term which *Isaiah* (5/5) uses in his account of the unproductive vineyard and its abandonment: "I will take away the hedge thereof, and it shall be eaten up." A different, but apparently related word is found in *Job* (1/10), where Satan protests, "Hast not thou made an hedge about him, and about his house, and about all that he hath on every side?" In Jesus' parable of the husbandman who rented his vineyard (*Matthew* 21/33), the familiar vineyard hedge is mentioned, but the evidence that it was a hedge of thorns is circumstantial only. A beautiful vine allegory is found in the 80th *Psalm,* and from the context we may reasonably assume that the hedges referred to in the 12th and 13th verses were well studded with thorns and spikes. "Why hast thou then broken down her hedges, so that all they which pass by the way do pluck her? The boar out of the wood doth waste it, and the wild beast of the field doth devour it." Wild boars are amongst the most dangerous and destructive of animals, and their rooting propensities would require creeping thorns as well as climbing ones to repel them effectively. A warning against damaging hedges is sounded in *Ecclesiastes* (10/8): "Whoso breaketh an hedge, a serpent shall bite him." Snakes commonly make their homes in shady undergrowth where they are unlikely to be disturbed by enemies.

The bramble bush is so translated from one Greek and two Hebrew words, the latter elsewhere being rendered thorn. The bramble mentioned in the tree parable in the 9th chapter of *Judges* is believed to have been the buckthorn. The challenge of this bush, "Let fire come out of the bramble, and devour the cedars of Lebanon," is interesting in view of a corresponding connection with fire elsewhere. *Luke* (6/44) explains, "For of thorns men do not gather figs, nor of a bramble bush gather they grapes." The Greek word here translated bramble bush is identical with that used in several New Testament passages to designate the burning bush of Mount Sinai, where God appeared to Moses, (*Exodus* 3/2). One of these references is in *Acts* (7/30): "There appeared to him (Moses) in the wilderness of mount Sinai an angel of the Lord in a flame of fire in a bush."

The sanctity of fire is one of the oldest of religious credos, pre-

[167]

served to this day in the burning of church candles, the transference of the ceremonial torch, and the constantly burning light on a venerated shrine. In other religions, notably the Parsee and Hindu, its sacred nature is more directly revered. Mystics have beheld visions while gazing subjectively into flickering flames, and who among us has not lost consciousness of the outer world when sitting before a blazing hearth on a wintry night. The Bible frequently associates fire with divinity, as in the 18th *Psalm,* and in the description of the Pentecostal cloven tongues of fire in the 2nd chapter of *Acts.*

Whether an esoteric meaning is conveyed in the account of the burning bush of Sinai, which burnt without being consumed, is a matter of opinion, but there is ample evidence that thorns were a regular source of firewood. Anyone who has burnt dry dead thorn bushes, and has listened to the sharp spasmodic sizzling and crackling of their brief blaze, will recognize the aptness of the comparison of *Ecclesiastes* (7/6): "For as the crackling of thorns under a pot, so is the laughter of the fool." Another reference to the use of thorns as fuel for cooking occurs in *Psalms* (58/9): "Before your pots can feel the thorns, he shall take them away." *Isaiah* (33/12) tells of the use of thorns to feed the prolonged fire necessary to calcine lime from bones, shells or rock: "The people shall be as the burnings of lime; as thorns cut up shall they be burned in the fire." This passage suggests a systematic collection of firewood, and receives support from *Nahum* (1/10): "For while they be folden together as thorns . . . they shall be devoured as stubble fully dry." *Amos* (2/1) threatens Moab "because he burned the bones of the king of Edom into lime."

So matted and tangled were the thorn thickets that the only practical way to clear them was by burning. Their inflammability is recognized in the first fire prevention law (*Exodus* 22/6): "If fire break out, and catch in thorns, so that the stacks of corn, or the standing corn, or the field, be consumed therewith; he that kindled the fire shall surely make restitution." Acceptance of the impenetrable nature of thorn thickets, and recognition of fire as the only effective agent of destruction, is well expressed in 2 *Samuel* (23/6-7): "But the sons of Belial shall be all of them as thorns thrust away, because they cannot be taken with hands: but the man that shall touch them must be fenced (margin: fitted) with iron and the staff of a spear; and they shall be utterly burned with fire in the same place." Two passages suggest the short-lived nature of a thorn fire: *Psalms* (118/12) says of the wicked, "They are quenched as the fire of thorns," and *Isaiah* (10/17) proclaims, "And the light of Israel shall be for a fire, and his Holy One for a flame: and it shall burn and devour his thorns and his briers in one day."

A suggestion that thorn branches were the forerunners of barbed wire entanglements in armed conflict may be read in *Isaiah* (27/4): "Who would set the briers and thorns against me in battle? I would go through them, I would burn them together."

Sound agricultural advice is given the careless Judean farmers by *Jeremiah* (4/3): "Break up your fallow ground, and sow not among thorns," and he follows it (12/13) by prediction of a grimmer harvest, "They have sown wheat, but shall reap thorns." Hundreds of years later, Jesus spoke of this annual menace to farming: "And some (seed) fell among thorns; and the thorns sprung up, and choked them (*Matthew* 13/7).

With the prevalence of thorns in Palestine, both in natural thickets and in planned hedges, we should naturally expect to find references to the painful pricks of its spikes. Solomon's warning in *Proverbs* (26/9), "As a thorn goeth up into the hand of a drunkard, so is a parable in the mouth of fools," may have been inspired by his observation of a vineyard owner who had quaffed too heavily of his new wine, and lurching homeward had fallen against his own thorn hedge, injuring his hand in grasping for support, thus suggesting to the philosophic monarch that a beneficial structure or idea may inflict self-injury on the careless or ignorant user. *Ezekiel* (28/24) refers to the menace of thorns in these words: "And there shall be no more a pricking brier unto the house of Israel, nor any grieving thorn of all that are round about them." In a much debated passage in 2 *Corinthians* (12/7) Paul coins an expression which has become proverbial: "There was given to me a thorn in the flesh ... lest I should be exalted above measure."

Much speculation surrounds the classification of the thorns with which the Roman soldiery tormented Jesus: "And when they had platted a crown of thorns, they put it upon his head, and a reed in his right hand: and they bowed the knee before him, and mocked him, saying, Hail, King of the Jews!" (*Matthew* 27/29). These thorns have the same Greek name as those in the parable of the sower of the seed, referred to earlier. Two species, *Zizyphus Spina-Christi* (jujube) and *Paliurus Spina-Christi* (buckthorn) have been named after the incident, but their size and structure would appear to make the plaiting of a small circlet a difficult matter. Old Roman coins show some of the Emperors wearing spiked crowns, so the thorns may have been chosen to resemble a royal diadem, and not to cause pain. Laurel leaves made up the traditional chaplet of the conqueror, and a thorny plant resembling laurel may have been used.

There remains one plant, not usually listed amongst Bible weeds, but being apparently included in that category by the context: "Thus judgment springeth up as hemlock in the furrows of the field" (*Hosea* 10/4). *Rosh* is the Hebrew word here translated hemlock, and *rosh* has already been reviewed in the herb chapter, under its more common rendering of wormwood. The plant *Hosea* referred to must have been one which germinated and sprouted rapidly, and while it may have been a domesticated variety the general association of *rosh* with the dark side of life rather suggests a weed.

CHAPTER 16

Plant Pests and Disease

WHEN JEHOVAH wrathfully expelled Adam and Eve from the garden of Eden, presumably the serpent was evicted as well. Eternal enmity was decreed between man and the serpent. Many insects go through the caterpillar stage, a stage which resembles the snake in shape and movement, and the insect world has furnished a perpetual and never vanquished threat to man's food supply, an unconquerable plague which has dogged man's agricultural footsteps, or in Bible language "bruised his heel," since the dawn of cultivation.

The locust, under various names, was the most dreaded invader that a farming people could suffer under. *Joel*, both literally and symbolically, devotes much of his brief prophecy to a description of the devastation wrought on a smiling countryside by this cursed and hated insect pest. Some of the imagery used by *Joel* is duplicated in *Revelation*, and an excerpt therefrom (9/7-9) serves as a key to the longer and more detailed quotation. "And the shapes of the locusts were like unto horses prepared unto battle; . . . their teeth were as the teeth of lions, and they had breastplates, as it were breastplates of iron; and the sound of their wings was as the sound of chariots of many horses running to battle." In the following passage, summarized from the *Book of Joel*, the same descriptions will be observed.

"Hear this, ye old men, and give ear, all ye inhabitants of the land. . . Tell ye your children of it, and let your children tell their children, and their children another generation. That which the palmerworm hath left hath the locust eaten; and that which the locust hath left hath the cankerworm eaten; and that which the cankerworm hath left hath the caterpillar eaten. Awake, ye drunkards, and weep; and howl, all ye drinkers of wine, because of the new wine; for it is cut off from your mouth. For a nation is come up upon my land, strong, and without number, whose teeth are the teeth of a lion, and he hath the cheek teeth of a great lion. He hath laid my vine waste, and barked my fig tree: he hath made it clean bare, and cast it away; the branches thereof are made white . . . The field is wasted, the land mourneth; for the corn is wasted: the new wine is dried up, the oil languisheth. Be ye ashamed, O ye husbandmen; howl, O ye vinedressers, for the wheat and for the barley; because the harvest of the field is perished. The vine is dried up, and the fig tree languisheth; the pomegranate tree, the palm tree also, and the apple tree, even all the trees, are withered: . . . Alas for the day! . . . . Is not the meat cut off before our eyes . . . . The seed is rotten . . . the garners are laid desolate, the barns are broken down; for the corn is withered. How do the beasts groan! the herds of cattle are perplexed, because they have no pasture; yea, the flocks of sheep are made desolate. . . . A day of darkness and of gloominess, a day of clouds and of thick darkness. . . . A fire devoureth before them; and behind them a flame burneth: the land is as the garden of Eden before them, and behind them a desolate wilderness; yea, and nothing shall escape them. The appearance of them is as the appearance of horses; and as horsemen, so shall they run. Like the noise of chariots on the tops of mountains shall they leap, like the noise of a flame of fire that devoureth the stubble, as a strong people set in battle array. Before their face the people shall be much pained; all faces shall gather blackness. They shall run like mighty men; they shall climb the wall like men of war; and they shall march every one on his ways, and they shall not break their ranks: neither shall one thrust another; they shall walk every one in his path: and when they fall upon the sword, they shall not be wounded. They shall run to and fro in the city; they shall run upon the wall, they shall climb up upon the houses; they shall enter in at the windows like a thief. The earth shall quake before them; the heavens shall tremble: the sun and the moon shall be dark, and the stars shall withdraw their shining. . . . Then will the Lord . . . pity his people .. And I will restore to you the years that the locust hath eaten, the cankerworm, and the caterpillar, and the palmerworm, my great army which I sent among you."

Only those who have seen at first hand the utter and complete destruction which locusts inflict on growing things, have heard the noise of their wings and watched the movements of their mass body, can understand how literally true is this description of *Joel*. In similar, but simpler, language, Moses threatened Pharaoh: "Else, if thou refuse to let my people go, behold, tomorrow will I bring the locusts into thy coast: and they shall cover the face of the earth, that one cannot be able to see the earth: and they shall eat the residue of that which is escaped, which remaineth unto you from the hail, and shall eat every tree which groweth for you out of the field: and they shall fill thy houses, and the houses of all thy servants, and the houses of all the Egyptians" (*Exodus* 10/4-6).

Solomon, a great naturalist, tells of their habits: "The locusts have no king, yet go they forth all of them by bands" (*Proverbs* 30/27) while *Isaiah* (33/4) adds,"Your spoil shall be gathered like the gathering of the caterpillar: as the running to and fro of locusts shall he run upon them." *Psalms* (109/23) refers to the influence of wind on the unstable insects: "I am tossed up and down as the locust." *Nahum* (3/15-17) adds to our information: "It shall eat thee up like the cankerworm: make thyself many as the cankerworm, make thyself many as the locusts . . . the cankerworm spoileth, and fleeth away. Thy crowned are as the locusts, and thy captains as the great grasshoppers, which camp in the hedges in the cold day, but when the sun ariseth they flee away, and their place is not known where they are."

Locusts, palmerworms, cankerworms, grasshoppers and caterpillars, all may be regarded as belonging to the same general family, and sometimes indicating the various stages of growth of the insect. Nine Hebrew words designate various types, or degrees of bodily development, of the locust. As usual, the English translation is loose. Sometimes cankerworm is translated instead of caterpillar from the same root word, while caterpillar and locust interchange as the rendering of two native terms. One "locust" original is elsewhere anglicized as "spear" and "shadowing," the latter a vivid testimony to the sky-darkening clouds of locusts: "Woe to the land shadowing with wings" (*Isaiah* 18/1).

The locust is normally a passive solitary insect, but under swarm influence its metabolism changes, it becomes nervous and restless, and gregarious mass instinct takes over the individual. Swarms occasionally travel long distances, some having been encountered by ships a thousand miles from land, while an enormous collection estimated as filling out a two thousand square mile area has been observed crossing the Red Sea. The larvae resemble the parents except for wings, while their destructive capacity equals that of the mature insects. The eggs are laid in holes in the soil and in about seven weeks the larvae become active, countless millions in an infested area creeping and wriggling over the doomed vegetation with a common general orientation. Unorganized destruction is a hopeless futile task. Experience has shown that the young cannot move over a smooth surface, so screens serve to divert the moving mass towards the ends, where pits trap huge quantities; the pits are covered with earth before they fill up and the screens are moved to a new location adjoining empty pits, where the process is repeated. There appears to be no Bible evidence that this counter measure was used against young locusts, although there are many references to ditches and pits being dug, the purpose of some being left unexplained.

It's an ill wind that blows nobody good, and even locusts had their uses. Much of the modern dietary taste remains under the influence of the old Mosaic category of clean and unclean food. The tendency has been to remove the taboo on animals such as the pig and the rabbit, but on the other hand there are foods certified clean and edible by Moses which majority opinion rejects. Here we find the locusts. "Yet these may ye eat of every flying creeping thing that goeth upon all four, which have legs above their feet, to leap withal upon the earth: even these of them ye may eat; the locust after his kind, and the bald locust after his kind, and the beetle after his kind, and the grasshopper after his kind" (*Leviticus* 11/21-22).

The Revised Version substitutes "cricket" for "beetle," but the native word makes but this single appearance, so identification is speculative. The only scriptural reference to locust-eating is the Gospel statement that the food of John the Baptist was locusts and wild honey. Bedouin Arabs are reported to eat locusts, boiling them in saltwater or frying them in butter; the flavor is said to resemble shrimp.

It was natural that the depredations of the locust family should loom so large that the ravages of other field and garden pests appeared negligible, and there is little mention of other harmful species. Our word "worm" translates six Hebrew and two Greek wrigglers, and from the context and alternative renderings in other passages, maggots, serpents, moth larvae, and crawlers yielding scarlet dye, are indicated as well as plant pests. The familiar earthworm appears to be missing, notwithstanding the reference in *Micah* (7/17): "They shall move out of their holes like worms of the earth." A marginal note offers "creeping things" for "worms," while the Revised Version substitutes "crawling things." These variants might still specify earthworms, but the theory is weakened by the appearance of the same Hebrew word in *Deuteronomy* (32/24), "with the poison of serpents of the dust."

There are two specific instances where worms damage or destroy plants, the better known being related in *Jonah* (4/7): "But God prepared a worm when the morning rose the next day, and it smote the gourd that it withered." The other is in *Deuteronomy* (28/39): "Thou shalt plant vineyards, and dress them, but shalt neither drink of the wine, nor gather the grapes; for the worms shall eat them." The insignificance of the worm is used by several writers to symbolize man's low estate. "But I am a worm and no man," confesses the humiliated David (*Psalms* 22/6). Both the Authorized and Revised Versions fail to do justice to the text of *Job* (25/6), where two different types of Hebrew worms occur in the original: "How much less man, that is a worm? and the son of man, which is a worm?" The moth larva seems to be designated in *Isaiah* (51/8): "For the moth shall eat them up like a garment, and the worm shall eat them like wool."

Scarlet and crimson dye was processed from the bodies of the female insect *Coccus ilicus*, which frequented the bark of the ilex tree; the one Hebrew name designates both the worm and the dye colors. In modern times we do the same with cochineal, a coloring made from the dried bodies of the insect *coccus cacti*, which lives on the Mexican cactus.

Two snails crawl across Bible pages: the first one, in *Leviticus* (11/30), receives lone mention among a list of unclean reptiles and animals and is considered to have been some sort of a sand lizard. A different snail, considered an ancestor of our common snail or slug, appears in *Psalms* (58/8): "As a snail which melteth, let every one of them pass away." The allusion is thought to refer to the slimy trail in the wake of the snail.

The ravages of field mice are implied in the sixth chapter of 1 *Samuel*. The Philistines had defeated the Israelites and captured the ark of the covenant, but the ark proved bad joss and calamity befell the populace wherever it was displayed, so in desperation they returned it to the Israelites, and on the advice of the priests and diviners included five golden emerods (hemorrhoids) and five golden mice as a trespass offering. The replicas were to ward off a recurrence of the twin plagues. The land of the Philistines was the wheat bowl of Canaan, and the mice had apparently ruined the crops: "your mice that mar the land" (1 *Samuel* 6/5). The only other references to mice are where they are branded, along with the snail, as unclean, and a denunciation by *Isaiah* (66/17) of the custom of eating them in idolatrous rites. A variety of dormouse is considered edible in parts of Asia.

The Bible refers to a form of crop blight which is always mentioned under the dual term of blasting and mildew, in that order. Blasting would seem to have been the cause of which mildew was the result. The derivation of the Hebrew word for mildew signifies "paleness" or "yellowness," and the word is translated "paleness" in a passage describing the pallor occasioned by great pain (*Jeremiah* 30/6). In one of his dreams, Pharaoh saw "seven ears (of corn), withered, thin, and blasted with the east wind" (*Genesis* 41/23). The Hebrew farmer was as wind-conscious as the skipper of a sailing ship. The east wind, howling sand-laden from the arid desert, meant crop ruin. *Ezekiel* (17/10), speaking of the vine, says, "Being planted, shall it prosper? shall it not utterly wither, when the east wind toucheth it?" The same weather lore is used by *Hosea* (13/15): "Though he be fruitful among his brethren, an east wind shall come, the wind of the Lord shall come up from the wilderness, and his spring shall become dry, and his fountain shall be dried up."

It would appear that mildew designated the pale, withered appearance of the crops after being blasted with the east wind, rather than that it denoted a particular plant disease. The Old Testament sometimes depicts Jehovah in the role of the god of fertility, and his displeasure is evinced in agricultural calamities for which he takes full responsibility: "I smote you with blasting, and with mildew, and with hail, in all the labors of your hands; yet ye turned not to me, saith the Lord" (*Haggai* 2/17). Israel was a stubborn race, prepared to absorb a lot of punishment: "I have withholden the rain from you . . . I have smitten you with blasting and mildew; when your gardens and your vineyards and your fig trees and your olive trees increased, the palmerworm devoured them: yet have ye not returned unto me, saith the Lord" (Amos 4/7-9.) The 28th chapter of *Deutoronomy* recites the punishments which a vengeful Jehovah will inflict on a disobedient

people, and agricultural disasters take up a large part of this long re-
cital. One verse, the 22nd, reveals the fear of the malign east wind in
the minds of the people: "The Lord shall smite thee with a consump-
tion, and with a fever, and with an inflammation, and with an extreme
burning, and with the sword (margin: drought) and with blasting, and
with mildew; and they shall pursue thee until thou perish."

CHAPTER 17

Laws, Regulations, and Customs

THE EGYPTIANS were an agricultural people and they were a regimented people. The periodic flooding of the Nile was the governing factor in Egyptian farming, and forced the early Pharaohs to establish a strong central control over irrigation. In order that the intricate system of water supply and water rights, together with timely cultivation, should be of national benefit rather than a prey to selfish individualism, a bureaucratic farm administration enforced a planned agricultural system. Religion and carnival, woven into the pattern of seasonal activity, added spiritual and sensual attraction to the cultivator's regime.

The tribesmen of Canaan were also good farmers, but they were rugged individualistic ones, impatient of all authority other than the patriarchal bond. The local gods sent rain or withheld it according to their whim, and each district had its own Baal (lord, master) who was indifferent or antagonistic to other Baals elsewhere. The prestige of the tribal god was tied to the fertility of woman, livestock and plant, and worship and festival in the groves of the deity were more spontaneous and orgiastic than in the formal temples of Egypt.

When Moses led the Israelites into the first lap of the long journey towards the Promised Land, he already knew the reputation of Canaan. Traffic was constant between Egypt and its northern neighbor. Moses had been reared in the upper circles of a totalitarian dictatorship, and his disagreement with Pharaoh was religious and political rather than social and economic. Moses was dignified, precise, orderly, bureaucratic, and the Mosaic Law reveals the discipline of his methodical mind. Emotionally and spiritually he was a Hebrew, but intellectually he was closer to the rulers of Egypt than to the turbulent and impulsive proletariat of Israel. "Moses was learned in all the wisdom of the Egyptians, and was mighty in words and in deeds. And when he was full forty years old, it came into his heart to visit his brethren the children of Israel" (*Acts* 7/22-23). He foresaw the influence which

Canaan folkways, both religious and secular, would exert on the freed serfs under his charge, and once the Israelites were well clear of the Egyptian border, but were still mentally conditioned by Egyptian ordinance, custom, and tradition, the great lawgiver, inspired by Jehovah, established the authoritarian code known by his name.

It is regrettable that the Mosaic Law, a system which has proven to be thoroughly sound and practical in many of its regulations, not only for the Jewish people but throughout the world, should confine itself to how, and ignore why. Explanation being absent, speculation is permissible. The influence of Egypt, both positive and negative, is evident. The Babylonian Code of Hammurabi, promulgated six centuries before that of Moses, had comparable edicts. Divine purpose, translated into human terms, is the hard center of the legislation. Some of the ordinances, meaningless to modern thought, may have propaganda value. Moses knew that the greatest peril his charges and their descendants faced in Canaan was not the hostility and armed opposition of the tribes they were to displace. The peoples of Canaan were kin to the Hebrews, the same ancestral blood flowing through their veins. The Egyptians had always been foreigners, in blood, and in culture, and in religion. It was the ideology of Canaan which Moses feared more than its warriors, the ideology which the patriarchs had tolerated and sometimes shared. At this distance, it appears that practical and logical regulations were sometimes supplemented with apparently meaningless parallel ordinances, to emphasize the danger of diluting the purity of the Chosen People with an alien strain: "For thou art an holy people unto the Lord thy God, and the Lord hath chosen thee to be a peculiar people unto himself, above all the nations that are upon the earth" (*Deuteronomy* 14/2).

We do not have to go back to 1491 B.C. to study the psychology and propaganda of a nation convinced of its manifest destiny as a divinely appointed leader. The track of history is scarred with the marks of peoples, religions and ideologies who insisted on their right to a place in the sun. The tragedy of Israel lay in the debasing of the goal of spiritual leadership into a material quest for power and riches. Whether the exclusiveness of the society of the old worshippers of Jehovah preserved and strengthened their theocracy set in a pagan world, or whether their ultra-nationalism and self-superiority infuriated and brought reprisal from neighboring nations, there is no doubt but that their tactics were those guaranteed not to win friends nor influence people. "Take heed to thyself, lest thou make a covenant with the inhabitants of the land whither thou goest, lest it be for a snare in the midst of thee" (*Exodus* 34/12).

Whatever the purpose and reasoning behind the rulings of the Mosaic legislation, conjecture must remain speculative. Each command may have deeper significance than we realize, for in spite of our vaunted scientific civilization we know but little of nature's laws and harmonies and warning signs. Research must also make allowance for the mutilation of the original sacred text by additions or deletions, deliberate or involuntary, on the part of later scribes and authorities, and the further distortion in translation to another language.

Man started his biblical career with one taboo only: the fruit of the tree of the knowledge of good and evil was the sole entry on the prohibited list. Other plants were edible: "And God said, Behold, I have given you every herb bearing seed, which is upon the face of all the earth, and every tree, in the which is the fruit of a tree yielding seed; to you it shall be for meat" (*Genesis* 1/29). It was a vegetarian's world; there is no mention of meat diet. We first read of clean and unclean beasts in Jehovah's commandment to Noah: "Of every clean beast thou shalt take to thee by sevens, the male and his female; and of beasts that are not clean by two, the male and his female" (*Genesis* 7/2). In the first chapter of the same book, all created animal life is extolled by God as very good. Six chapters later animals are segregated into clean and unclean. When, and by whom, was the differentiation established? It is not until the promulgation of the Mosaic code that Divine sanction is claimed for hygienic classification of living creatures.

The last verse of the eighth chapter establishes the Divine sequence upon which all agricultural organization rests. "While the earth remaineth, seedtime and harvest, and cold and heat, and summer and winter, and day and night shall not cease." A few verses later (9/2-4) we come to the authorized extension of man's diet into animal meat: "And the fear of you and the dread of you shall be upon every beast of the earth, and upon every fowl of the air, upon all that moveth upon the earth, and upon all the fishes of the sea: into your hand are they delivered. Every moving thing that liveth shall be meat for you: even as the green herb have I given you all things. But flesh with the life thereof, which is the blood thereof, shall ye not eat."

Here is an echo of the first chapter of *Genesis,* where all creation is good, and discrimination is a meaningless word; clean and unclean categories are unknown and unadmissible, and all living creation below man is permissible food; only blood is prohibited, not because it is unclean but because it is vital rather than material. This is further stressed in *Deuteronomy* (12/23): "Only be sure that thou eat not the blood: for the blood is the life; and thou mayest not eat the life with the flesh." An understanding of this postulation gives a new meaning to the many blood references in both the Old and the New Testaments.

The patriarchs seem to have got along with a minimum of laws and regulations, and it is not until after the Exodus that we find a multitude of "thou shalts" and "thou shalt nots." The agricultural foundation of the Hebrew state was theocratic: "The land shall not be sold for ever; for the land is mine; for ye are strangers and sojourners with me" (*Leviticus* 25/23). The Revised Version substitutes "The land shall not be sold in perpetuity." David corroborates this in the opening words of the 24*th Psalm*: "The earth is the Lord's and the fulness thereof." This was the cornerstone of the commonwealth, safeguarded by the fiftieth or Jubilee year provision which abrogated all alien title and possession of family land. The ninety-nine-year lease clause under which the United States was granted bases in British possessions, in exchange for destroyers, is a relic of this law of limitations. The philosophy and economic doctrine of Henry George, better known as Single Tax, is based on this divine premise.

Many theorists in many lands offer diverse diagnostic opinions on the causes of the trials and tribulations which beset this old world, and each generation is presented with streamlined versions of ancient panaceas, while the patient, man, and the long-suffering soil of the family homestead, earth, increasingly rely on narcotics and stimulants, with results ephemeral and regressive. Jesus warned the materialistic and dogmatic Pharisees of His time, while realizing the futility of expecting that His words would be heeded: "Ye are they which justify yourselves before men; but God knoweth your hearts: for that which is highly esteemed among men is abomination in the sight of God. . . And it is easier for heaven and earth to pass, than one tittle of the law to fail" (*Luke* 16/15-17). The Master referred to the Mosaic Law and the later revelations of the prophets. "And he said, If they hear not Moses and the prophets, neither will they be persuaded though one rose from the

[181]

dead" (*Luke* 16/31). These are unequivocal words.

"For in six days the Lord made heaven and earth, the sea, and all that in them is, and rested the seventh day; wherefore the Lord blessed the sabbath day, and hallowed it." So ends the fourth commandment in *Exodus* (20/11). Seven is the sabbatical number, the sacred number of Scripture, and the Mosaic social economy used seven as its working digit. A septennial period was a basic time unit, when contracts expired or were renewed, and obligations were fulfilled or wiped out. Seven such units, forty-nine years, completed a cycle, and the fiftieth year was celebrated as a year of jubilee. The Hebrew word for jubilee, *yobel,* means "ram's horn" or "trumpet," and the mass blowing of horns inaugurated this year of freedom and rest. Much of the fabric of Jewish life was woven round the mystical number seven, and awareness of this is essential to a better understanding of many Bible events. Seven was the standard trading count, as is our dozen, and it also indicated completeness in a class or group sense.

Man lives by the soil, and agricultural practices and requirements are always woven into the mythology, religion and folkways of a nation. The twenty-fifth chapter of *Leviticus* lays down the system and schedule of farm economy for the Hebrew race, and on this earthy foundation much of Jewish ritual and ceremony lies. "And the Lord spake unto Moses in mount Sinai, saying, Speak unto the children of Israel, and say unto them, When ye come into the land which I give you, then shall the land keep a sabbath (Hebrew: rest) unto the Lord. Six years thou shalt sow thy field, and six years thou shalt prune thy vineyard, and gather in the fruit thereof; but in the seventh year shall be a sabbath of rest unto the land, a sabbath for the Lord: thou shalt neither sow thy field, nor prune thy vineyard. That which groweth of its own accord of thy harvest thou shalt not reap, neither gather the grapes of thy vine undressed: for it is a year of rest unto the land. And the sabbath (rest) of the land shall be meat for you; for thee, and for thy servant, and for thy maid, and for thy hired servant, and for thy stranger that sojourneth with thee, and for thy cattle, and for the beasts that are in thy land, shall all the increase thereof be meat . . . . And if ye shall say, What shall we eat the seventh year? behold, we shall not sow, nor gather in our increase: then I will command my blessing upon you in the sixth year, and it shall bring forth fruit for three years. And ye shall sow the eighth year, and eat yet of old fruit

[182]

until the ninth year; until her fruits come in ye shall eat of the old store.... And thou shalt number seven sabbaths of years unto thee, seven times seven years; and the space of the seven sabbaths of years shall be unto thee forty and nine years. Then shalt thou cause the trumpet of the jubile to sound on the tenth day of the seventh month, in the day of atonement shall ye make the trumpet sound throughout all your land. And ye shall hallow the fiftieth year, and proclaim liberty throughout all the land unto all the inhabitants thereof: it shall be a jubile unto you; and ye shall return every man unto his possession, and ye shall return every man unto his family. A jubile shall that fiftieth year be unto you: ye shall not sow, neither reap that which groweth of itself in it, nor gather the grapes in it of thy vine undressed. For it is the jubile; it shall be holy unto you: ye shall eat the increase thereof out of the field. In the year of this jubile ye shall return every man unto his possession. And if thou sell ought unto thy neighbor, or buyest ought of thy neighbor's hand, ye shall not oppress one another: according to the number of years after the jubile thou shalt buy of thy neighbor, and according unto the number of years of the fruits he shall sell unto thee: according to the multitude of years thou shalt increase the price thereof, and according to the fewness of years thou shalt diminish the price of it: for according to the number of the years of the fruits doth he sell unto thee."

When the tribes settled in Canaan, a piece of ground was allotted each family as their property, by the grace of God and subject to obeying His commandments. "And the Lord spake unto Moses,.... saying, Speak unto the children of Israel, and say unto them, When ye are passed over Jordan into the land of Canaan; then ye shall drive out all the inhabitants of the land from before you.... and ye shall dispossess the inhabitants of the land, and dwell therein: for I have given you the land to possess it. And ye shall divide the land by lot for an inheritance among your families: and to the more ye shall give the more inheritance, and to the fewer ye shall give the less inheritance: every man's inheritance shall be in the place where his lot falleth;.... But if ye will not drive out the inhabitants of the land from before you.... it shall come to pass, that I shall do unto you, as I thought to do unto them " (*Numbers* 33/50-56).

The original allotment of each family thus became their permanent property (under God) and could not be permanently alienated.

The Bible speaks of land being sold and redeemed, but actually the transaction was a lease, usually paid in a lump sum beforehand. The price depended on the interval between the sale and the year of jubilee, the maximum of forty-nine years commanding the highest amount. Provision was made for the land to be bought back into the family in inter-jubilee years. "If thy brother be waxen poor, and hath sold away some of his possession, and if any of his kin come to redeem it, then shall he redeem that which his brother sold. And if the man have none to redeem it, and himself be able to redeem it; then let him count the years of the sale thereof, and restore the overplus unto the man to whom he sold it; that he may return unto his possession. But if he be not able to restore it to him, then that which is sold shall remain in the hand of him that hath bought it until the year of jubile: and in the jubile it shall go out, and he shall return unto his possession" (*Leviticus* 25/25-28).

This ruling applied to country property. Houses within a walled city, if sold, could not be redeemed more than twelve months after date of sale, and if not redeemed within the year became the absolute property of the new owner, and no longer subject to the law of jubilee.

In the *Book of Ruth* there is an interesting account of the redeeming of ancestral land, and the close relationship between the law of property and the law respecting a wife or widow is apparent. The book opens with the report of a famine in the Bethlehem district of Canaan, in consequence of which a farmer named Elimelech along with his wife Naomi and their two sons left their parched acres and moved over into Moab, which had escaped the dearth. Shortly after settling in their new home, Elimelech died, and the two boys married local Moab girls, Ruth and Orpah. Ten years later Naomi's two sons also passed away, and the griefstricken woman decided to return to her home town, which had by this time recovered its agricultural prosperity. Her daughters-in-law offered to go with her, but she dissuaded them. Orpah decided to remain in Moab, but Ruth insisted on accompanying Naomi and sharing her fortune for good or ill. So, the two women crossed the Jordan into Judea. ". . . And they came to Bethlehem in the beginning of barley harvest. And Naomi had a kinsman of her husband's, a mighty man of wealth, of the family of Elimelech; and his name was Boaz. And Ruth the Moabitess said unto Naomi, Let me now go to the field, and glean ears of corn

after him in whose sight I shall find grace. And she said unto her,
Go, my daughter. And she went, and came, and gleaned in the field
after the reapers: and her hap was to light on a part of the field belonging unto Boaz....Then said Boaz unto his servant that was set over
the reapers, Whose damsel is this? And the servant that was set over
the reapers answered and said, It is the Moabitish damsel that came
back with Naomi."

Naomi's sad return had made local news...."all the city was
moved"....and Boaz had heard of the young foreign widow who
had forsaken her land and her kindred to follow her mother-in-law
to a country notorious for its suspicion of strangers. Ruth's altruistic
action had already made Boaz well disposed towards her, and when
he saw the girl his kindness was spurred by new born physical attraction. He warned his reapers not to molest her but to give her *carte
blanche* and unobtrusively to drop sufficient corn to enable her to
fill her basket. He invited Ruth to share the midday meal in the
field, and encouraged her to continue gleaning on his acres. "So
she kept fast by the maidens of Boaz to glean unto the end of barley
harvest and of wheat harvest; and dwelt with her mother-in-law.
Then Naomi her mother-in-law said unto her, My daughter, shall
I not seek rest for thee, that it may be well with thee?" This expression did not indicate solicitude on the part of Naomi for Ruth's
strenuous harvest labors; if we turn to *Ruth* (1/9), we note that the
phrase to "seek rest" was a synonym for getting married: "The Lord
grant you that ye may find rest, each in the house of her husband."

The third chapter tells of the technique which Ruth used on
Boaz, under her mother-in-law's instruction, which fanned her elderly
admirer's ardor into matrimonial channels, and brings us to the
description of the redeeming of the land of a kinsman, recounted in
the last chapter of Ruth. "Then went Boaz up to the gate, and sat
him down there: and, behold, the kinsman of whom Boaz spake came
by; unto whom he said Ho, such a one! turn aside, sit down here.
And he turned aside, and sat down. And he took ten men of the elders
of the city, and said, sit ye down here. And they sat down. And he
said unto the kinsman, Naomi, that is come again out of the country
of Moab, selleth a parcel of land, which was our brother Elimelech's:
and I thought to advertise thee, saying, Buy it before the inhabitants,
and before the elders of my people. If thou wilt redeem it, redeem

[185]

it: but if thou wilt not redeem it, then tell me, that I may know: for there is none to redeem it besides thee; and I am after thee. And he said, I will redeem it."

Then Boaz played his trump card, and to undertstand the game it is necessary to read part of the law of inheritance, as explained in *Deuteronomy* (25/5 ff.). "If brethren dwell together, and one of them die, and have no child, the wife of the dead shall not marry without unto a stranger: her husband's brother (margin: next kinsman) shall go in unto her, and take her to him to wife, and perform the duty of an husband's brother unto her. And it shall be, that the firstborn which she beareth shall succeed in the name of his brother which is dead, that his name be not put out of Israel. And if the man like not to take his brother's wife, then let his brother's wife go up to the gate unto the elders, and say, My husband's brother refuseth to raise up unto his brother a name in Israel, he will not perform the duty of my husband's brother. Then the elders of the city shall call him, and speak unto him: and if he stand to it, and say, I like not to take her; then shall his brother's wife come unto him in the presence of the elders, and loose his shoe from off his foot, and spit in his face, and shall answer and say, So shall it be done unto that man that will not build up his brother's house. And his name shall be called in Israel, The house of him that hath his shoe loosed."

"Then said Boaz, What day thou buyest the field of the hand of Naomi, thou must buy it also of Ruth the Moabitess, the wife of the dead, to raise up the name of the dead upon his inheritance. And the kinsman said, I cannot redeem it for myself, lest I mar mine own inheritance; redeem thou my right to thyself; for I cannot redeem it. Now this was the manner in former time in Israel concerning redeeming and concerning changing, for to confirm all things; a man plucked off his shoe, and gave it to his neighbor: and this was a testimony in Israel. Therefore the kinsman said unto Boaz, Buy it for thee. So he drew off his shoe. And Boaz said unto the elders, and unto all the people, Ye are witnesses this day, that I have bought all that was Elimelech's, and all that was Chilion's and Mahlon's, of the hand of Naomi. Moreover, Ruth the Moabitess, the wife of Mahlon, have I purchased to be my wife, to raise up the name of the dead upon his inheritance."

The eighteenth word in this last paragraph, "it" (verse 5) is italicized in the Bible, and it appears to have been incorrectly interpolated, for verses 9-10 clearly indicate that Boaz bought the land from Naomi, but purchased Ruth. The inclusion of Ruth in the transaction evidently frightened off the kinsman, and the expression "lest I mar mine own inheritance" refers either to some legal technicality, or perhaps to interference with other marriage plans or to possible domestic discord.

The law of jubilee applied to transactions other than land, as the 25th chapter of *Leviticus* reveals. A man could buy a servant, and the latter then became his property. If of foreign blood, the servant and his or her descendants remained slaves in perpetuity, but if they were Israelites they were freed in the year of jubilee, and even while serving rated preferred treatment over gentile serfs. It is considered by many authorities that the 25th chapter of *Leviticus* represents a late and modified version of the Mosaic law, and that the original injunctions are more accurately set forth in passages such as *Exodus* (21/2): "If thou buy an Hebrew servant, six years he shall serve: and in the seventh he shall go out free for nothing."

This much more liberal treatment, together with further evidence of a spirit of amity and goodwill, is corroborated in *Deuteronomy* (15/12). Six verses later we read: "It shall not seem hard unto thee, when thou sendest him away free from thee; for he hath been worth a double hired servant to thee, in serving thee six years." This allusion to a double hired servant is explained by *Isaiah* (16/14): "Within three years, as the years of an hireling . . ." which informs us that the contract for a hired servant expired at the end of three years while a purchased serf served six. The opening verses of this 15th chapter of *Deuteronomy* also command a remission of debts every seventh year, except towards foreigners.

Human nature being what it is, man's selfishness and mercenary interests gradually whittled away the more generous terms of the original dispensation, while paying lip service to the form. Freeing a serf who had labored for fifty years was freeing a worn-out hulk, who had become more of a liability than an asset. Granting liberty to a lot of slaves at the end of a mere six years was encouraging subversive activity, reasoned the ancestors of the Pharisees. *Jeremiah* (34/8-17) tells of an occasion when the letter of the sabbatical law was observed but the spirit violated. "This is the word that came unto Jeremiah from the

Lord . . . that every man should let his manservant, and every man his maidservant, being an Hebrew or an Hebrewess, go free; that none should serve himself of them, to wit, of a Jew his brother. Now when all the princes, and all the people, which had entered into the covenant, heard that every one should let his manservant, and every one his maidservant, go free . . . . then they obeyed, and let them go. But afterwards they turned, and caused the servants and the handmaids, whom they had let go free, to return, and brought them into subjection for servants and for handmaids."

With the biting sarcasm which the exasperated Jehovah sometimes uses towards his problem children, the Lord retaliates: "Ye have not hearkened unto me, in proclaiming liberty, every one to his brother, and every man to his neighbor: behold, I proclaim a liberty for you, saith the Lord, to the sword, to the pestilence, and to the famine; and I will make you to be removed into all the kingdoms of the earth." *Ezekiel* (46/16-17) relates a modification of one of the provisions of the law of jubilee, weighted in favor of the nobility. When a prince deeded a property to his son, the son retained permanent title. When a servant was the beneficiary, the title reverted to the prince in the jubilee year.

The laws of the sabbatical year and of jubilee served three main purposes. They ensured a periodic rest and building up period for the soil. Also, a man remained anchored to his land, in thought if not always in deed and in person; one's inheritance was assured and could not be permanently alienated. And finally, there was a continuous pressure towards maintaining the status quo, with a periodic levelling-off of the inevitable inequalities in personal wealth and possessions.

There is hardly any Bible evidence to enable us to judge to what extent the provisions of the sabbatical and jubilee holidays were observed. Jewish writers indicate that the law was more honored in the breach than in the observance. Non-scriptural authors furnish a few clues: Tacitus, the Roman historian, complains of Jewish idleness every seventh year; Josephus tells us that warlike preparations were outlawed each sabbatical year. Some modern opinion, negating the promise of a triple harvest each seventh year, considers that the fallow year did not apply to all the land, but that each section had its own seven year cycle, differing from neighboring ones, so that approximately only one seventh of the total arable land would be out of cultivation each year.

This, of course, is contrary to both the spirit and the letter of the ordinance, which was based on a divine agricultural (and presumably meteorological) cycle, and not on human land management.

When we leave the long range policies of the farming sections of the Mosaic code and come to examine the short term schedules and the practical details, we are again confronted with the mystical number seven. "Remember the sabbath day, to keep it holy. Six days shalt thou labor, and do all thy work: but the seventh day is the sabbath of the Lord thy God: in it thou shalt not do any work, thou, nor thy son, nor thy daughter, thy manservant, nor thy maidservant, nor thy cattle, nor thy stranger that is within thy gates: for in six days the Lord made heaven and earth, the sea, and all that in them is, and rested the seventh day: wherefore the Lord blessed the sabbath day, and hallowed it" (*Exodus* 20/8-11).

In English, the words "sabbath" and "holy" and "hallowed" have a strong religious significance, any secular meaning being overshadowed by the sacred. Yet the Hebrew etymology does not necessarily carry these overtones, although no doubt they acquired the same aura of righteousness as the English equivalents, in the process of time. The word "sabbath" is associated with cessation, rest, putting down or putting away. The Hebrew word for "holy" and "hallowed" denotes to "set apart." It was applied to unclean things as well as to revered ones. The people of Israel were set apart from other nations, just as the tribe of Levi was set apart from the other tribes. A passage from *Leviticus* (11/44) takes on a changed meaning when "set apart" is substituted for "holy" and "sanctified," as is permissible from the etymology: "For I am the Lord your God: ye shall therefore sanctify yourselves, and ye shall be holy; for I am holy."

Even this weekly day of rest, which has impressed its relaxation on the physical and psychological tension of myriads of people in all ages, suffered at the hands of the ancient Jews. In righteous indignation, *Nehemiah* (13/15-17) recounts, "In those days saw I in Judah some treading wine presses on the sabbath, and bringing in sheaves, and lading asses; as also wine, grapes, and figs, and all manner of burdens, which they brought into Jerusalem on the sabbath day: and I testified against them in the day wherein they sold victuals. There dwelt men of Tyre also therein, which brought fish, and all manner of ware, and sold on the sabbath unto the children of Judah, and in Jerusalem. Then I contended with the nobles of Judah, and said unto them, What evil thing is this that ye do, and profane the sabbath day?" Nehemiah did more than testify and contend, for he ordered the city gates to be closed before the sabbath commenced, and when the farmers and hucksters congregated outside the gates, Nehemiah threatened "If ye do so again, I will lay hands on you." This one-man forerunner of the Lord's Day Alliance triumphed, for "from that time forth came they no more on the sabbath."

Leviticus (19/19) commands, "Thou shalt not let thy cattle gender with a diverse kind: thou shalt not sow thy field with mingled seed: neither shall a garment mingled of linen and woolen come upon thee." Adulteration or adultery in any form is one of the most denounced sins of the Mosaic law. For a people divinely set apart from the rest of mankind, while exposed to personal and commercial contact with an unsympathetic majority, such rules of daily living had a sound psychological and propaganda value, for they reinforced the consciousness of the Hebrews with constant reminders of their exclusiveness and racial purity. Yet they must have had a deeper meaning, and also a practical commonsense application. Modern thinking and values have repudiated practically all stigma attached to adulteration and heterogeneity, and the only relic is the legal and ecclesiastical censure of adultery.

The mixed seed ban is amplified in *Deuteronomy* (22/9), "Thou shalt not sow thy vineyard with divers seeds: lest the fruit (Hebrew: fulness) of thy seed which thou hast sown, and the fruit of thy vineyard, be defiled." This last word "defiled" has the same meaning of "set apart" as the words "holy," "hallowed" and "sanctified," in the Hebrew text. The next verse reads, "Thou shalt not plow with an ox and an ass together," while the following one broadens the corresponding Levitical injunction, "Thou shalt not wear a garment of divers sorts, as of woolen and linen together." As a practical example, an undergarment of mixed wool and cotton can be much more irritating to a sensitive skin than one of all wool or all cotton, so this rule may be a personal note based on Moses' experience.

Whatever deeper significance may underlie these laws of homogeneity, their ulterior purpose seems to have been to strengthen the race-consciousness of the Israelites by creating a mental aversion to any mixing or adulteration which could symbolically typify racial or religious tolerance or uncritical association with foreign elements. Fifteen hundred years later, the apostle Paul preached the same doctrine: "Be ye not unequally yoked together with unbelievers; for what fellowship hath righteousness with unrighteousness? . . . . what part hath he that believeth with an infidel? . . . . Wherefore come out from among them, and be ye separate, saith the Lord, and touch not the unclean thing" (2 *Corinthians* 6/14-17).

The significance of the taboo against mixed seed becomes clearer when we realize that the Hebrews used the same word to designate the seed of plants and the seed of man; indeed, the word "seed" meaning "human progeny," as for example "Abraham's seed," is much commoner than the botanical variety. In the New Testament the Greek word *sperma* has the same broad application. One of the minor regulations applying to seed covers its status after being in contact with the body of an unclean animal: "And if any part of their carcase fall upon any sowing seed which is to be sown, it shall be clean. But if any water be put upon the seed, and any part of their carcase fall thereon, it shall be unclean unto you" (*Leviticus* 11/37-38). This may indicate that seed was sprouted in water to ensure germination before being planted.

As the nation got further away in years and in principles from the pioneer days, tenant farming and the employment of farm managers began to weaken the hold of the old family farm. David established Jonathan's crippled son Mephibosheth on a crown farm, and appointed one of Saul's former servants, Ziba, as manager of the estate, which apparently was to be run on a share basis. "Thou therefore, and thy sons, and thy servants, shall till the land for him, and thou shalt bring in the fruits . . . . but Mephiboseth thy master's son shall eat bread alway at my table. Now Ziba had fifteen sons and twenty servants" (2 *Samuel* 9/10). Solomon leased out land on a cash basis: "Solomon had a vineyard at Baal-hamon; he let out the vineyard unto keepers; every one for the fruit thereof was to bring a thousand pieces of silver . . . . thou, O Solomon, must have a thousand, and those that keep the fruit thereof two hundred" (*Song of Solomon* 8/11-12).

There are parts of the Old Testament which shock our sense of ethics, yet there are humanitarian provisions which put our modern economic practices to shame; for example, the agricultural portion allotted to the poor and the needy. "And when ye reap the harvest of your land, thou shalt not wholly reap the corners of thy field, neither shalt thou gather the gleanings of thy harvest. And thou shalt not glean thy vineyard, neither shalt thou gather every grape of thy vineyard; thou shalt leave them for the poor and stranger" (*Leviticus* 19/ 9-10). *Deuteronomy* (24/19-22) adds: "When thou cuttest down thine harvest in thy field, and hast forgot a sheaf in the field, thou shalt not go again to fetch it: it shall be for the stranger, for the fatherless, and for the widow . . . . When thou beatest thine olive tree, thou shalt not go over the boughs again . . . . and thou shalt remember that thou wast a bondman in the land of Egypt: therefore I command thee to do this thing." Under the later scribes, legislation was enacted which standardized the production of the corner at one-sixtieth that of the field, and the owner was allowed to reap the whole field provided he set aside one-sixtieth of the grain reaped. This was tithe-free, as were the gleanings.

While the farmer was enjoined to leave a residue for the indigent, this did not give the lower classes the right to glean when and where they pleased. The consent of the owner was necessary and poor relatives and retainers got first choice. When Ruth proposed to her mother-in-law that she should glean, she said, "Let me now go to the field, and glean ears of corn after him in whose sight I shall find grace" (*Ruth* 2/2). A few verses later the overseer tells Boaz that Ruth had requested, and been granted, permission to glean. Ruth's first day's gleaning amounted to about a bushel of barley, but this was much above the average as Boaz had privately instructed the reapers, "Let her glean even among the sheaves, and reproach her not: and let fall also some of the handfuls of purpose for her, and leave them, that she may glean them." Probably the reapers regarded the usual gleaner as a nuisance who got in their way and impeded them in their work.

Passers-by could pluck corn or fruit at will to satisfy hunger: "When thou comest into thy neighbor's vineyard, then thou mayest eat grapes thy fill at thine own pleasure; but thou shalt not put any in thy vessel. When thou comest into the standing corn of thy neighbor, then thou mayest pluck the ears with thine hand; but thou shalt not move a sickle unto thy neighbor's standing corn" (*Deuteronomy* 23/ 24-25). On one recorded occasion Jesus and His disciples availed themselves of this privilege. "And it came to pass on the second sabbath after the first, that he went through the corn fields; and his disciples plucked the ears of corn, and did eat, rubbing them in their hands.

And certain of the Pharisees said unto them, Why do ye that which is not lawful to do on the sabbath days?" (*Luke* 6/1-2). The Pharisees did not question the right of the disciples to trespass or to help themselves to somebody else's grain, but objected to sabbath breaking. Another concession to the underprivileged was the right to eat the field produce of the sabbatical fallow year: "But the seventh year thou shalt let it (the land) rest and lie still; that the poor of thy people may eat: and what they leave the beasts of the field shall eat. In like manner thou shalt deal with thy vineyard, and with thy oliveyard" (*Exodus* 23/11).

The Mosaic code covers damage to crops, and injury to or by farm animals. "If an ox gore a man, or a woman, that they die: then the ox shall be surely stoned, and his flesh shall not be eaten; but the owner of the ox shall be quit. But if the ox were wont to push with his horn in time past, and it hath been testified to his owner, and he hath not kept him in, but that he hath killed a man or a woman; the ox shall be stoned, and his owner also shall be put to death" (*Exodus* 21/28-29). The next verse indicates that under extenuating circumstances the death penalty on the owner might be waived by payment of a fine; lesser injury was also remitted by payment of money. "And if a man shall open a pit, or if a man shall dig a pit, and not cover it, and an ox or an ass fall therein; the owner of the pit shall make it good, and give money unto the owner of them; and the dead beast shall be his. And if one man's ox hurt another's, that he die; then they shall sell the live ox, and divide the money of it; and the dead ox also they shall divide. Or if it be known that the ox hath used to push in time past, and his owner hath not kept him in; he shall surely pay ox for ox; and the dead shall be his own (*Exodus* 21/33-36).

Deuteronomy (25/4) enjoins, "Thou shalt not muzzle the ox when he treadeth out the corn." And the apostle Paul philosophizes on this (1 *Corinthians* 9/9-10): "For it is written in the law of Moses, Thou shalt not muzzle the mouth of the ox that treadeth out the corn. Doth God take care for oxen? Or saith he it altogether for our sakes? For our sakes, no doubt, this is written," somewhat smugly concludes the apostle.

The 22nd chapter of *Exodus* covers penalties for sheep and cattle stealing, animal trespass, and faulty care of loaned livestock. The Mosaic law, unduly harsh in some respects according to our standards, took a much milder view of cattle-rustling than did the ranchers of the American west. The stolen animal had to be replaced in kind, under double or quintuple indemnity according to the offense. Poetic justice was decreed on the man who permitted his animal to graze on his neighbor's choice crop: "If a man shall cause a field or vineyard to be eaten, and shall put in his beast, and shall feed in another man's field; of the best of his own field, and of the best of his own vineyard, shall he make restitution" (*Exodus* 22/5).

The Mosaic law is an early model of formal organization and legal ordinances governing much of the social, economic and religious life of the Israelites. However, its orderliness does not extend to its documentary presentation, and often a long sequence covering the ramifications of one phase of life is interrupted by an irrelevant law affecting a totally different subject. Thus, sandwiched between the penalty for seduction of a married slave woman, and an injunction outlawing witchcraft and fortune-telling, we find a gardening maxim: "And when ye shall come into the land, and shall have planted all manner of trees for food, then ye shall count the fruit thereof as uncircumcised: three years shall it be as uncircumcised unto you: it shall not be eaten of. But in the fourth year all the fruit thereof shall be holy to praise the Lord withal. And in the fifth year shall ye eat of the fruit thereof." (*Leviticus* 19/23-25).

The agricultural basis of Hebrew life is implicit in the coincidence of the outstanding activities of the growing season with the timing of the three most sacred festivals, commemorating historic episodes in Jewish history: the Passover, with its memories of release from Egyptian bondage, Pentecost celebrating the giving of the law at Mount Sinai, and the Feast of Tabernacles symbolizing the pilgrimage to the Promised Land. The Passover occurred in March or April, depending on the phase of the moon, and set farming into full swing after the rainy season; barley was ripening and figs were in blossom. Pentecost, fifty days later, marked the harvesting of the grain crops, while the Feast of Tabernacles, also movably set according to the moon, took place in September-October, with an agricultural significance comparable to our Thanksgiving Day.

The scriptural text is a farmer's almanac: "In the fourteenth day of the first month at even is the Lord's passover . . . . seven days ye must eat unleavened bread . . . . when ye . . . . shall reap the harvest

thereof, then ye shall bring a sheaf of the firstfruits of your harvest unto the priest: and he shall wave the sheaf before the Lord . . . . and ye
shall offer that day when ye wave the sheaf an he lamb without blemish
of the first year for a burnt offering unto the Lord. And the meat offering thereof shall be two tenth deals of fine flour mingled with oil, ...
and the drink offering thereof shall be of wine . . . . and ye shall eat
neither bread, nor parched corn, nor green ears, until the selfsame day
that ye have brought an offering unto your God . . . . and ye shall
count . . . . from the day that ye brought the sheaf of the wave offering
. . . . fifty days . . . . and ye shall offer a new meat offering unto the
Lord . . . . two wave loaves . . . . of fine flour . . . . baken with leaven:
they are the first fruits unto the Lord . . . Also in the fifteenth day of the
seventh month, when ye have gathered in the fruit of the land, ye shall
keep a feast unto the Lord seven days . . . . and ye shall take you on the
first day the boughs of goodly trees, branches of palm trees, and the
boughs of thick trees, and willows of the brook; and ye shall rejoice before the Lord your God seven days" (*Leviticus* 23/5-40). *Exodus* (23/
15-16) terms these three occasions the feast of unleavened bread, the
feast of harvest and the feast of ingathering, respectively. The middle
one, on account of pressure of essential farm duties, was confined to one
day. The first and last were lengthy affairs.

Tithing, the offering of the tenth part of one's product or increase
to the deity or temporal representative, is of remote antiquity, and was
common in Babylon, Egypt, Persia and Arabia as well as in Canaan.
The original tithe is believed to have been an offering to the gods of a
tenth of the spoils of war. The Mosaic law gives explicit instructions regarding the practice, but long before Moses tithing was customary in
Canaan. After the great battle of the kings, in which Sodom was looted,
Abram rescued Lot and his family, together with much booty, from
one of the raiding bands, and on returning was met by "Melchizedek,
king of Salem . . . . the priest of the most high God . . . . and . . . .
Abram . . . . gave him tithes of all" (*Genesis* 14/18-20). In the concluding verses of the 28th chapter of *Genesis*, Jacob offers a conditional
tithe to Jehovah: "And Jacob vowed a vow, saying, If God will be with
me, and will keep me in this way that I go, and will give me bread to
eat, and raiment to put on, so that I come again to my father's house
in peace; then shall the Lord be my God: . . . . and of all that thou shalt
give me, I will surely give the tenth unto thee."

The detailed system of tithing laid down by Moses, including further tithing of the tithe, became more involved and punctilious under the bureaucratic hierarchy, and brought forth Jesus' withering attack: "Woe unto you, Pharisees! for ye tithe mint and rue and all manner of herbs, and pass over judgment and the love of God" (*Luke* 11/42).

The principle underlying the Hebrew law of tithe is laid down in the concluding verses of the book of *Leviticus*: "And all the tithe of the land, whether of the seed of the land, or of the fruit of the tree, is the Lord's: it is holy unto the Lord. And if a man will at all redeem ought of his tithes, he shall add thereto the fifth part thereof." This portion of the Lord's was ordered to be given to the priestly tribe of Levi, who in view of their consecrated work had no share in the worldly inheritance possessed by the other tribes. The Levites in turn were ordered to tithe their grant, and give it to the high priest for his support, so that dignitary was entitled to a one per-cent share of the income of the people of Israel (*Numbers* 18/21-28).

In order that tithing should not share the unpopular regard which surrounds most taxation and forced levies, the tendering of tithes was accompanied by a festive banquet, composed of the edible produce of the tithe, so that it was "on the house" of the receiving priest. Should the farmer's homestead be remote from the Levite center, "If the way be too long for thee, so that thou art not able to carry it; or if the place be too far from thee, which the Lord thy God shall choose to set his name there . . . then shalt thou turn it into money, and bind up the money in thine hand, and shalt go unto the place which the Lord thy God shall choose: And thou shalt bestow that money for whatsoever thy soul lusteth after, for oxen, or for sheep, or for wine, or for strong drink, or for whatsoever thy soul desireth: and thou shalt eat there before the Lord thy God, and thou shalt rejoice, thou, and thine household, and the Levite that is within thy gates" (*Deuteronomy* 14/24-27).

This liberal dispensation doubtlessly took a lot of sting out of the burden of tithe. Every third year the tithing feast was held in the farmer's own home, the local poor and needy being invited as well as the Levites; the host was ordered to take a vow, declaring he had not withheld any of the tithe, an easy thing to get away with under the circumstances: "Then thou shalt say before the Lord thy God, I have brought away the hallowed things out of mine house, and also have given them unto the Levite, and unto the stranger, to the fatherless,

[196]

and to the widow, according to all thy commandments, which thou hast commanded me: I have not transgressed thy commandments, neither have I forgotten them. I have not eaten thereof in my mourning, neither have I taken away ought thereof for any unclean use, nor given ought thereof for the dead" (*Deuteronomy* 26/13-14). This vow was evidently drawn up by a legal mind, for there are few loopholes.

The treasuries of absolute monarchs usually have a rapid turnover, and that of the rulers of Israel was no exception. The traditional respect, and the long conditioning of the public mind, to tithing suggested an extension of the principle as an effective way to raise royal revenue. The Pharaohs, long experienced in such matters, had set a precedent, described in the Egyptian section of the chapter on foreign influences. When the Israelites clamored for a king "like all the nations," Samuel (whose advice was not altogether disinterested) warned them: "He will take the tenth of your seed, and of your vineyards, and give to his officers, and to his servants . . .He will take the tenth of your sheep" (1 *Samuel* 8/15-17). While many monarchs, and particularly Solomon, raised huge sums through various imposts, there is only circumstantial evidence that tithing was enforced by the crown.

Royal prerogative to the first crop of tender grass may be inferred from *Amos* (7/1): "Thus hath the Lord God shewed unto me; and, behold, he formed grasshoppers (margin: green worms) in the beginning of the shooting up of the latter growth; and, lo, it was the latter growth after the king's mowings. And it came to pass, that when they had made an end of eating the grass of the land . . . ." The idea is speculative, and the passage may refer simply to the first hay-cutting in the royal fields.

As happened to many of the Mosaic ordinances, which demanded more than lip service and formalism, tithing became neglected. Jehovah, through his prophet *Malachi* (3/8-10) complains, "Will a man rob God? Yet ye have robbed me. But ye say, Wherein have we robbed thee? In tithes and offerings . . . . Bring ye all the tithes into the storehouse, that there may be meat in mine house, and prove me now herewith, saith the Lord of hosts, if I will not open you the windows of heaven, and pour you out a blessing, that there shall not be room enough to receive it."

On two other occasions we read of rulers who reintroduced the tithe system, which apparently had lapsed. The 31st chapter of 2 *Chron-*

icles tells how King Hezekiah collected an enormous stockpile, which perhaps included retroactive contributions: "The tithe of all things brought they in abundantly . . . . and laid them by heaps. In the third month they began to lay the foundation of the heaps, and finished them in the seventh month." A hierarchy of rulers and overseers and storekeepers guarded and rationed the supplies. The king did pretty well for himself too, for "Hezekiah had exceeding much riches and honor: and he made himself treasuries for silver, and for gold, and for precious stones." When Nehemiah (10/37-38) set about reorganizing the Jewish state in Jerusalem, after the return from Babylon, he set the tithe wheels in motion. During his temporary absence in Babylon the presumably unpopular tribute was stopped, and on his return Nehemiah complained, "And I perceived that the portion of the Levites had not been given them; for the Levites and the singers, that did the work, were fled every one to his field. Then contended I with the rulers, and said, Why is the house of God forsaken? and I gathered them together, and set them in their place. Then brought all Judah the tithe of the corn and the new wine and the oil unto the treasuries" (*Nehemiah* 13/10-12). Inasmuch as the books of the Old Testament were edited by the priestly class, historical accounts of popular opposition to payment of tithes have probably been censored.

Besides tithe, the husbandman had to pay many other tributes of his production, one of the most important being the first fruits. Jehovah assured Aaron, the high priest, "All the best of the oil, and all the best of the wine, and of the wheat, the firstfruits of them which they shall offer unto the Lord, them have I given thee. And whatsoever is first ripe in the land, which they shall bring unto the Lord, shall be thine . . . . Every thing devoted in Israel shall be thine. Every thing that opens the matrix in all flesh, which they bring unto the Lord, whether it be of men or beasts, shall be thine: nevertheless, the firstborn of man shalt thou surely redeem, and the firstling of unclean beasts shalt thou redeem" (*Numbers* 18/12-15). Many other offerings, both obligatory and freewill, were ordained for the farmer. Naturally, a decline in the moral and ethical standards of the priesthood would be reflected in popular reluctance to contribute tithes. The priests were the accredited representatives of the divine landowner, Jehovah, and this contributory system could only prosper while God's laws were nationally revered. In a year of crop failure there would be little enthusiasm to share meager supplies with a corrupt priesthood.

Deuteronomy (27/17) warns, "Cursed be he that removeth his neighbor's landmark," and Solomon cautions against this on two occasions (*Proverbs*: 22/28; 23/10). *Job,* in the 24th chapter, rages against the social injustice of his time: "Some remove the landmarks; they violently take away flocks, and feed thereof. They drive away the ass of the fatherless, they take the widow's ox for a pledge." *Job,* whose book dates from the 7th to the 4th century B.C., "was the greatest of all the men of the east," but "he was perfect and upright, and one that feared God and eschewed evil." So, in all ages, laws enacted for the general good are violated for individual profit.

From an empiric stand, the selection of Palestine for the establishment of a theocratic state seems to have foredoomed the experiment to failure, insofar as the material interests of the Hebrew community were concerned. Yet the leaven of the pioneer monotheistic principles implanted in Canaan has provided the ferment which has spread throughout much of the civilized world. Freedom from surrounding pressure, whether vindictive or seductive, appears to be a prerequisite for the successful development of a closed colony devoted to religious, political and economic doctrines differing radically from those of neighboring communities. Yet such is human nature that the very absence of competitive ideology and adverse environment may encourage mental and physical lethargy and smugness, a fertile soil for the seeds of decay.

The Mosaic law offered the children of Israel a well charted path to material success and spiritual harmony, but, in just as clear and unequivocal words, it guaranteed ruin and damnation to lawbreakers. The 26th chapter of *Leviticus* and the 28th of *Deuteronomy* are full of details of the most virulent catastrophes booked for the breakers of the law. There was no middle road, nor did Jesus, fifteen hundred years later, offer one. "No man can serve two masters .... Ye cannot serve God and mammon." (What of today? Has agricultural science and mechanized farming relegated into oblivion the ancient laws of the Books of Moses?) "And thy heaven that is over thy head shall be brass, and the earth that is under thee shall be iron. The Lord shall make the rain of thy land powder and dust: from heaven shall it come down upon thee, until thou be destroyed .... and thou shalt grope at noonday, as the blind gropeth in darkness" (*Deuteronomy* 28/23, 24, 29).

The stupidity, followed by the tragedy, of the American Dust Bowl is very modern history, and the lure of three dollar wheat is rapidly undoing the conservation measures of recent years. The grapes of wrath are still bitter. "Thou shalt carry much seed out into the field, and shalt gather but little in: for the locust shall consume it.... all thy trees and fruit of thy land shall the locust consume" (*Deuteronomy* 28/38, 42). 1933 was not only the nadir of the United States' biggest bust. It was the high of a ten year period for grasshopper ravages; the bill for twenty-three affected States was nearly sixty million dollars. The estimated total losses caused by insect damage in the United States in one year would finance the Marshall Plan for four years. The billion dollar chemical industry, aided and abetted by the powerful resources of orthodox agricultural science, keeps forcing production and variety at the expense of quality and vitality. The soil is regarded as a chemical testtube, insect and disease ravages a challenge to deadlier poisons (with a fingers-crossed attitude towards the health of the propaganda-dazed consumer), while mechanized farming and gardening beckons big business, and elbows poor husbandman Adam out of his home-made garden of Eden.

Are we getting away with it? Are the old agricultural laws of Jehovah a dead letter? Not according to Jesus: "Verily I say unto you, Till heaven and earth pass, one jot or one tittle shall in no wise pass from the law, till all be fulfilled" (*Matthew* 5/18).

CHAPTER 18

Good Husbandry

THE SOMEWHAT old-fashioned word "husbandry" has an interesting background in its original biblical versions. The Greek word is *georgion,* a husbandman being a *georgos.* Virgil's *Georgics* praised country life, and modern words such as geography, geology and geometry are derived from the same Greek root; the earliest use of geometry was in land measurement. *Adamah* is the Hebrew word for husbandry; Adam was the primeval husbandman, and his name means "of the ground."

The agricultural mind of Jehovah is evident in His explanation of the manner in which the original Canaanite inhabitants were to be displaced by the invading Israelites. An urban or a war-minded deity would be inclined to make a clean sweep of the aboriginals, replacing each heathen farmer with a Hebrew one. Jehovah realized that the long period of Egyptian bondage, followed by forty years of nomadic wandering in the desert, meant that most of His protégés would be deficient in farming skill and knowledge, so He arranged that they should infiltrate gradually into Canaan, learning land management and agricultural wisdom from the example of the native cultivators, and only then supplanting them. Also, God did not consider the Hebrew forces adequate to both drive out the tribes of Canaan and properly cultivate the occupied land. Here Jehovah is not depicted in his later role of invincible Lord of battles. "I will send hornets before thee, which shall drive out the Hivite, the Canaanite, and the Hittite, from before thee. I will not drive them out before thee in one year; lest the land become desolate, and the beast of the field multiply against thee. By little and little I will drive them out from before thee, until thou be increased, and inherit the land" (*Exodus* 23/28-30).

According to the Bible, the success or failure of the agriculture of the Hebrews was in direct ratio to spiritual devotion or lack thereof, rather than being the outcome of husbandry practices. However,

[201]

the relationship between God and His people was of the most personal and practical kind, and through His prophets and lawgivers He furnished detailed instruction and education embracing mundane as well as metaphysical wisdom. In the concluding verses of his 28th chapter, *Isaiah* credits the Lord as being professionally expert in farm practice: "For his God doth instruct him (the plowman) to discretion, and doth teach him. This also cometh from the Lord of hosts, which is wonderful in counsel, and excellent in working."

Jehovah spoke to a farming people in farming terms. There is nothing cabalistic in *Deuteronomy* (11/13-17): "And it shall come to pass, if ye shall hearken diligently unto my commandments, which I command you this day, to love the Lord your God, and to serve him with all your heart and with all your soul, that I will give you the rain of your land in his due season, the first rain and the latter rain, that thou mayest gather in thy corn, and thy wine, and thine oil. And I will send grass in thy fields for thy cattle, that thou mayest eat and be full. Take heed to yourselves, that your heart be not deceived, and ye turn aside, and serve other gods, and worship them. And then the Lord's wrath be kindled against you, and he shut up the heaven, that there be no rain, and that the land yield not her fruit; and lest ye perish quickly from off the good land which the Lord giveth you."

The basic foundation of theocratic husbandry was observance of the septennial fallow year; there was to be a complete cessation of all agricultural activities each sabbatical year. Strangely, we find no thought given to the psychology inherent in a year of national idleness; it seems incomprehensible that Deity, knowing man's innate flair for mischief when bored with nothing to do, did not make provision for compensatory occupation.

Solomon, who was a thrifty farmer himself, advises the husbandman to give priority to getting his fields cultivated and planted before tackling the less productive requirement of building a home: "Prepare thy work without, and make it fit for thyself in the field; and afterwards build thine house" (*Proverbs* 24/27). This advice is still taken literally by many farmers whose barns and implements are their first love, their dwellings being subordinate.

From the Philistines, who were of energetic Phoenician strain, the Israelites learnt some of their most important lessons in efficient land use. History credits the early Phoenicians with the discovery of terracing and contour farming, necessitated by their hilly terrain and the sequence of long dry spells followed by heavy downpours of rain. The terraced mountainsides where flourished the vineyards of Judah and Israel owed their pattern to the earlier developments of the Philistines, and had little in common with the viticultural methods of Egypt and Babylon. Both Philistia and Israel were sufficiently strong to resist domination by the other, so a balance of power equilibrium developed, periods of friendly intercourse and association being interrupted by border incidents and war.

Fertilizing of the soil to maintain and increase its production is a very ancient practice, probably as old as magic fertility rites and sacrifices to deity for the same purpose. North American Indians planted fish in their corn hills, while the bird droppings in Chile served the aborigines as soil manure long before the white man commercialized guana. The first reference to manuring the soil is found in an Accadian tablet, a tablet that was old when Abraham was young. The ancient Romans were adept in handling and storing manure so that its valuable contents were preserved. When they transplanted cabbage, they used seaweed for fertilizer. Green manuring and crop rotation were in common practice. Modern application of organic fertilizers is not a new discovery; rather is it a revival of an age-old custom, going back thousands of years, back of authenticated history into the shadowland of mythology.

Our streamlined sophisticated civilization buries its dead in street clothing, with cheeks rouged and hair carefully brushed. Need we sneer at our remote ancestors who included hunting equipment and food in the grave of the deceased. For such a long and uncertain journey, only food which would not soon spoil or deteriorate seemed of value, and what could be better than cereal grain. In due course the enriched soil returned a bumper crop of barley and oats, and the spirit of the departed was doubly blessed. Gradually the association of burial with a good crop yield led to the practice of immolating one of the tribe, or a slave or captive, to ensure a bountiful harvest. The sacrifice of the firstborn, either in person or by a redeeming symbol, probably stems from the same root.

The old Anglo-Saxon word "dung" is used throughout the Bible to translate several Hebrew names which designate different forms and stages of animal excrement. Thus the phrase, "I have given thee

[203]

cow's dung for man's dung, and thou shalt prepare thy bread there-with" (*Ezekiel* 4/15), when referred to the native script, tells a num-ber of things. First of all we get two different words which designate animal and human excrement respectively. The context, describing the eking out of provisions during a siege and famine, indicates that cows' droppings were commonly used for fuel, but Jehovah's command to use human ordure for this purpose shocked the ritualistic Ezekiel. In eastern countries where wood is scarce, dried animal droppings are collected and sold as fuel in modern times.

Strangers visiting the East are invariably warned not to eat local green vegetables, and to boil or chlorinate all drinking water. It is general practice in the Orient to manure crops with human as well as with animal droppings. Rather surprisingly, the Mosaic law with its emphasis on hygiene omits instructions for the collection and use of manure. From a passage in *Deuteronomy* (23/12-14) it is permissible to infer that only animal manure was used to fertilize Hebrew farms and gardens. "Thou shalt have a place also without the camp, whither thou shalt go abroad: and thou shalt have a paddle upon thy weapon; and it shall be, when thou wilt ease thyself abroad, thou shalt dig therewith, and shalt turn back and cover that which cometh from thee. For the Lord thy God walketh in the midst of thy camp, to deliver thee, and to give up thine enemies before thee; therefore shall thy camp be holy: that he see no unclean thing in thee, and turn away from thee."

The various Hebrew words translated "dung" have different desig-nations: human excrement; animal excrement; intestinal secretions of slaughtered animals; animal manure spread as fertilizer and compost. The expression in 2 *Kings* (6/25), "the fourth part of a cab of dove's dung," is considered by some Hebrew students to be an erroneous ren-dering. In Arabic the same word denotes chick pea and pigeon drop-pings, and this type of vetch, which flourishes in the Levant, would seem to be more appropriate.

There is no doubt about the fertilizing use of animal manure, whether applied directly to the fields or composted. Some passages suggest that the bodies of slain enemies were used as organic fertilizer. 2 *Kings* (9/37) is graphic, if gruesome: "And the carcase of Jezebel shall be as dung upon the face of the field in the portion of Jezreel; so that they shall not say, This is Jezebel." Referring to the dead Midianites,

Psalms (83/10) relates, "They became as dung for the earth." The word *as* in this passage is italicized, and is not in the original. Jeremiah has four references to dung, and from the context we deduce that manure was not dug in nor plowed under, but merely spread on the surface of the field. "They shall not be . . . . buried: but they shall be as dung upon the face of the earth" (*Jeremiah* 16/4). A parallel passage is in (25/33). (9/22) is similar: "The carcases of men shall fall as dung upon the open field." The last of Jeremiah's references suggests the use of bones as fertilizer: "They shall bring out the bones of the kings of Judah, and the bones of his princes, and the bones of the priests, and the bones of the prophets, and the bones of the inhabitants of Jerusalem, out of their graves: and they shall spread them . . . . they shall be for dung upon the face of the earth" (8/1-2).

In *Isaiah* (25/10) we get the first glimpse of a compost pile. "Moab shall be trodden down under him, even as straw is trodden down for the dunghill." The Revised Version changes the end of the sentence into "trodden down in the water of the dunghill." The Hebrew word translated dunghill is *Madmenah*, and three biblical settlements bore this name or synonymous variants. Madmenah was a Benjamite village north of Jerusalem, Madmannah was a town in southern Judea, while Madmen was located in Moab. What significance can we draw from this? No self-respecting community would allow their town to be officially known as dunghill, and Madmen is historically bracketed with Heshbon, royal city of the Amorites and famous for its grapes. Compost as a place name would carry no slur, and these three widely separated places may have specialized in compost making, selling the finished product to local farmers and vineyard owners.

The Hebrew word rendered "straw" in the foregoing passage from *Isaiah* does not appear elsewhere in the Bible. A different native word denotes the straw used by the Israelites to make bricks in Egypt, the straw fed horses, etc. The composted straw may have included waste vegetable products other than grain stalks. In the East fibrous plant refuse is strewn along roadways near compost piles, where it is macerated by the feet of oxen and the wheels of carts, as well as by passers-by. When sufficiently broken up it is moved to the compost pile. Treading straw in liquid manure would both reduce its bulk and permeate it with valuable animal waste products.

[205]

The most direct reference to composting comes from Jesus (*Luke*: 14/34-35): "Salt is good: but if the salt have lost his savor, wherewith shall it be seasoned? It is neither fit for the land, nor yet for the dung-hill; but men cast it out." Substitute "compost-pile" for "dunghill" and the reference becomes clear, for much potentially valuable fertilizer which is unsuited for direct application to the soil becomes transformed into good humus in the compost process. If the dunghill Jesus referred to had been a garbage pile or the city dump, the allusion would be meaningless.

This reference to salt deserves explanation. In small quantities salt was used as a soil treatment, and to hasten decomposition of dung in the compost heap. Too large a mixture was held to produce steril-ity, as exemplified on the shores of the Dead Sea. Abimelech used a scorched earth policy when he captured Shechem (*Judges* 9/45): "He took the city, and slew the people that was therein, and beat down the city, and sowed it with salt." The Jews considered that salt exposed to the damp Mediterranean air lost its virtue; such sodden salt was useless either as a seasoning or a soil agent.

The Mosaic code ordered the ashes of the sacrificial altar fire, rich in organic residue of the sacrifices as well as in wood ash, to be col-lected by the officiating priest and removed to a specified dump. "And he shall put off his garments, and put on other garments, and carry forth the ashes without the camp unto a clean place" (*Leviticus* 6/11). "And the skin of the bullock, and all his flesh, with his head, and with his legs, and his inwards, and his dung, even the whole bullock shall he carry forth without the camp unto a clean place, where the ashes are poured out, and burn him on the wood with fire: where the ashes are poured out shall he be burnt" (*Leviticus* 4/11-12). The Hebrew term denoting "clean place" in the foregoing passages is sig-nificant, the word "clean" being the same as that used elsewhere to define clean animals and clean food in contrast to unclean animals, prohibited food, etc. Thus ashes could be removed by anyone from the ashheap without incurring the penalties for impurity.

From other texts we may infer that ashes were spread over the fields for their value in promoting plant growth: "He scattereth the hoarfrost like ashes" (*Psalms* 147/16); "He has cast me into the mire, and I am become like dust and ashes" (*Job* 30/19); "Ye shall tread down the wicked, for they shall be ashes under the soles of your feet"

(*Malachi* 4/3). These passages do not furnish proof of the agricultural use of ashes, but they are suggestive of this use. The Talmud is more specific. "They lay dung to moisten and enrich the soil; dig about the roots of trees; pluck up the suckers; take off the leaves; sprinkle ashes; and smoke under the trees to kill vermin."

Another Talmud passage tells us of the use of blood as fertilizer. The blood of the sacrifice, poured out before the altar, flowed away through an underground channel to a sump outside the city wall. Here it was sold to gardeners for manuring the soil, on payment of a trespass offering, without which its use for common purposes was prohibited, as the blood retained the sanctity of dedication at the altar.

Our short-sighted policy of setting fire to straw, leaves, and other dry plant refuse instead of composting them was equally prevalent in biblical times. The burning of stubble was a favorite metaphor of the prophets of old, and the fate of the wicked was often symbolized as a flash fire. Anyone who has seen a field of grass, tinder dry after long drought, suddenly roar into brief flame as the tongues of fire race across it, will appreciate *Joel's* picturesque simile, "They leap like the noise of a flame of fire that devoureth the stubble." There was an excuse for the burning of straw by the Israelites; fuel was a constant problem, and anything combustible was pressed into service to provide heat for cooking. The oven of scripture was a pit dug in the ground, usually in the centre of the house; it was lined with clay and had an underground vent surfacing beyond the house wall. When not in use it was covered over, but when burning it presented a hazard to the people of the house, especially to the children. Great heat was generated in this crude device. Jesus, speaking of the oven and its fuel says (*Matthew* 6/30), " .... the grass of the field, which to-day is, and tomorrow is cast into the oven."

While there is no direct evidence that agricultural practices were regulated in accordance with the phases of the moon, or planetary aspects, there is a considerable amount of circumstantial data. Occult customs were widespread among the Israelites, and constituted part of the sacred religions of neighboring peoples. The Chaldeans are believed to have been the originators of astrology in historical times, and Abram's home town was Ur of the Chaldees. The Jewish calendar was lunar, not solar, and the new moon had particular significance.

[207]

The Hebrew words designating moon and new moon are interchangeable with those signifying month. In many passages the days of the new moon, sabbaths, and the days of solemn feasts are linked together as set apart, with special sacrifices ordained.

Psalms (81/3-4) proclaims, "Blow up the trumpet in the new moon, in the time appointed, on our solemn feast day. For this was a statute for Israel, and a law of the God of Jacob." Specially appointed priests scanned the hilly horizon from the top of mount Olivet for the first glimpse of the new moon and lit a huge bonfire there when its crescent form was discerned, that moment marking the legal commencement of a new month. The neighboring and unfriendly Samitarians, however, decided to subvert the works of Jewish precision, and they set off a decoy bonfire on a nearby hill before the astronomical portents justified, causing more confusion in the timetable of Judea than the hit and miss application of modern daylight-saving time. The Jews decided to discontinue the bonfire. It is not surprising that the ordained celebration of a particular time, regulated by lunar astronomy, should gradually begin to take on an aura of sanctity around the more tangible timepiece.

Jeremiah unsuccessfully attempted to discourage moon worship amongst the Jews who had migrated to Egypt, part of the remnant left after the Babylonian deportations. The agricultural influence of the moon may be read into the reply of the heretical Jews to the prophet: "As for the word that thou hast spoken unto us in the name of the Lord, we will not hearken unto thee. But we will certainly do whatsoever thing goeth forth out of our own mouth, to burn incense unto the queen of heaven, and to pour out drink offerings unto her, as we have done, we, and our fathers, our kings, and our princes, in the cities of Judah, and in the streets of Jerusalem: for then had we plenty of victuals, and were well, and saw no evil. But since we left off .... we have wanted all things, and have been consumed .... by the famine" (*Jeremiah* 44/16-18).

Popular belief in the malevolent power of the moon is indicated in *Psalms* (121/6): "The sun shall not smite thee by day, nor the moon by night." Modern words such as "lunatic" and "moonstruck" testify to the persistence of the idea, and that animals react to some influence of the full moon is indisputable. In his *Epistle to the Galatians* (4/10) Paul reproves them for observing favorable and unfavorable astrological periods, while in his address to the *Romans* (14/5), written two years later, the Apostle appears to tolerate the practice.

The 3rd chapter of *Ecclesiastes* may be read with or without occult and mystical significance. "To every thing there is a season, and a time to every purpose under heaven: a time to be born, (*Hebrew*: to bear) and a time to die; a time to plant, and a time to pluck up that which is planted." The chapter continues enumerating many more such contrasts. The 15th verse is hard to explain rationally: "That which hath been is now; and that which is to be hath already been; and God requireth that which is past." Several Hebrew words are translated into English as "time" or "times," but the one which occurs so often in the first eight verses of the chapter is used on at least two occasions elsewhere (*Esther* 1/13; 1 *Chronicles* 12/32) in what appears to be an astrological or occult sense.

One passage in the Bible seems to indicate that Moses believed in the influence of the moon on plant growth. In *Deuteronomy* (33/13-14) we read: "Blessed of the Lord be his land, for the precious things of heaven, for the dew, and for the deep that coucheth beneath, and for the precious fruits brought forth by the sun, and for the precious things put forth by the moon" (Hebrew: "thrust forth by the moons"). The plural form probably means successive phases or cycles of the moon. While the English version uses "precious fruits" and "precious things" respectively, the Hebrew original employs the same word, and it recurs again in *Song of Solomon* (4/13; 4/16), where it is rendered "pleasant fruits," with the literal meaning unmistakable. So, we have to find an explanation of the phrase "the precious fruits thrust forth by the moons." Two meanings are plausible; that fruits ripen successively with the passage of the (lunar) months, or, planting and harvesting in accordance with the phases and aspects of the moon.

Arboriculture gets scant mention in Scripture, yet the popularity and abundant yield of fruit trees and vines in Canaan denotes advanced knowledge and skill on the part of the husbandmen. "Six years thou shalt sow thy field, and six years thou shalt prune thy vineyard," ordained Jehovah, according to *Leviticus* (25/3), and the language seems to indicate that pruning was just as commonplace and routine as sowing. *Isaiah* (2/4) and *Micah* (4/3) tell of the peacetime conversion of spears into pruning hooks, while *Joel* (3/9-10) sounds the call to arms: "Prepare war, wake up the mighty men, let all the men of war draw near; let them come up: beat your plowshares into swords, and your pruning hooks into spears: let the weak say, I am strong." In the three foregoing passages, it is always the spear which doubles with the pruning hook, the heavier sword with the plowshare. Only one instance of the actual use of a pruning hook on a bush is recorded, and then its action is destructive rather than beneficial: "For afore the harvest, when the bud is perfect, and the sour grape is ripening in the flower, he shall both cut off the sprigs with pruning hooks, and take away and cut down the branches" (*Isaiah* 18/5).

Solomon, announcing the arrival of spring, mentions the singing of birds as one of the harbingers (*Song of Solomon* 2/12). The words "of birds" are italicized, and do not appear in the Hebrew, which merely states that the time of singing is come. The same Hebrew word denotes pruning and singing, so some authorities contend that pruning is the correct translation.

In Jesus' parable of the true vine (*John* 15/2) he says, "Every branch that beareth fruit, he purgeth it, that it may bring forth more fruit. Now ye are clean through the word which I have spoken unto you." Different tenses of the same Greek word are here translated "purgeth" and "clean," and the Revised Version substitutes "cleanseth" for "purgeth." The Master may have meant pruning, or disbudding, or some other technic.

Paul was a tent-maker before he became a missionary, and he was also a gardener. We are indebted to him for the sole biblical mention of grafting; it was a process with which he was evidently thoroughly familiar, and he knew, or assumed, that his correspondents in Rome had skilled fruit growers amongst them. Apparently there was dissension between the former Jewish and Gentile adherents to the new Christian church in the capital city; Jewish converts had founded the religious movement in Rome, but later Gentile members found the admixture of Jewish orthodoxy in the new faith distasteful. "For I speak to you Gentiles, inasmuch as I am the apostle of the Gentiles, I magnify mine office: if by any means I may provoke to emulation them which are my flesh (Jews) and might save some of them .... For if the firstfruit be holy, the lump is also holy: and if the root be holy, so are the branches. And if some of the branches be broken off, and thou, being a wild olive tree, were graffed (grafted) in among them, and with them partakers of the root and fatness of the olive tree; boast not against the branches. But if thou boast, thou bearest not the root, but the root thee. Thou wilt say then, The branches were broken off, that I might be graffed in. Well: because of unbelief they were broken off, and thou standest by faith. Be not highminded, but fear. For if God spared not the natural branches, take heed lest he also spare not thee.... For if thou wert cut out of the olive tree which is wild by nature, and were graffed contrary to nature into a good olive tree: how much more shall these, which be the natural branches, be graffed into their own olive tree?" (*Romans* 11/13-24).

Isaiah (17/10), who merits the title of gardening prophet as much as Solomon deserves to be called the gardening king, gives us the only scriptural reference to setting slips. "Therefore shalt thou plant pleasant plants, and shalt set it with strange slips."

Good husbandry is an art, learnt slowly and painstakingly from contact with the soil and plants and animals. Its secrets seldom get into print, and the husbandmen of the Bible have left us little of their "green finger" lore in the pages of Holy Writ. Then, as now, it was the eye of the master which fattened his cattle and produced the choicest crops.

CHAPTER 19

Flocks and Herds

THE PATRIARCHS counted their wealth in cattle and sheep and goats, and by any standards, ancient or modern, they were big business. Numerous livestock was synonymous with much wealth, and one of the Hebrew words translated "cattle" is in other passages rendered "substance" and "possessions." Only the industrial age separates us from a like correspondence, for "cattle" is a corruption of the older "chattle."

Early in the Bible we come across the first shepherd: "And Abel was a keeper of sheep . . . . and . . . . brought . . . . an offering unto the Lord . . . of the firstlings of his flock and of the fat thereof. And the Lord had respect unto Abel and to his offering" (*Genesis* 4/2-4). We have no account of the fate of Abel's sheep, following the death of their master at the hands of Cain. The next link is in *Genesis* (4/20): "And Adah bare Jabal: he was the father of such as dwell in tents, and of such as have cattle." The nomadic association is evident. According to the genealogy, Jabal was a sixth generation descendant of Cain, so livestock raising must have lapsed during the Abel-Jabal interval. Again the record fades until the Flood wiped out man and beast from the earth, except for Noah and his breeding stock. Generation succeeded generation for hundreds of years, but the Bible confines itself to tracing the family tree; background interests and occupations remain blank until Abram restores history and geography and cattle to the sacred pages.

We find Abram leaving Ur of the Chaldees, in the Mesopotamian plain, and journeying with his wife and relatives westward towards Canaan, and then, because of famine there, southward into Egypt. It was not until he was established in Pharaoh's favor that we read of his vast cattle holdings: "He had sheep, and oxen, and he asses, and men-servants, and maidservants, and she asses, and camels" (*Genesis* 12/16). The catalog gives a low rating to the human stock. Evidently the cattle did well on Egyptian pasture and grain, for Abram and company left

Egypt "very rich in cattle, in silver, and in gold." We infer that the silver and gold were dividends from the sale of livestock, meat, and wool to the subjects of Pharaoh. Apparently the Canaan grazing grounds were inferior to those by the lush banks of the Nile, and we learn of the increasing importance of the junior partner: "And Lot also, which went with Abram, had flocks, and herds, and tents. And the land was not able to bear them, that they might dwell together: for their substance was great, so that they could not dwell together. And there was a strife between the herdmen of Abram's cattle and the herdmen of Lot's cattle . . . . And Abram said unto Lot . . . . separate thyself, I pray thee, from me . . . . and Lot journeyed east: and they separated themselves the one from the other. Abram dwelled in the land of Canaan, and Lot dwelled in the cities of the plain, and pitched his tent toward Sodom" (*Genesis* 13/5-12).

Although Abram and Lot had parted company and agreed to disagree, they remained bound by nomad traditions of mutual assistance when threatened. Lot became involved in an early world war and was taken captive when the city of Sodom was overrun. Abram, who in the interval had entered into a new cattle partnership, assembled his confederates and with an armed troop of over three hundred household servants rescued Lot (*Genesis* 14). Another nomad tradition is hospitality to strangers, a code still observed by Bedouins of the desert, and Abram set a worthy precedent, related in the opening verses of the 18th chapter of *Genesis*. "He sat in the tent door in the heat of the day; and he lift up his eyes and looked, and, lo, three men stood by him: and when he saw them, he ran to meet them from the tent door, and bowed himself toward the ground, and said, My Lord, if now I have found favor in thy sight, pass not away, I pray thee, from thy servant: let a little water, I pray you, be fetched, and wash your feet, and rest yourselves under the tree: and I will fetch a morsel of bread, and comfort ye your hearts: after that ye shall pass on: for therefore are ye come to your servant. And they said, So do, as thou hast said." The morsel of bread turned out to be a prime young calf, killed and dressed for the occasion, served with new baked bread and butter and milk.

The patriarchs had a canny habit of passing off an attractive wife as a sister, when their nomad wanderings took them into the territory of strangers. Presumably desert morality insisted that a man's sister must be wooed with formal recognition of the brother's personal and civil rights, whereas a good-looking wife could be acquired by the simple process of making her a widow. Abram practiced this deception on at least two occasions, in Egypt (*Genesis* 12/13) and in Philistine territory (20/2). Apparently Sarah was a willing accomplice, and the duplicity paid off handsomely in increasing Abram's cattle holdings. Sarah, Abram's wife, was also his half-sister (*Genesis* 20/12), so this dual relationship offered a sop to any pangs of conscience. King Abimelech proved to be a more honorable man than Abram, and he reproached him, "What have I offended thee, that thou hast brought on me and on my kingdom a great sin? Thou hast done deeds unto me that ought not to be done." Although he had had no intimacy with Sarah, "Abimelech took sheep, and oxen, and menservants, and womenservants, and gave them unto Abram, and restored him Sarah his wife .... And unto Sarah he said, Behold, I have given thy brother a thousand pieces of silver: behold, he is to thee a covering of the eyes, unto all that are with thee, and with all other: thus she was reproved."

Kings as well as commoners owned large flocks and herds, indeed regal status was somewhat dependent on the extent of cattle holdings. Abimelech seems to have been a generic name for Philistine kings, comparable to Pharaoh in Egypt and Caesar in Rome. A later Abimelech had the same sister trick pulled on him by Abraham's son Isaac. "And there was a famine in the land, beside the first famine that was in the days of Abraham. And Isaac went unto Abimelech king of the Philistines unto Gerar .... and the men of the place asked him of his wife; and he said, She is my sister; for he feared to say, She is my wife; lest, said he, the men of the place should kill me for Rebekah; because she was fair to look upon. And it came to pass, when he had been there a long time, that Abimelech king of the Philistines looked out at a window, and saw, and behold, Isaac was sporting with Rebekah his wife. And Abimelech called Isaac, and said, Behold, of a surety she is thy wife: and how saidst thou, she is my sister? And Isaac said unto him, Because I said, lest I die for her. And Abimelech said, What is this that thou hast done unto us? one of the people might lightly have lien with thy wife, and thou shouldest have brought guiltiness upon us. And Abimelech charged all his people, saying, He that toucheth this man or his wife shall surely be put to death" (*Genesis* 26/1-11).

Isaac continued to reside with the Philistines in peace and prosperity, and settled down to raise grain for his animals and household: "And Isaac sowed in that land, and received in the same year an hundredfold . . . . and the man waxed great, and went forward, and grew until he became very great: for he had possession of flocks, and possession of herds, and great store of servants: and the Philistines envied him" (*Genesis* 26/12-14). Later in this chapter may be found the first evidence of the curse which has plagued the Jewish people throughout their history, anti-semitism; anti-hebrewism would be more correct, for most of the people of the Bible were Semitic themselves. "And Abimelech said unto Isaac, Go from us, for thou art much mightier than we." The later similarity of Pharaoh's reaction is striking. "And the children of Israel were fruitful, and increased abundantly, and multiplied, and waxed exceeding mighty; and the land was filled with them. Now there arose up a new king over Egypt, which knew not Joseph. And he said unto his people, Behold, the people of the children of Israel are more and mightier than we: come on, let us deal wisely with them; lest they multiply, and it come to pass, that, when there falleth out any war, they join also unto our enemies" (*Exodus* 1/7-10).

In a minor way in Philistia and in a major way in Egypt, a handful of herdsmen driven by drought from their regular pasture grounds were amicably received in foreign territory. After they settled in their new home, their acumen and hard work raised their economic status above that of their hosts, while their fecundity indicated a change of balance from a minority to a majority race. Meanwhile they resisted assimilation and closely preserved their religious and social customs. Economic and political pressure created shortages and friction. Friendship and tolerance turned to hate and suspicion. The resentment of the native sons and daughters, fanned by nationalistic priests and politicians, sowed the seeds of an incipient pogrom.

One of the principal causes of friction among Canaan herders was disputed water rights. The first instance to come to our attention is in *Genesis* (21/25): "And Abraham reproved Abimelech because of a well of water, which Abimelech's servants had violently taken away. And Abimelech said, I wot not who hath done this thing: neither didst thou tell me, neither yet heard I of it, but to day." The matter was settled peaceably, and perhaps Abraham discovered that his own herdsmen had aggravated the controversy, for "Abraham took sheep and oxen, and gave them unto Abimelech; and both of them made a covenant." Much impressed by the incident, "Abraham planted a grove in Beer-sheba, (the well site) and called there on the name of the Lord" (*Genesis* 21/33).

Years later, Isaac ran into similar well trouble in the same district. In the period intervening after Abraham's departure, the Philistines had filled in the wells; no reason is given, but the Philistines' main farming interests lay in corn and orchards, rather than cattle raising, and they probably figured that the apparent absence of wells would discourage nomadic herdsmen, whose flocks were a menace to the grain fields and vineyards. Isaac's herdsmen discovered the old well sites which Abraham had dug, and re-excavated them, which immediately provoked local opposition, for "the herdmen of Gerar did strive with Isaac's herdmen, saying, the water is our's" (*Genesis* 26/20). Isaac pursued a policy of appeasement and kept on digging wells which the natives promptly claimed. He named one well Esek (contention) and another Sitnah (hatred). Eventually Isaac's industry wore down the Philistines, and he was left in peace with his latest well which he named Rehoboth (room): "and he said, For now the Lord hath made room for us, and we shall be fruitful in the land."

Jacob carried on the pastoral tradition, for while "Esau was a cunning hunter, a man of the field . . . . Jacob was a plain man, dwelling in tents" (*Genesis* 25/27). Ostensibly because she disliked the local girls, but actually to save her son Jacob from Esau's revenge, Rebekah persuaded Isaac to send Jacob to Mesopotamia (Padan Aram), to his uncle's farm, where she hoped he might marry one or more of his cousins. Jacob's arrival at his destination discloses an interesting pastoral scene, related in the 29th chapter of *Genesis*. "Then Jacob went on his journey, and came into the land of the people of the east. And he looked, and behold a well in the field, and, lo, there were three flocks of sheep lying by it; for out of that well they watered the flocks: and a great stone was upon the well's mouth. And thither were all the flocks gathered: and they rolled the stone from the well's mouth, and watered the sheep, and put the stone again upon the well's mouth in his place." Jacob greeted the shepherds, and found he was near his journey's end, and that one of his cousins would soon be arriving to water her father's sheep. While awaiting her appearance, Jacob, an experienced sheep-herder used to hard work in the cool Canaan hills, criticized the lethargy of the easy-going shepherds of the Mesopotamian plain, "and he said, Lo, it is yet high day, neither is it time that the cattle should be gathered together: water ye the sheep, and go and feed them. And they said, We cannot, until all the flocks be gathered together, and till they roll the stone from the well's mouth; then we water the sheep. And while he yet spake with them, Rachel came with her father's sheep: for she kept them."

Rachel proved to be a very attractive girl, so Jacob displayed his gallantry and his brawn by rolling back the heavy stone single-handed, and watering Rachel's flock. Meanwhile the excited Rachel ran to her father to tell the news, and Laban, who later proved himself to be a shrewd, selfish farmer, decided that Jacob would be a valuable and cheap asset in the sheep business. So it proved, and Jacob's infatuation for Rachel deprived him of his native hardheadedness for many years, to Laban's advantage. The cunning old man kept stringing Jacob along, and it was not until Rachel's continued barrenness began to cool Jacob's ardor that he recognized his uncle's duplicity. When Rachel unexpectedly bore him a son, Jacob commenced to shape his plans towards eventually moving his growing establishment back to Canaan.

In the meantime, he decided to get some of his own back, and towards the end of the 30th chapter we read of occult fertility rites, whereby Jacob gradually acquired the greater and better part of Laban's flocks. Both Jacob's wives were versed in local magic, and they probably revealed the secrets to Jacob, for they too despised their father's meanness. During an absence of Laban and his sons in the sheep-shearing season, Jacob, with the concurrence of his wives, decided that the time was propitious for a hasty departure, and as rapidly as he could drive his large herds of cattle they headed for Canaan. Rachel added insult to injury by stealing her father's household images, probably figuring that their absence would defeat the power of any revenge her father might plan.

The enraged Laban pursued the fleeing caravan and overtook it a week later, by which time his anger had cooled to reproach for Jacob's unceremonious decampment. When Laban upbraided Jacob with stealing his household gods, Jacob, who knew nothing of Rachel's theft, told him to search the whole caravan, and even authorized him to kill whoever was found with the idols. The quick-witted Rachel, using an age old subterfuge, tricked the old man into accepting her innocence, and consequently the images could not be located. The futile search ended, Jacob's long suppressed sense of injustice boiled over, and in his tirade to Laban we learn many interesting details of the life of a shepherd. "This twenty years have I been with thee; thy ewes and thy she goats have not cast their young, and the rams of thy flock have I not eaten. That which was torn of beasts I brought not unto thee; I bare the loss of it; of my hand didst thou require it, whether stolen by day, or stolen by night. Thus I was; in the day the drought consumed me, and the frost by night; and my sleep departed from mine eyes. Thus have I been twenty years in thy house; I served thee fourteen years for thy two daughters, and six years for thy cattle: and thou hast changed my wages ten times" (*Genesis* 31/38-41).

The shepherd had responsible as well as arduous and lonely duties. It was no task for a weakling, or a casual laborer. Rugged physique, strength and skill to circumvent and beat off predatory animals, and to rescue sheep who had fallen into pits and crevices, keen knowledge and observance of nature to constantly search out pasture and water, and shelter the flock from approaching storms, and veterinary skill to treat injured animals and assist in the lambing and kidding season, all were requisites of the good shepherd. It was a solitary life, with a monotonous if ample diet. For a religiously inclined man it provided the environment and the leisure for prayer and meditation, and called for devotion and sacrifice of one's comfort to helpless charges.

The Mosaic law legalized and modified practices which were old in Jacob's time, and which he cast up at Laban. In *Exodus* (22/10-13) we read, "If a man deliver unto his neighbor an ass, or an ox, or a sheep, or any beast, to keep; and it die, or be hurt, or driven away, no man seeing it: then shall an oath of the Lord be between them both, that he hath not put his hand unto his neighbor's goods; and the owner of it shall accept thereof, and he shall not make it good. And if it be stolen from him, he shall make restitution to the owner thereof. If it be torn in pieces, then let him bring it for witness, and he shall not make good that which was torn." Presumably the labor and time involved in bringing a mauled carcase from the distant pasture grounds to Laban's farm outweighed the value of the animal, and Jacob preferred to stand the loss rather than go to the trouble of furnishing evidence.

The shepherd was expected to tally his sheep frequently, and this was accomplished by having the leader of the flock, a ram or he-goat, pass through a narrow gate or opening beside which stood the shepherd with a rod in his hand, and as the imitative sheep followed the leader the shepherd touched each lightly with the rod and kept his count. This monotonous task, always necessary after an attack by wild animals or a storm or a panic among the sheep, lulled the sleep-starved shepherd into drowsiness which he had to fight to overcome. The mental sheep-counting prescribed to sufferers from insomnia probably derives from the ancient shepherd's experience. Our modern expression, "to pass under the rod," also stems from this old sheep tally, to which there are several Bible references. "And concerning the tithe of the herd, or of the flock, even of whatsoever passeth under the rod, the tenth shall be holy unto the Lord" (*Leviticus* 27/32): "In the cities of Judah shall the flocks pass again under the hands of him that telleth them" (*Jeremiah* 33/13); "And I will cause you to pass under the rod" (*Ezekiel* 20/37).

After Jacob returned to Canaan he continued to rear sheep and cattle, but as he grew too old for active work he sent his sons to tend the flocks while he stayed home. It was while Joseph was on an extended trip to the remote pasture grounds that he was sold by his jealous brothers to the Midianites and carried to Egypt. Here he found many fine cattle but few or no sheep, "for every shepherd is an abomination unto the Egyptians" (*Genesis* 46/34). This Egyptian aversion to sheep is confirmed in *Exodus* (8/26): "And Moses said .... we shall sacrifice the abomination of the Egyptians to the Lord our God: lo, shall we sacrifice the abomination of the Egyptians before their eyes, and will they not stone us?" Moses was referring to the Hebrew custom of sacrificing a lamb or a kid.

Unfortunately, the Israelite sojourn in Egypt is virtually unreported in Egyptian records, or if it is the account is drastically different from the Bible version. Modern authorities are not in agreement regarding the dynasties which occupied the throne of Pharaoh from the time of Joseph until Moses. Some investigators claim that the Hyksos or Shepherd Kings ruled Egypt when Jacob and his family arrived, and that these Semitic invaders welcomed their distant brethren from Canaan. The Hyksos were unpopular and their rule was finally overthrown. It is speculative whether this abhorrence of sheep indicates that the foreign Shepherd Kings had been expelled, and that this revulsion against shepherds was a popular reaction, or whether the

Hyksos had military control of Egypt but that resentment and resistance against them still smoldered amongst the populace, and that accordingly Pharaoh and his advisers considered it tactful to isolate the sheep-tending Israelites in a restricted area.

When Jacob and his family arrived in Egypt, Joseph coached them: "I will go up, and shew Pharaoh, and say unto him, My brethren, and my father's house, which were in the land of Canaan, are come unto me; and the men are shepherds, for their trade hath been to feed cattle; and they have brought their flocks, and their herds, and all that they have. And it shall come to pass, when Pharaoh shall call you, and shall say, What is your occupation? That ye shall say, Thy servants' trade hath been about cattle from our youth even until now, both we, and also our fathers: that ye may dwell in the land of Goshen" (*Genesis* 46/31-34). The inference here is that the land of Goshen was a cattle reserve. Evidently the immigrants impressed Pharaoh as competent stockmen, for he told Joseph, "If thou knowest any men of activity among them, then make them rulers over my cattle" (*Genesis* 47/6).

When Moses fled from Pharaoh's vengeance and escaped to Midian, he displayed a gallantry towards some fair shepherdesses he met there which surpassed Jacob's prowess in Padan Aram. "Moses fled from the face of Pharaoh, and dwelt in the land of Midian: and he sat down by a well. Now the priest (margin: or prince) of Midian had seven daughters: and they came and drew water, and filled the troughs to water their father's flock. And the shepherds came and drove them away: but Moses stood up and helped them, and watered their flock" (*Exodus* 2/15-17). The grateful Midianite offered the refugee a home, and "Moses kept the flock of Jethro his father in law, the priest of Midian: and he led the flock to the backside of the desert, and came to the mountain of God, even to Horeb. And the angel of the Lord appeared unto him in a flame of fire out of the midst of a bush" (*Exodus* 3/1-2). Jehovah told him of his new mission, and Moses' sheep-tending days were over; no doubt there were times during the forty years wandering in the desert when he would willingly have traded his unruly charges for Jethro's docile sheep.

Meanwhile, in the land of Uz, northeast of Midian, another great cattle baron proudly counted his living wealth. "His substance also was seven thousand sheep, and three thousand camels, and five hundred yoke of oxen, and five hundred she asses, and a very great household; (margin: husbandry). so that this man was the greatest of all the men of the east" (*Job* 1/3). This assessment may have been correct in the time of Job and Moses (about 1500 B.C.), but six hundred years later Job's cattle holdings would have been considered modest.

2 *Kings* (3/4) tells us "Mesha king of Moab was a sheepmaster, and rendered unto the king of Israel an hundred thousand lambs, and an hundred thousand rams, with the wool." This was an annual tribute and enormous flocks must have been kept to furnish the necessary number of animals to Israel. This Mesha was the author of the famous Moabite stone, discovered in Dibon in Moab in 1868, and now in the Louvre in Paris. The deciphered inscription on this stone confirms Mesha's subjugation, but claims that later the role was reversed. The Hagarites were another group who had very extensive cattle holdings; they were defeated by the trans-Jordan Israelites, who "took away their cattle; of their camels fifty thousand, and of sheep two hundred and fifty thousand, and of asses two thousand" (1 *Chronicles* 5/21).

Job, after his great vicissitudes, resumed cattle raising and did so well that in the 12th verse of the last chapter we learn that "the Lord blessed the latter end of Job more than his beginning, for he had fourteen thousand sheep, and six thousand camels, and a thousand yoke of oxen, and a thousand she asses." Rather remarkably, each of these figures represents an exact doubling of the original stock. Unfortunately, Job is flockless and herdless throughout most of his tale, so we learn little of pastoral interest, but the first verse of the 30th chapter refers to the dogs which herded his flocks. In a passage in *Isaiah* (56/9-11) we find a shepherd's contemptuous criticism of poorly trained sheep dogs: "All ye beasts of the field, come to devour, yea, all ye beasts in the forest. His watchmen are blind: they are all ignorant, they are all dumb dogs, they cannot bark; sleeping, lying down, loving to slumber. Yea, they are greedy dogs which can never have enough, and they are shepherds that cannot understand: they all look to their own way, every one for his gain, from his quarter."

The value of ancient sheep dogs lay not only in their assistance to the shepherd in herding flock, but equally in their ability to detect, drive off and, if necessary, kill wild animals threatening the sheep. Savage beasts were a constant menace. David started his career as

GARDENING IN THE BIBLE

a shepherd, and when Saul showed scepticism at David's challenging of the giant Goliath, the lad replied, "Thy servant kept his father's sheep, and there came a lion, and a bear, and took a lamb out of the flock: and I went out after him, and smote him, and delivered it out of his mouth: and when he arose against me, I caught him by his beard, and smote him, and slew him. Thy servant slew both the lion and the bear" (1 *Samuel* 17/34-36).

When a killer was tracked down, a posse of shepherds was organized to destroy the animal. "Like as the lion and the young lion roaring on his prey, when a multitude of shepherds is called forth against him, he will not be afraid of their voice, nor abase himself for the noise of them" (*Isaiah* 31/4). *Amos* (3/12), himself a shepherd, probably wrote from first hand experience of the lion menace: "As the shepherd taketh out of the mouth of the lion two legs, or a piece of an ear."

The responsibility of a shepherd towards his flock, and the natural habits of sheep, are two similes used time and again throughout the Bible to typify the relationship between God and man. The 34th chapter of *Ezekiel* is entirely pastoral and contains scores of allusions to shepherds and their flocks. It could have been written only by a man who had lived a shepherd's life, and equally it was addressed to a sheep raising people. Indeed most of the prophets freely employ sheep similes and metaphors.

So responsible and onerous were the shepherd's duties that hired help was seldom used, unless the servant was a tried and trusted retainer. The owner and his family were the usual custodians, there being only one instance in the Old Testament where the flock was turned over to a deputy, and on this occasion the shepherd was sent by his father to bear a gift to the king (1 *Samuel* 17/20). This innate sense of responsibility, shared by many Israelites, made the sheep parables particularly telling. Jesus used it to full advantage. "I am the good shepherd: the good shepherd giveth his life for the sheep. But he that is an hireling, and not the shepherd, whose own the sheep are not, seeth the wolf coming, and leaveth the sheep, and fleeth: and the wolf catcheth them, and scattereth the sheep. The hireling fleeth, because he is an hireling, and careth not for the sheep. I am the good shepherd" (*John* 10/11-14).

The spread of cultivation in Palestine, the disruptive influence

[222]

of other countries, and the ravages of war and captivity had all but destroyed the old patriarchal traditions in Jesus' time, but the responsibility of the good shepherd towards his sheep was uncompromised. The hireling would not and could not take it. We think of sheepherding as a tame, monotonous, safe task, but in the lonely Palestine hills, beset by savage animals, it was a job for a he-man, and the Master's saying, "The good shepherd giveth his life for the sheep," was strictly true, for sometimes wild animals killed the sheep-tender.

The Christian church has adopted the phraseology and the comparisons concerning the shepherd and the sheep to a greater extent than any other parable offered by Jesus. Our word "pastor," denoting a minister of religion, is synonymous with "shepherd," and is so used in the opening verses of the 23rd chapter of *Jeremiah,* and in *Ephesians* (4/11). The apostle Paul, in *Hebrews* (13/20), acclaims "our Lord Jesus, that great shepherd of the sheep." Our church services, our prayers, and our hymns constantly use the language of the shepherd. City dwellers who have never seen a sheep, far less a shepherd, fervently intone," The Lord is my shepherd; I shall not want. He maketh me to lie down in green pastures: he leadeth me beside the still waters" (*Psalms* 23/1-2), and confess "All we like sheep have gone astray; we have turned every one to his own way" (*Isaiah* 53/6). The Paschal lamb, "without spot or blemish," has been one of the most sacred of Jewish sacrifices since the sojourn in Egypt, and the early Christians identified Christ with this sacrificial lamb. "John seeth Jesus coming unto him, and saith, Behold the Lamb of God, which taketh away the sin of the world" (*John* 1/29). *Revelation* is particularly rich in this symbolism. The comparison is not to the gentle and innocent nature of the lamb, but to its ancient token of sacrifice and redemption.

Sheep flock across the pages of Scripture, and provide a revealing source for study of the natural background of the Bible. Jesus, in the 10th chapter of *John,* condenses into a pastoral paragraph a fund of sheep lore. "Verily, verily, I say unto you, He that entereth not by the door into the sheepfold, but climbeth up some other way, the same is a thief and a robber. But he that entereth in by the door is the shepherd of the sheep. To him the porter openeth; and the sheep hear his voice: and he calleth his own sheep by name, and leadeth them out. And when he putteth forth his own sheep, he goeth before them, and the sheep follow him: for they know his voice. And a stranger will they not follow, but will flee from him: for they know not the voice of strangers."

The sheepfold or sheepcote was usually a large walled but roofless enclosure, used in the shearing season, to corral a flock which was awaiting sale or had been sold, as shelter if severe weather was expected, or for hand-feeding if pasture failed. The patriarchs erected a sheepfold when they found permanent or semi-permanent grazing grounds. There is an interesting background to the first mentioned biblical one, in the 32nd chapter of *Numbers*. The long residence in Egypt had apparently weakened the traditional attachment to sheep and cattle raising, and many of the Hebrews looked to urban occupations and dirt farming as an easier and more profitable way of life.

However, the tribes of Reuben and Gad, along with a segment of the sons of Manasseh, kept up the sheep tradition, and when they left Egypt they took their "flocks and herds, even very much cattle" (*Exodus* 12/38). In spite of the hardships of the main body of the pilgrims, the shortage of water and the absence of all food except manna, it appears that the cattle survived and prospered, for when the expedition arrived in what is now Trans-Jordan, the men of Reuben, Gad and Manasseh decided that insofar as they were concerned, the Promised Land had been reached (*Numbers* 32). "Now the children of Reuben and the children of Gad had a very great multitude of cattle: and when they saw the land of Jazer, and the land of Gilead, that, behold, the place was a place for cattle.... said they.... let this land be given unto thy servants for a possession, and bring us not over Jordan.... we will build sheepfolds here for our cattle, and cities for our little ones." Jehovah, and Moses, bitterly opposed this fragmentation, but a compromise was worked out whereby the animals and the children remained in Gilead, while the men of war continued with the other tribes to assist in conquering the Canaanites.

We find the Israelites leaving Egypt with huge flocks and herds, and forty years later arriving at the Jordan with extensive cattle stocks. The 31st chapter of *Numbers* tells of the pillage of the Midianites, and that "the booty ... was six hundred thousand and seventy thousand and five thousand sheep, and threescore and twelve thousand beeves, and threescore and one thousand asses." Yet the Israelites were several million in number and had been meat-starved for many years, so even this huge total of sheep and cattle would last the hungry hordes less than a month. Presumably the two and a half cattle tribes added some of the better Midianite animals to their breeding stock, but it seems likely that their main holdings were the descendants of Egyptian animals. While the Bible makes no mention of it, it is possible that the route of the cattle tribes diverged from that of the main body led by Moses, liaison being maintained. Had the cattle been accessible, the half-starved Israelites would doubtlessly have slaughtered them for food, particularly in view of the great shortage of water for the people themselves. The sheep and cattle herders probably trekked from pasture ground to pasture ground, and in the long period lost a sense of identity with the main body.

When the tribes finally settled down in the Promised Land there was antagonism and bad feeling between the Trans-Jordan settlers who retained their nomadic instincts, and the main body who went in for agriculture and husbandry and commerce. The government, the priesthood and the scribes remained in Canaan proper; the semi-secession of the cattle tribes always rankled, and when the Trans-Jordanites built an altar to Jehovah in their own territory the main tribes threatened war, for they suspected heresy. The famous Song of Deborah (*Judges* 5/16-17) reproaches the sheepmen who chose partition: "Why abodest thou among the sheepfolds, to hear the bleatings of the flocks. For the divisions of Reuben there were great searchings of heart. Gilead abode beyond Jordan."

Sheepherding in Palestine proper no longer carried the prestige of patriarchal times, and this explains the comparative absence of reference to large flocks and herds in the subsequent history of Israel. A brief summary of the later history of the range-riding cattlemen is given in the 5th chapter of 1 *Chronicles*. "The sons of Reuben, and the Gadites, and half the tribe of Manasseh, of valiant men, men able to bear buckler and sword, and to shoot with bow, and skilful in war .... they made war with the Hagarites .... and the Hagarites were delivered into their hand .... and they took away their cattle .... and they dwelt in their steads until the captivity .... unto the entering in of the wilderness from the river Euphrates .... mighty men of valor, famous men .... and they transgressed against the God of their fathers, and went a whoring after the gods of the people of the land .... and the God of Israel stirred up the spirit of Pul, king

[225]

of Assyria, and the spirit of Tilgath-pilneser king of Assyria, and he carried them away." These independent cattlemen were fierce desert warriors but they fell before the organized war machine of Assyria, and being east of the Jordan were the earliest of the ten tribes of Israel to be deported eastward, and subsequently disappear from recorded history.

In Jesus' time flocks were comparatively small and sheepfolds were communal affairs sheltering several flocks, having a permanent custodian. The Master's statement, "He calleth his own sheep by name, for they know his voice," was quite true; Levant shepherds to this day train sheep to recognize individual names, and the response is as effective as with a well trained dog. The eastern shepherd leads his flock, and encourages and controls them by addressing the leaders by name, the rest of the animals docilely following these "principal of the flock" (*Jeremiah* 25/34-36). This bond between the shepherd and the sheep ensured against loss by vocal theft, but a change in shepherds must have thrown a lot of work and training on the new man; probably the shepherd retained his flock leaders wherever he went, just as he took his sheep dogs.

What the pressing of the vintage was to the husbandman, the time of sheep-shearing was to the shepherd. A session of hard work, but with gay company rather than the normal solitude, followed by celebration and feasting. In David's freebooting days, while he led a guerilla band, he once sent some of his hungry followers to cash in on the traditional bounty and hospitality dispensed at shearing time. "There was a man in Maon, whose possessions were in Carmel: and the man was very great, and he had three thousand sheep, and a thousand goats; and he was shearing his sheep in Carmel. (We observe here the reduction in the holdings of an outstanding sheepmaster, from the days of Job.) Now the name of the man was Nabal: and the name of his wife Abigail: and she was a woman of good understanding, and of a beautiful countenance: but the man was churlish and evil in his doings .... And David heard in the wilderness that Nabal did shear his sheep. And David sent out ten young men, and .... said .... Get you up to Carmel, and go to Nabal, and greet him in my name: and .... say to him .... Peace be both to thee, and peace be to thine house, and peace be unto all that thou hast. And now I have heard that thou hast shearers; now thy shepherds which were with us, we hurt them not, neither was there ought missing unto them, all the while they were in Carmel.... Wherefore let the young men find favor in thine eyes: for we come in a good day: give, I pray thee, whatsoever cometh to thine hand unto thy servants, and to thy son David" (1 *Samuel* 25/2-8).

At this distance it is hard to judge the merits of the case, and a knowledge of the customs of the era would be essential. Nowadays this would be classed as a racket, and we have many instances where a gang gives unwanted "protection" to legitimate business and then demands a reward, or else! David's henchmen were decidedly anarchistic: "David .... escaped to the cave Adullam .... And every one that was in distress, and every one that was in debt, and every one that was discontented, gathered themselves unto him; and he became a captain over them: and there were with him about four hundred men" (1 *Samuel* 22/1-2). Nabal greeted David's envoys with the cordiality which a Wall Street financier would tender a Communist delegation demanding a dividend cut to finance the *Daily Worker* on the grounds that the paper had refrained from attacking his holding companies. "Who is David? and who is the son of Jesse? there be many servants now a days that break away every man from his master. Shall I then take my bread, and my water, and my flesh that I have killed for my shearers, and give it unto men, whom I know not whence they be?" (25/10-11).

When David's emissaries returned empty-handed, he armed his band and vowed immediate death not only to Nabal but to his family, his shearers and everyone connected with him. Hearing of the danger, Abigail intercepted David and bought him off with generous gifts of food and wine, and apologized for her husband's action. When Abigail returned she found Nabal celebrating the end of shearing: "And Abigail came to Nabal; and, behold, he held a feast in his house, like the feast of a king; and Nabal's heart was merry within him, for he was very drunken" (1 *Samuel* 25/36).

Another festive sheepshearing is related in 2 *Samuel* (13/24-29): "And Absalom came to the king, and said, Behold now, thy servant hath sheepshearers; let the king, I beseech thee, and his servants, go with thy servant." David demurred on the ground of the expense which such a large number of guests would impose, but finally agreed that his sons, including Amnon, might attend. Two years previously Amnon had seduced Tamar, Absalom's sister, and then thrown her aside; Amnon thought that Absalom had forgotten, or forgiven, the incident, and went to the shearing feast in good heart. In the midst of the celebration, when Amnon was "merry with wine," Absalom's servants stabbed him at a prearranged signal, and he fell dead. A different kind of shearing-house tragedy is told in 2 *Kings* (10/12-14); the Hebrew term used for shearing-house in this last passage means "tie-house" or "binding house," the reference being to the practice of tying the sheep's legs prior to shearing.

In a rather obscure text in *Jeremiah* (43/10-12) we read that "Nebuchadnezzar the king of Babylon, my servant .... shall array himself with the land of Egypt, as a shepherd putteth on his garment." Evidently shepherds wore a distinctive garb. They carried slings for defense and attack, the sling from which David launched the stone which killed Goliath being the weapon with which he was most proficient, and for which he turned down the armor and sword proffered by Saul. "And he took his staff in his hand, and chose him five smooth stones out of the brook, and put them in a shepherd's bag which he had, even in a scrip; and his sling was in his hand: and he drew near unto the Philistine .... And the Philistine said unto David, Am I a dog, that thou comest to me with staves?" (1 *Samuel* 17/40, 43). Had the slingshots missed or failed to disable Goliath, it is obvious that David intended to rely on his shepherd's staff to overthrow the armor-laden giant, probably by tripping him. David had killed lions and bears with the same weapons, and was fully confident of his ability to use them effectively.

History is full of accounts of light mobile units, using guerilla tactics, discomfiting heavily armed opponents relying on orthodox warfare. The shepherd's staff must have been a multi-purpose implement. *Zechariah* (11/7) tells of a shepherd using two staffs when he fed the flock. The shepherd's bag, or scrip, was a leather purse slung across the shoulder by a strap, and was normally used to carry food. Its peculiar shape is commemorated in the name of a common weed.

The Bible has several references to shepherds' shelters; sometimes these are called tents as in *Song of Solomon* (1/8) and *Isaiah* (38/12); from this latter mention we infer the flimsy and temporary nature of the erection. *Jeremiah* (33/12) and *Amos* (1/2) speak of the habitation of shepherds. *Zephaniah* (2/6) prophesies, "The sea coast shall be dwellings and cottages for shepherds, and folds for flocks." The word "cottages" in this last quotation means "cut out of the rock or earth," and may designate caves formerly eroded by the sea. Most of these words used for translating shepherds' shelters are applied in a loose and inexact manner, and we may surmise that the divines who translated our Bible had their thoughts fixed more on the heaven above than on the earth beneath.

Apart from regular flocks of sheep it was common practice for a family to buy a lamb and raise it. Naturally, tender-hearted persons got so attached to the little animal that instead of butchering it for mutton at maturity they kept it as a household pet. Nathan's parable to David (2 *Samuel* 12/1-4) describes such an incident in tender terms: "The poor man had nothing, save one little ewe lamb, which he had bought and nourished up: and it grew up together with him, and with his children; it did eat of his own meat, and drank of his own cup, and lay in his bosom, and was unto him as a daughter." Kind shepherds sometimes raised a delicate or orphaned little lamb, giving it personal attention: "He shall gather the lambs with his arm, and carry them in his bosom" (*Isaiah* 40/11).

The Canaan sheep are believed to have been the fat-tailed variety the swollen tail being specified as a sacrificial offering: it is still considered a delicacy in Asia Minor. The word "rump," used in the Authorized Version in texts such as *Exodus* (29/22), is rendered "fat tail" in the Revised Version. Sometimes fat-tailed sheep suffer acutely from over development of their appendage, and devices to support the weight are required.

An enormous amount of wool must have been processed yearly in Palestine, yet the Bible tells little about it. *Ezekiel* (27/18) identifies Damascus in Syria as an export center of white wool. The Hebrews too must have been meticulous in the standards applying to the higher grades of wool, for the purity and whiteness of the fleece is used for comparison in the most sacred references: "I beheld . . . . the Ancient of days . . . . whose garment was white as snow, and the hair of his head like the pure wool" (*Daniel* 7/9), and "One like unto the Son of man . . . . his head and his hairs were white like wool, as white as snow" (*Revelation* 1/13-14). *Psalms* (147/16) uses a similar phrase, "He giveth snow like wool." The cleansing prescription, "cedar wood and scarlet and hyssop," specified in *Leviticus* (14/4), has the mysterious scarlet ingredient identified as scarlet wool by Paul in his *Epistle to the Hebrews* (9/19).

Proverbs (31/13) lauds the model housewife, "She seeketh wool, and flax, and worketh willingly with her hands," while Hosea (2/5) condemns the courtesan whose lovers supply her with wool and flax and other requirements. It would appear that both the virtuous and the shameless one did their own spinning and weaving. The ban of *Ezekiel* (44/17) on the wearing of woolen garments while carrying out the sacred offices of the priesthood is explained as a hygienic precaution in the succeeding verse: "They shall not gird themselves with anything that causeth sweat." Perhaps the prophet had come unpleasantly close to the woolen garments of the shepherds (34/3), and the odor arising from long periods without bathing and from enforced sleeping in their clothes remained an offensive memory.

Sheep give wool while goats furnish hair. Goats' hair was specified as the material of which the eleven curtains of the tent of the tabernacle were to be woven (*Exodus* 26/7), while *Exodus* (36/15) stipulated that each curtain was to measure thirty cubits by four cubits (52 feet by 7 feet). Goats' hair was also woven into garments and tent furnishings (*Numbers* 31/20). In a passage presaging the patriotic fervor of a wartime knitting bee, *Exodus* (35/26) relates, "And all the women whose hearts stirred them up in wisdom spun goats' hair." The occasion was the construction and ritualistic decoration of the tabernacle. Superficially, the verse seems to indicate that the more erudite and spiritually advanced women did the spinning; however, an examination of supplementary texts, for example *Exodus* (31/1-6), suggests that the Israelites were not generally skilled in handicrafts, which was understandable in view of their Egyptian serfdom, but that there were a few divinely inspired artisans, and that Jehovah facilitated the rapid learning of craftsmanship by the hands of willing and consecrated workers.

"I have called by name Bezaleel . . . . and I have filled him with the spirit of God, in wisdom, and in understanding, and in knowledge, and in all manner of workmanship, to devise cunning works, to work in gold, and in silver, and in brass, and in cutting of stones, to set them, and in carving of timber, to work in all manner of workmanship . . . . and in the hearts of all that are wise hearted I have put wisdom, that they may make all that I have commanded thee." Apparently the hair

[230]

of black goats was most suited for weaving into tent cloths and tabernacle furnishings: "I am black, but comely, O ye daughters of Jerusalem, as the tents of Kedar, as the curtains of Solomon" (*Song of Solomon* 1/5). This goat hair would appear to have been long stranded, of fine glossy texture, possibly from an angora type of goat. "Behold, thou are fair, my love: . . . . thy hair is as a flock of goats, that appear from mount Gilead" (*Song of Solomon* 4/1).

When we think of a sack we visualize a coarse burlap woven from jute or hemp. Our word "sack" is a direct link with Bible language, and comes from the Hebrew *saq* and the Greek *sakkos;* there the resemblance ceases, for the ancient sack was woven of coarse goats' or camels' hair. This fabric is the sackcloth which is commonly associated with ashes in scriptural scenes of mourning and desolation. Sackcloth, like tent cloth, was black: "The sun became black as sackcloth of hair" (*Revelation* 6/12), and "I clothe the heavens with blackness, and I make sackcloth their covering" (*Isaiah* 50/3). The sombre color of sackcloth and its coarse texture made it appropriate for mourning and repentance, not only amongst the Jews but generally throughout the East. When Nineveh, the Assyrian capital, accepted Jonah's warning, the king cast off his royal robes and ordained, "Let man and beast be covered with sackcloth" (*Jonah* 3/8). The hair shirt of the medieval ascetic, and of some modern monastic orders, had its counterpart amongst the austere prophets of the Canaan hills.

The use of skins as clothing is first reported in the garden of Eden, the tailoring being credited to Jehovah: "Unto Adam also and to his wife did the Lord God make coats of skins, and clothed them" (*Genesis* 3/21). There is no clue to the skins used, but five verses further on we read that Abel was a keeper of sheep, so sheepskin is a permissible surmise. "Rams' skins died red" were specified as a covering for the tent of the tabernacle (*Exodus* 26/14). *Deuteronomy* (18/4) enjoined that the priestly Levites should be given "the first of the fleece of thy sheep," while *Job* (31/20) speaks of the destitute whom he has helped and "warmed with the fleece of my sheep." In New Testament times the use of sheepskins as clothing was regarded conventionally as branding the wearers uncivilized and poverty-stricken: "They wandered about in sheepskins and goatskins; being destitute, afflicted, tormented . . . in dens and in caves of the earth" (*Hebrews* 11/37-38).

Bible flocks usually included goats as well as sheep, and the leader of the flock was as likely to be a he-goat or buck as a ram. In mixed flocks the most powerful male fought his way to leadership, and a goat usually won the honors. "Be as the he goats before the flocks," encourages *Jeremiah* (50/8) as he tells the Jews to break away from Babylon, and again in (51/40) he singles out the he-goat, "I will bring them down like lambs to the slaughter, like rams with he-goats." In *Ezekiel* (34/17-18) the contrast is again drawn, to be followed by mention of a habit which has irked many a farmer: "And as for you, O my flock, thus saith the Lord God; Behold, I judge between cattle and cattle, between the rams and the he-goats. Seemeth it a small thing unto you to have eaten up the good pasture, but ye must tread down with your feet the residue of your pastures? and to have drunk of the deep waters, but ye must foul the residue with your feet?" Substituting the marginal alternatives for the first sentence, we get, "I judge between the small cattle of lambs and kids, and cattle, between the rams and the great he goats."

Several different Hebrew words are translated into English as "cattle," while the same word appears elsewhere in the Bible as "flock" or "herd" or "possession." The Israelites called sheep and goats "small cattle," and used different terms from that designating bovine stock, but the translators ignored this. To further complicate livestock identification, a native word rendered into English as "lamb" was applied to the young of the goat as well as of the sheep. *Exodus* (12/5) furnishes a good example: "Your lamb shall be without blemish, a male of the first year: ye shall take it out from the sheep, or from the goats."

A proverb says, "Give a dog a bad name and you might as well hang it." The goat was put on the wrong side of the fence very early in Bible history, and has never managed to live it down. In Egypt the goat was deified and worshipped, along with the calf, and when the Israelites attempted to revert to these forms of idolatry both they and their images were denounced and damned. The worthy translators of the Authorized Version slapped on some more black paint, as we discover in examining *Leviticus* (17/7): "They shall no more offer their sacrifices unto devils, after whom they have gone a whoring," and 2 *Chronicles* (11/15), where we are told that king Rehoboam "ordained him priests for the high places, and for the devils, and for the calves which he had made." The devils in these two passages are correctly rendered "he-goats" in the Revised Version, with a marginal alternative "satyrs." The same word is translated "goat" and "kid," dozens of times in other texts of the Authorized Version, as well as appearing as "he goat," "hairy," and "rough."

Satyr, and Pan, half goat, half man, was a Greek and not an Egyptian creation, but mythology and idolatry often have international relations. The Mosaic law classed the goat as a clean animal and suitable for sacrifice, but it was generally assigned to the sin offering, and by association of ideas became a black goat if not a black sheep. The scapegoat service, on the annual day of atonement, further branded the unfortunate goat. At this solemn ceremony, described in the 16th chapter of *Leviticus,* two goats were presented by the high priest as a sin offering for all the people. Lots were cast, and one was dedicated to Jehovah, the other to Azazel. The Authorized Version renders this latter word "scapegoat," while the Revised Version retains the Hebrew original, but the true meaning and significance of this mysterious word never has been discovered. As the ritual proceeded, the "Jehovah" goat was sacrificed for a sin offering, after which, in the words of the Bible, "Aaron shall lay both his hands upon the head of the live goat, and confess over him all the iniquities of the children of Israel, and all their transgressions in all their sins, putting them upon the head of the goat, and shall send him away by the hand of a fit man into the wilderness: and the goat shall bear upon him all their iniquities unto a land not inhabited: and he shall let go the goat in the wilderness."

Probably Jesus' parable in *Matthew* (25/31-46) has done more to discredit goats among Christians than all of the Old Testament slurs. "When the Son of man shall come in his glory, and all the holy angels with him, then shall he sit upon the throne of his glory; and before him shall be gathered all nations: and he shall separate them one from another, as a shepherd divideth his sheep from the goats: and he shall set the sheep on his right hand, but the goats on the left. Then shall the King say unto them on his right hand, Come, ye blessed of my Father, inherit the kingdom prepared for you from the foundation of the world . . . . Then shall he say also unto them on the left hand, Depart from me, ye cursed, into everlasting fire, prepared for the devil and his angels."

If anyone considers that Bible propaganda has not injured the reputation of the goat, let him consider the effect of the biblical discrimination in favor of the right hand and against the left. Right is

[233]

synonymous with justice and correctness and in accordance with the law of God and man. The Anglo-Saxon meaning of left was worthless, and we speak of a left-handed compliment or a left-handed marriage. The modern political meaning adds further complications. While goats and sheep have superficial resemblances, their nature is radically different. Sheep are timid, docile, stupid, imitative followers. Goats are alert, independent, intelligent, headstrong, mischievous. The contrast is very marked. Sheep are uncritical mass followers, goats rugged individualists.

However, the goat had admirers even among the Jews, and no less an authority than king Solomon acclaims the graceful animal: "There be three things which go well, yea, four are comely in going: a lion which is strongest among beasts, and turneth not away for any; a greyhound; an he goat also; and a king, against whom there is no rising up" (*Proverbs* 30/29-31). Elsewhere in the same book the monarch reveals his knowledge of practical farming: "Be thou diligent to know the state of thy flocks, and look well to thy herds . . . . the lambs are for thy clothing, and the goats are the price of the field. And thou shalt have goats' milk enough for thy food, for the food of thy household, and for the maintenance of thy maidens" (27/23, 26-27).

The patriarchs were inveterate cattle raisers as well as herders of sheep and goats. Ranges were wide, pasture was normally good and abundant, and men were few. Up to the time of David and Solomon we find many references to cattle, but later they dwindle off as Israel became a field and garden-minded people. The loose use of the word "cattle" has already been mentioned, and reference to the concordance is necessary to distinguish cattle in the specialized modern meaning.

Egypt was famous for its cattle, and it is likely that it was mostly Egyptian stock which Abram took with him when he left Egypt after his first visit there (*Genesis* 13/2). He had covered a lot of ground before reaching Egypt and had passed through a time of famine, so we may surmise that he was travelling light when he reached the land of Pharaoh. For all his wealth and large retinue, Abram took a leading part in handling and knowing his stock, and when unexpected guests arrived, "Abram ran into the herd, and fetcht a calf tender and good, and gave it unto a young man; and he hasted to dress it" (*Genesis* 18/7). The patriarch selected a choice animal and caught it, but let a servant do the butchering and dressing.

Great men considered it their duty and their privilege to give personal attention to their herds. Saul, first king of Israel, went right back to cattle tending after his coronation, and when danger threatened his craven subjects, he drafted an army with a cattleman's harsh logic. The Ammonites had besieged the Hebrew city of Jabesh Gilead, and the city fathers had sent messengers for help: "And, behold, Saul came after the herd out of the field; and Saul said, What aileth the people that they weep? and they told him the tidings of the men of Jabesh. And the Spirit of God came upon Saul when he heard those tidings, and his anger was kindled greatly. And he took a yoke of oxen, and hewed them in pieces, and sent them throughout all the coasts of Israel by the hands of messengers, saying, Whosoever cometh not forth after Saul and after Samuel, so shall it be done unto his oxen. And the fear of the Lord fell on the people, and they came out with one consent" (1 *Samuel* 11/5-7). Here we note the great value placed on oxen, and the keen psychology of Saul in threatening loss of the farmers' prize possession rather than employing personal threats, which might have antagonized his newly created subjects. One of the great Hebrew prophets, Elisha, was plowing with twelve yoke of oxen, when the mantle of destiny fell on him (1 *Kings* 19/19).

Cattle were so highly esteemed in ancient Egypt that they were associated with and symbolized in the images of some of the senior gods and goddesses. Apis, the sacred bull of Memphis, was held to be a reincarnation of the great god Osiris, and Hathor, queen of heaven, was cow-headed. Calf or bull worship persisted throughout the history of Israel from the Exodus to the final disappearance of the ten tribes into Assyria, and it was probably during the sojourn in Egypt that this cult was adopted by the Israelites. Neither Aaron's golden calf, nor king Rehoboam's twin calves, were presented, or accepted, as pagan idols, but were sincere, if misguided, attempts to bring down to earth the mystical concept of Jehovah.

Transcendental and incorporeal monotheism is an elusive concept even in our day, and the human attributes of anger, jealousy, revenge and hate with which the Old Testament frequently clothes Jehovah are only a degree removed from His representation in symbolic statuary. The ordaining of consecrated animal sacrifices to God must have lent support to the adherents of the Golden Calf. It was not until the latter part of the 8th century B. C. that calf worship was emphatically denounced, and about the same time the potency of animal sacrifices to deity was criticized.

Every countryman has seen a herd of cows wading in a shallow stream or pond on a hot day. Cattle have done this throughout the ages, and four thousand years ago it was a familiar sight to the rulers of Egypt. "Pharaoh dreamed: and, behold, he stood by the river. And, behold, there came up out of the river seven well favored kine and fat-fleshed; and they fed in a meadow. And, behold, seven other kine came up after them out of the river, ill favored and leanfleshed; and stood by the other kine on the brink of the river. And the ill favored and lean-fleshed kine did eat up the seven well favored and fat kine. So Pharaoh awoke" (*Genesis* 41/1-4). (Kine is an old Anglo-Saxon word for cows.) Interpretation of this dream raised Joseph from a prison cell to occupancy of the governor's palace, from whence he superintended the royal acquisition of all Egyptian livestock in return for enough grain to keep the ex-cattle owners alive. While Pharaoh and his successors probably farmed out to tenants and managers much of this huge herd and its progeny, the title to these animals and most of the income derived from them remained crown rights.

When the Pharaoh of the Exodus refused to release the Israelites, and plagues were inflicted on him to force his acquiescence, the first four—water turned to blood, frogs, flies and lice—were more in the nature of annoyances and inconveniences than catastrophes, and it was the common people who bore the brunt of the plagues rather than the monarch, ensconced in his luxurious palace with an army of servants to minister to his comfort. The fifth plague, the death of all the cattle of Egypt, hit Pharaoh himself where it hurt, and much of his wealth and farm economy was wiped out. In *Exodus* (9/3, 6) we read, "Behold, the hand of the Lord is upon thy cattle which is in the field, upon the horses, upon the asses, upon the camels, upon the oxen, and upon the sheep .... and the Lord did that thing on the morrow, and all the cattle of Egypt died: but of the cattle of the children of Israel died not one."

It would appear that this total destruction of Egyptian cattle was exaggerated, for further on in this same chapter, prior to the plague of hail, Moses addressed Pharaoh, "Send therefore now, and gather thy cattle, and all that thou hast in the field; for upon every man and beast which shall be found in the field, and shall not be brought home, the hail shall come down upon them, and they shall die. He that feared the word of the Lord among the servants of Pharaoh made his servants and his cattle flee into the houses: and he that regarded not the word of the Lord left his servants and his cattle in the field." The Hebrew word denoting livestock in general is used in all the foregoing cattle references. The final plague, the slaughter of the firstborn, again took its toll of the supposedly extinct Egyptian cattle. "At midnight the Lord smote all the firstborn in the land of Egypt.... and all the first born of cattle" (*Exodus* 12/29). The word used here for cattle differs from the earlier mentioned, and signifies large cattle, cows and bulls and oxen.

Pharaoh's concern about the loss of his cattle is evident in *Exodus* (10/24, 26): "And Pharaoh called unto Moses, and said, Go ye, serve the Lord; only let your flocks and your herds be stayed: let your little ones also go with you.... And Moses said, Our cattle also shall go with us; there shall not an hoof be left behind."

Two Hebrew kings are reputed to have had large herds, but no detail is given, and probably their holdings were relatively small compared to the great nomad chiefs. In *Ecclesiastes* (2/7) Solomon boasts, "I had great possessions of great and small cattle above all that were in Jerusalem before me." King Uzziah, the lover of husbandry, "had much cattle, both in the low country and in the plains" (2 *Chronicles* 26/10). Evidently Saul came to realize that his duties as a monarch interfered with his cattle breeding, so he appointed "Doeg, an Edomite, the chiefest of the herdmen" (1 *Samuel* 21/7). This office was one of the highest in the new kingdom, for the same book (22/9) speaks of "Doeg the Edomite, which was set over the servants of Saul." David, Saul's successor, had two chief herdsmen: "Over the herds that fed in Sharon was Shitrai, the Sharonite; and over the herds that were in the valleys was Shaphat" (1 *Chronicles* 27/29). Two verses later we read, "Over the flocks was Jaziz the Hagerite." The Hagarites were the great sheep-raising tribe who were conquered by the Reubenites. Evidently the early kings had no patriotic scruples about hiring foreigners as their chief officers and superintendents, and while political reasons may have influenced their choice, it is also likely that competent and trustworthy cattlemen were becoming increasingly scarce among the Israelites.

The priestly order of Levites had special cities allotted to them

[237]

and literally lived in the center of a cattle ring. "And the Lord spake unto Moses . . . . saying, Command the children of Israel, that they give unto the Levites . . . . cities to dwell in; and . . . . suburbs for the cities round about them. And the cities shall they have to dwell in; and the suburbs of them shall be for their cattle, and for their goods, and for all their beasts. And the suburbs . . . . shall reach from the wall of the city and outward a thousand cubits round about" (*Numbers* 35/1-4). Besides the grazing requirements of their own domestic stock, the Levites required a lot of corral space to accommodate those animals tendered by the laity as sacrifices and offerings.

It is natural to wonder at the purpose served by these huge flocks of sheep and goats, and herds of cattle. Bible history tends to concentrate on national leaders and celebrities, both religious and secular; the patriarchs were tribal chieftains who lived to great age, and during their lifetime they retained authority over all their descendants. Polygamy and concubinage were customary, and only the prolific woman attained honored status in her husband's menage and amongst her associates. Slaves and serfs of both sexes were acquired, and their progeny multiplied also.

Shortly after Abram settled in Canaan, we read (*Genesis* 14/14): "And when Abram heard that his brother was taken captive, he armed his trained servants, born in his own house, three hundred and eighteen and pursued them unto Dan." Members of this mobile troop would be selected for their youth, agility and skill with arms, and would constitute only a fraction of the total domestic establishment, which probably contained as many more males below and over fighting age, as well as a large female staff. These were house servants and did not include many sheep and cattle tenders out on the ranges. A very conservative estimate would put one thousand people in Abram's retinue, and it should be taken into account that at this time Abram was childless with only one wife, and was a comparative newcomer to the district. Later tribal chiefs, with scores of contemporary direct descendants maintaining branch households and working cooperatively in the community, had to make provision for many thousand of blood kin and retainers, providing food and clothing and tents, the raw material being furnished by the flocks and herds. When a nomad tribe moved to new pasture grounds, camels and asses and oxen provided the transportation.

There were no country stores, and the strict code of hospitality required that all the makings be at hand to whip up a worthy repast for unexpected guests, or provide the greater luxuries for a ceremonial feast. The patriarch Job "had seven sons and three daughters.... and a very great household," so seven thousand sheep was not an excessive number for his establishment. The family was very socially minded and entertained lavishly: "His sons went and feasted in their houses, every one his day; and sent and called for their three sisters to eat and to drink with them" (*Job* 1/4). When fortune smiled once more on Job, "then came there unto him all his brethren, and all his sisters, and all they that had been of his acquaintance before, and did eat bread with him in his house" (*Job* 42/11). It is no wonder that his livestock holdings had to be doubled.

Long before Moses regularized with strict formality the offering of sacrifices to Jehovah, his ancestors had, with equal devotion if less ritual, laid the firstborn of their flocks on a crude altar. It was Jehovah's acceptance of Abel's meat sacrifice and His rejection of Cain's vegetable offering which led to Abel's murder.

The craving of the early Israelites for animal meat is implicit in a passage in *Deuteronomy* (12/20): "When the Lord thy God shall enlarge thy border, as he hath promised thee, and thou shalt say, I will eat flesh, because thy soul longeth to eat flesh; thou mayest eat flesh, whatsoever thy soul lusteth after." The ancient Hebrews were a flesh-eating race. Agricultural activity was transient and spasmodic. Large flocks and herds were required to ensure adequate progeny, sufficient to satisfy the appetites of hard-working pastoral people. Even the drain of sacrificial animals was considerable. Major celebrations and feast days traditionally demanded bounty of meat and drink to the whole nation.

Young goats were esteemed for their meat, and we read of many instances where a kid was prepared as a delicacy for guests. In *Genesis* (27/9) Rebekah tells Jacob, "Go now to the flock, and fetch me from thence two good kids of the goats; and I will make them savory meat for thy father, such as he loveth." The elder brother of the prodigal reproaches his father, "Thou never gavest me a kid, that I might make merry with my friends" (*Luke* 15/29). Three times the Mosaic law admonishes, "Thou shalt not seethe a kid in his mother's milk." The reason for this injunction remains speculative.

[239]

Sacrifices, both regular and extraordinary, took a heavy toll of livestock during the dynastic period. The 35th chapter of 2 *Chronicles* describes an outstanding passover celebration during the reign of king Josiah: "There was no passover like to that kept in Israel from the days of Samuel the prophet; neither did all the kings of Israel keep such a passover as Josiah kept." The king must have had huge flocks, for "Josiah gave to the people, of the flock, lambs and kids, all for the passover offerings . . . . to the number of thirty thousand, and three thousands bullocks: these were of the king's substance." Lesser dignitaries contributed a further seven thousand six hundred sheep and goats and eight hundred oxen.

As David triumphantly brought the ark of the covenant to Jerusalem, "When they that bare the ark of the Lord had gone six paces, he sacrificed oxen and fatlings" (2 *Samuel* 6/13). A few verses later, following the ceremonial installation of the ark in Jerusalem, we read, "He dealt among all the people, even among the whole multitude of Israel, as well to the women as men, to every one a cake of bread, and a good piece of flesh, and a flagon of wine." When David numbered his subjects, the census revealed over a million and a half able-bodied men, fit for war, and two tribes, Levi and Benjamin, were not included. This would appear to indicate a total population of at least five million. Making allowance for oriental exaggeration, we must still admit that the barbecue supplies to furnish even a million people with a "good piece of flesh" must have made heavy inroads into the king's livestock.

Solomon never did things by halves, and when he dedicated the Temple his celebration dwarfed his father's largesse. A long chapter, the 8th of 1 *Kings,* is devoted to the ceremony. "And king Solomon, and all the congregation of Israel, that were assembled unto him, were with him before the ark, sacrificing sheep and oxen, that could not be told nor numbered for multitude." His inaugural speech opens with a mixture of naiveté and brashness: "The Lord said that he would dwell in the thick darkness. I have surely built thee an house to dwell in, a settled place for thee to abide in for ever." When his address was finished, "Solomon offered a sacrifice of peace offerings, which he offered unto the Lord, two and twenty thousand oxen, and an hundred and twenty thousand sheep." The great occasion wound up with Solomon tendering a feast to all his subjects for "seven days and seven days, even fourteen days." There is no mention of commissariat detail, but the whole affair must have caused a noticeable diminution in the livestock of Israel.

In 1 *Kings* (4/23) we learn of the daily butchering for Solomon's household at the beginning of his reign, before he had had opportunity to develop the regal style to which he hoped to become accustomed: "Ten fat oxen, and twenty oxen out of the pastures, and an hundred sheep, beside harts, and roebucks, and fallowdeer, and fatted fowl." Details of the butchering, dressing and cooking of animals are remarkably meagre, considering the large amount of skilled labor that must have been employed in the culinary departments of large establishments. Egyptian art is prolific in illustrations of butchers killing cattle and fowl, dressing meat and cooking it. One drawing depicts a meat cutter sharpening his knife on a whetstone or steel, just as modern butchers do. Although they had large household staffs to call on, the patriarchs and their wives did not consider it beneath their dignity to dress and cook animals on special occasions.

Professional cooks get scant mention in the Bible, the only direct reference being in 1 *Samuel* (9/23-24). Here Samuel announces to the somewhat incredulous Saul that he is a man of destiny, and then the prophet entertains him at a small gathering, prior to anointing Saul first king of Israel. "And Samuel said unto the cook, Bring the portion which I gave thee, of which I said unto thee, Set it by thee. And the cook took up the shoulder, and that which was upon it, and set it before Saul. And Samuel said, Behold that which is left! (margin: reserved) set it before thee, and eat: for unto this time hath it been kept for thee since I said, I have invited the people." Apparently the shoulder was the cut reserved for the honored guest. In the preceding chapter, verse 13, Samuel warned the Israelites that the king they craved would take their daughters to be cooks. The Hebrew word which designates Samuel's "cook" is used elsewhere on many occasions as "guard." Possibly the cook was a trusted retainer who was responsible for seeing that no poisoned food reached his master. A good example of the use of this word may be found in *Genesis* (39/1): "And Joseph was brought down to Egypt; and Potiphar, an officer of Pharaoh, captain of the guard, an Egyptian, bought him of the hands of the Ishmeelites, which had brought him down thither." Potiphar was actually chief of the slaughter-men, who presumably doubled as executioners of convicted prisoners and as animal butchers.

[241]

Cattle and sheep and goats provided much more than meat, however. Milk and milk products were equally appreciated, and the reiterated description of Canaan as a land flowing with milk and honey served to spur the weary footsteps of the pilgrims towards journey's end. This attraction never palled, for more than seven hundred years later *Isaiah* (7/21-22) depicted a countryman's dream: "And it shall come to pass in that day, that a young man shall nourish a young cow, and two sheep; and it shall come to pass, for the abundance of milk that they shall give he shall eat butter: for butter and honey shall every one eat that is left in the land."

Not only cows and goats, but sheep and camels were milk producers. Besides Isaiah's reference to milch sheep, we have one by Moses in his song in the 32nd chapter of *Deuteronomy*: "Butter of kine, and milk of sheep." Butter and milk formed part of the repast offered his angelic guests by Abram (*Genesis* 18/8), and the same fare was treacherously served her victim by Jael, in one of the blackest episodes in Bible history. Sisera and his Canaanite army had been vanquished by the Israelites under Barak and Deborah, and Sisera fled to the tent of one of his supposed friends. Jael, the chief's wife, greeted him cordially: "Turn in, my lord, turn in to me; fear not. And when he had turned in unto her into the tent, she covered him with a mantle (margin: rug, or blanket). And he said unto her, Give me, I pray thee, a little water to drink; for I am thirsty. And she opened a bottle of milk, and gave him drink, and covered him" (*Judges* 4/18-19). When the weary man, feeling temporarily secure, sank into slumber, the murderess drove a tent spike through his temples, and went to greet his pursuers with the news. The victors lauded this infamous betrayal in a triumphant song, using an extraordinarily effective word arrangement. "Blessed above women shall Jael the wife of Heber the Kenite be, blessed shall she be above women in the tent. He asked water, and she gave him milk; she brought forth butter in a lordly dish. She put her hand to the nail, and her right hand to the workmen's hammer; and with the hammer she smote Sisera, she smote off his head, when she had pierced and stricken through his temples. At her feet he bowed, he fell, he lay down: at her feet he bowed, he fell: where he bowed, there he fell down dead" (*Judges* 5/24-27). Poor Sisera didn't have a chance— "The stars in their courses fought against Sisera" (5/20).

In the times of the Old Testament milk was a staple food, a he man's drink. Solomon starts the 5th chapter of his *Song* with a gourmand's gusto: "I am come into my garden, my sister, my spouse: I have gathered my myrrh with my spice; I have eaten my honeycomb with my honey; I have drunk my wine with my milk: eat, O friends; drink, yea, drink abundantly, O beloved." *Isaiah* (55/1) invites, "Come, buy wine and milk without money and without price." In foretelling the destruction of the nomadic Ammonites, *Ezekiel* (25/4) prophesies, "I will deliver thee to the men of the east for a possession, and they shall set their palaces in thee, and make their dwellings in thee: they shall eat thy fruit, and they shall drink thy milk." With the passage of time, bringing reduction in pasture grounds and dairy animals, and raising the cost of living, milk ceased to be a general drink and came to be regarded as a food for infants. Paul, addressing the *Hebrews* (5/12-13), reproves their incomprehension: " (Ye) are become such as have need of milk, and not of strong meat. For every one that useth milk is unskillful in the word of righteousness: for he is a babe." In 1 *Corinthians* (3/1-2) the apostle speaks in similar fashion: ". . . . even as unto babes in Christ. I have fed you with milk, and not with meat."

"Surely the churning of milk bringeth forth butter," observes farmer Solomon (*Proverbs* 30/33). While butter, as we know it, was obtained by pouring milk or cream in a skin bottle and agitating and kneading the contents, the biblical word butter more commonly designates curdled or coagulated milk. The keeping quality of butter in a hot climate was too brief for any but immediate use. It is believed that the Hebrew word for butter sometimes represented cream, a term which is not found in the English translation. *Job* (29/2, 6) lamenting the good old days, sighs, "Oh that I were as in months past, as in the days when God preserved me . . . . when I washed my steps with butter." His friend Zophar (20/17) speaks of "the rivers, the floods, the brooks of honey and butter." These references seem to indicate a liquid rather than a solid dairy product. In *Isaiah* (7/14-15) we find veiled symbolism in a remarkable prophecy: "Behold, a virgin shall conceive, and bear a son, and shall call his name Immanuel. Butter and honey shall he eat, that he may know to refuse the evil, and choose the good." A modern expression, and the inspiration for a passage in the Book of Common Prayer, derive from *Psalms* (55/21): "The words of his mouth were smoother than butter, but war was in his heart."

[243]

Cheese is mentioned but three times, and on each occasion a different Hebrew word is used. The most picturesque reference is in *Job* (10/10): "Hast thou not poured me out as milk, and curdled me like cheese?" When David was fighting Absalom and his troops were in temporary retreat, his weary men were hospitably received, and rested and fed by allies, who presented, among other things, "honey, and butter, and sheep, and cheese of kine." David was in the rich Transjordan cattle country. While munching this cheese, David must have thought back to his boyhood, when his father Jesse took him from tending the family flock, and sent him with a gift of ten cheeses to the captains of Saul's undermanned army, then engaged with the Philistines. It was on this opportune occasion that David unexpectedly distinguished himself by killing the giant Goliath (1 *Samuel* 17/18).

The derivation of this last-quoted "cheese" suggests "cuttings" or "slices" of cheese, or ten sections of curds. Cheese-making was primitive, and usually took the method of drying and curing curdled milk. The cheese of kine served to David and his soldiers may have been grated, for the etymology of the word means "to scrape." Job's variety probably was curds or cottage cheese.

CHAPTER 20

Draught, Pack, and Riding Animals

"WHEN THOU art come into the land which the Lord thy God giveth thee . . . . and shalt say, I will set a king over me, like as all the nations that are about me . . . . he shall not multiply horses to himself, nor cause the people to return to Egypt, to the end that he should multiply horses. . . . . Neither shall he multiply wives to himself . . . . neither shall he greatly multiply to himself silver and gold" (*Deuteronomy* 17/14-17). Jehovah knew the habits of kings, and He knew that power corrupts; the monarchs of Israel proved no exception. When David defeated the Syrian army, he captured "a thousand chariots, and seven hundred horsemen . . . . and David houghed all the chariot horses, but reserved of them for an hundred chariots" (2 *Samuel* 8/4). The injunction stated that kings were not to multiply horses, so David evidently assumed that one hundred was a safe low number. In any case he was not enthusiastic about this new fangled war weapon, for in *Psalms* (20/7) he says, "Some trust in chariots, and some in horses: but we will remember the name of the Lord our God."

His son and heir had no such scruples: "Solomon had forty thousand stalls of horses for his chariots . . . . barley also and straw for the horses (1 *Kings* 4/26, 28). On top of this, Solomon went into the war armament business in a big way: "Solomon had horses brought out of Egypt . . . . and they fetched up, and brought forth out of Egypt, a chariot for six hundred shekels of silver, and an horse for an hundred and fifty: and so brought they out horses for all the kings of the Hittites, and for the kings of Syria, by their means" (2 *Chronicles* 1/16-17).

Solomon was class-conscious, and he regarded horses as a prerogative of the nobility, and frowned on their use by plebeians: "There is an evil which I have seen under the sun, as an error which proceedeth from the ruler (Hebrew: "from before"; evidently a crack at David's more democratic regime). Folly is set in great dignity, and the rich sit in low place. I have seen servants upon horses, and princes walking as servants upon the earth" (*Ecclesiastes* 10/5-7). Three hundred years later Egyptian horses were still fashionable, and *Isaiah* (31/1,3) complains: "Woe to them that go down to Egypt for help; and stay on horses, and trust in chariots; and in horsemen, because they are very strong . . . . Now the Egyptians are men, and not God; and their horses flesh, and not spirit."

It is believed that the Hyksos or Shepherd Kings introduced the horse and the chariot into Egypt. Probably because of its late entry and unpopular sponsors, it never attained the sacred status which most Egyptian animals held in Nile mythology. From *Genesis* (47/15-17) we may assume that the horse was then in common use and employed on farms, a condition which never prevailed in Palestine: "All the Egyptians came unto Joseph, and said, Give us bread . . . . and Joseph said, Give your cattle . . . . and Joseph gave them bread in exchange for horses, and for the flocks, etc." When Joseph journeyed to Canaan to bury his father Jacob, "there went up with him both chariots and horsemen: and it was a very great company" (*Genesis* 50/9).

The first contingent of Jews who returned to Jerusalem from the Babylonian captivity brought back Mesopotamian horses along with other livestock. The totals are exactly detailed in *Ezra* (2/66) and *Nehemiah* (7/68), the equine herd being seven hundred and thirty-six. Persia was another horse-minded country and the nobility used horses for riding and hunting as well as for war. *Esther* (8/10) tells that royal decrees were sent by posts on horseback to the king's deputies in the provinces. Joram, king of Israel, also used couriers on horseback to carry despatches (2 *Kings* 9/18-19). *Habakkuk,* in his first chapter, pays an unwilling tribute to the Chaldeans, "that bitter and hasty nation . . . . they are terrible and dreadful . . . . their horses also are swifter than the leopards, and are more fierce than the evening wolves."

It is in *Isaiah* (28/28) that we find the solitary reference to the use of the horse in agriculture: "Bread corn is bruised; because he will not ever be threshing it, nor break it with the wheel of his cart, nor bruise it with his horsemen." An obscure allusion to horses in *Amos* (6/12) may have farming significance: "Shall horses run upon the rock? will one plow there with oxen?"

In the majestic passage where the Lord answers Job out of the whirlwind, we find a spirited description of a war horse: "Hast thou given the horse strength? hast thou clothed his neck with thunder? canst thou make him afraid as a grasshopper? the glory of his nostrils

[246]

is terrible. He paweth in the valley, and rejoiceth in his strength: he goeth on to meet the armed men. He mocketh at fear, and is not affrighted; neither turneth he back from the sword. The quiver rattleth against him, the glittering spear and the shield. He swalloweth the ground with fierceness and rage; neither believeth he that it is the sound of the trumpet. He saith among the trumpets; Ha, ha; and he smelleth the battle afar off, the thunder of the captains, and the shouting" (*Job* 39/19-25).

Spiritual and mythological horses are encountered in many places in the Bible, and while the prophets and seers who experienced and related these visions bear some of the most respected names in scripture, it is possible that the inspiration cannot be entirely disassociated from pagan rites. For example, " (Josiah) took away the horses that the kings of Judah had given to the sun, at the entering in of the house of the Lord . . . . and burned the chariots of the sun with fire" (2 *Kings* 23/ 11). While Elisha was holding his last conversation with Elijah, "It came to pass, as they still went on, and talked, that, behold, there appeared a chariot of fire, and horses of fire, and parted them both asunder; and Elijah went up by a whirlwind into heaven" (2 *Kings* 2/11). In the opening verses of the 6th chapters of *Zechariah* and *Revelation* respectively, there are accounts of symbolic horses, four in number. Black, and white, and red horses are common to each passage, but Zechariah's last horses are gristled and bay, while John's pale horse is the steed of death.

The best known mule of the Bible is probably the one ridden by Absalom, fleeing from David's victorious army (2 *Samuel* 18/9). "And Absalom rode upon a mule, and the mule went under the thick boughs of a great oak, and his head caught hold of the oak, and he was taken up between the heaven and the earth; and the mule that was under him went away." Mules appear early in the Authorized Version of the Bible: "This was that Anah that found the mules in the wilderness, as he fed the asses of Zibeon his father" (*Genesis* 36/24). This word "mules" is generally conceded to be a mistaken translation, and the Revised Version uses the preferred definition, "hot springs." The finder, Anah, is elsewhere referred to as Beeri, which literally means "well man," thus seeming to confirm the later translation.

"Thou shalt not let thy cattle gender with a diverse kind," commanded Jehovah in *Leviticus* (19/19), and this ruled out the breeding of mules, normally the offspring of an ass and a mare, and sterile themselves. There was a tendency amongst later Hebrews to comply strictly with the letter of the law, but to evade the spirit, and apparently it was considered legitimate to purchase imported mules, or get them in trade. Except for the doubtful reference in *Genesis,* there is no scriptural mention of mules until David's time. Mules appear in connection with Absalom's shearing feast (2 *Samuel* 13/29), where, after witnessing the assassination of Amnon, their brother, "all the king's sons arose, and every men gat him up upon his mule, and fled." Not only the king's sons, but the king too had a special mule, and when in the monarch's old age one of his sons, Adonijah, had himself proclaimed king, David had his favorite son Solomon set on the king's mule and ceremoniously anointed as the lawful successor. The evidence of David's well known mule bearing Solomon apparently convinced the somewhat bewildered populace, and they applauded the official heir. The tale is told in the first chapter of 1 *Kings.*

The mule of three thousand years ago was just as versatile and democratic as the modern one, whether she carried a king or a burden of earth as Naaman's did (2 *Kings* 5/17). Appearing later in Bible pages, but earlier genealogically than the mules of the king's sons, are the mules laden with provisions which brought bounty to David as he was bringing up the ark (1 *Chronicles* 12/40). From *Psalms* (32/9) we learn that David's mules were as stubborn and ornery as their descendants today: "Be ye not as the horse, or as the mule, which have no understanding: whose mouth must be held in with bit and bridle, lest they come near unto thee." 2 *Chronicles* (9/23-24) tells us that "all the kings of the earth" included mules amongst their gifts to Solomon, but we learn nothing of the use to which the monarch put them. David's and Solomon's era and the century following seems to have been the heyday of mules, for they get little notice thereafter and in the New Testament none at all. In the 5th century B. C., five hundred years after David, mules reappear in widely separated passages. *Ezra* (2/66) relates that the Babylonian exiles brought two hundred odd mules to Jerusalem, probably packing their belongings in the panniers of the mules. Esther, playing palace politics in Persia twenty-five years later, tells that "the posts that rode upon mules and camels went out, being hastened and pressed on by the king's commandment" (*Esther* 8/14). These Persian mules have a different Hebrew name from other biblical ones, a name which is elsewhere rendered dromedary and swift beast. A slightly earlier contemporary, Ezekiel, tells (27/14) of the mule trade from Togarmah (probably Armenia) to Tyre.

While the Bible is rich in animal life, individual beasts rarely get the spotlight of attention. No Bible animal has a personal name, yet we cannot doubt but that the ancient peoples named pet animals just as we do. Jesus confirms this: "He calleth his own sheep by name" (*John* 10/3). Yet here and there an animal steals the show from man. The serpent who cajoled Eve was a *bona fide* precedent for Balaam's talking ass. "And Balaam rose up in the morning, and saddled his ass, and went with the princes of Moab. And God's anger was kindled because he went: and the angel of the Lord stood in the way for an adversary against him. Now he was riding upon his ass, and his two servants were with him. And the ass saw the angel of the Lord standing in the way, and his sword drawn in his hand: and the ass turned aside out of the way, and went into the field: and Balaam smote the ass, to turn her into the way. But the angel of the Lord stood in a path of the vineyards, a wall being on this side, and a wall on that side. And when the ass saw the angel of the Lord, she thrust herself unto the wall, and crushed Balaam's foot against the wall: and he smote her again. And the angel of the Lord went further, and stood in a narrow place, where there was no way to turn either to the right hand or to the left. And when the ass saw the angel of the Lord, she fell down under Balaam: and Balaam's anger was kindled, and he smote the ass with a staff. And the Lord opened the mouth of the ass, and she said unto Balaam, What have I done unto thee, that thou hast smitten me these three times? And Balaam said unto the ass, Because thou hast mocked me: I would there were a sword in mine hand, for now would I kill thee. And the ass said unto Balaam, Am not I thine ass, upon which thou hast ridden ever since I was thine unto this day? was I ever wont to do so unto thee? And he said, Nay. Then the Lord opened the eyes of Balaam, and he saw the angel of the Lord standing in the way, and his sword drawn in his hand: and he bowed down his head, and fell flat on his face" (*Numbers* 22/21-31). We hear no more of this famous ass, but presumably Balaam respected her judgment thereafter.

For farm work, as a pack animal, and for sure-footed if slow transport, the ass outranked all other animals in the Holy Land. An ass and an ox were the minimum requirements for a self-supporting country

[249]

menage, and very often they remained the maximum. Nowadays the uninformed regard the ass as rather dull and stupid, but the ass of Bible times was rightly considered intelligent and dependable. *Proverbs* (26/3) speaks of "a whip for the horse, a bridle for the ass," implying that the latter was more tractable than his larger cousin.

Many a Bible tale commences, "He rose up and saddled his ass." Abraham is the first mentioned, and we read of his trip in the 22nd chapter of *Genesis,* which tells that the patriarch took his son Isaac along to offer him as a human sacrifice. Women, too, saddled their asses, and set out on missions that made history. One such was the Shunamite, "a great woman," according to 2 *Kings* (4/8), whose faith in Elisha's power restored her son to life. Another was Abigail, who later became David's wife: "And when Abigail saw David, she hasted, and lighted off the ass" (1 *Samuel* 25/23).

Finally, there was the ass of destiny, of whom *Zechariah* (9/9) had prophesied half a thousand years before the event: "Rejoice greatly, O daughter of Zion: shout, O daughter of Jerusalem: behold, thy King cometh unto thee: he is just, and having salvation: lowly, and riding upon an ass, and upon a colt the foal of an ass." The fulfillment is in the opening verses of the 21st chapter of *Matthew*: "And when they drew nigh unto Jerusalem .... then sent Jesus two disciples, saying unto them, Go into the village over against you, and straightway ye shall find an ass tied, and a colt with her; loose them, and bring them unto me. And if any man say ought unto you, ye shall say, The Lord hath need of them; and straightway he will send them. All this was done, that it might be fulfilled which was spoken by the prophet, saying, Tell ye the daughter of Sion, Behold, thy King cometh unto thee, meek, and sitting upon an ass, and a colt the foal of an ass. And the disciples went, and did as Jesus commanded them, and brought the ass, and the colt, and put on them their clothes, and they set him thereon. And a very great multitude spread their garments in the way; others cut down branches from the trees, and strawed them in the way."

The inference here is that the ass was an unpretentious poor man's steed, and in the Jerusalem of the Master's time, used to triumphant Roman cavalry, such a mount would be considered as that of a humble and unassuming man. It was not always so, for the men who rode asses in the time of the Judges were distinguished as rulers and law-givers. "Speak, ye that ride on white asses, ye that sit in judgment," says

Judges (5/10). In the 10th chapter of the same Book we read of Jair, a Gileadite, who "judged Israel twenty and two years. And he had thirty sons that rode on thirty ass colts, and they had thirty cities." White asses were evidently unusual, and reserved for the ruling classes; one of the Hebrew names designating ass comes from a root meaning "of ruddy color."

The ass makes an early appearance in Bible history, being listed among Abram's possessions when he resided in Egypt. In this passage in *Genesis* (12/16) he asses and she asses are tabulated separately, whereas the sheep and camels mentioned have no sex differentiation. The Hebrew words offer little help as they are loosely used in the English translation, but from comparative passages an inference may be drawn that the difference meant more than just male and female of the same breed.

It is usually considered that "Love thy neighbor and hate thine enemy" was an Old Testament dictum, and that it was not until the time of Jesus that love of enemies was enjoined. However, an example of the Golden Rule towards one's enemy may be found in *Exodus* (23/4-5): "If thou meet thine enemy's ox or his ass going astray, thou shalt surely bring it back to him again. If thou see the ass of him that hateth thee lying under his burden, and thou wouldest forbear to help him, thou shalt surely help with him." A similar injunction regarding the simpler moral problem of a brother's ass is in *Deuteronomy* (22/3-4). Evidently it was common for asses to stray, and it was while he was searching for a lost flock of his father's asses that Saul first met Samuel. Saul's extensive search is recounted in the 9th and 10th chapters of 1 *Samuel*. *Deuteronomy* (22/10) enjoins, "Thou shalt not plow with an ox and an ass together." Some commentators claim that this was because of the unequal size and strength of the two animals, but the context suggests that racial and religious exclusiveness outweighed humanitarian concern.

Stealing of asses was not uncommon, and the tenth commandment warns, "Thou shalt not covet thy neighbor's . . . . ass" (*Exodus* 20/17). In *Numbers* (16/15) Moses indignantly protests, "I have not taken one ass from them," and Samuel does likewise, "Behold, here I am . . . . whose ass have I taken?" (1 *Samuel* 12/3). *Job* (24/3) stigmatizes the usurers of the time: "They drive away the ass of the fatherless, they take the widow's ox for a pledge."

Isaiah, in two passages, tells us of the role of the ass in farming:

"The young asses that ear the ground shall eat clean provender" (30/24); and "Blessed are ye that sow beside all waters, that send forth hither the feet of the ox and the ass" (32/20). In a mystical passage (21/7) Isaiah speaks of "a chariot of asses."

In spite of the great service rendered to the people of Israel by the patient and willing ass, its end was proverbially ignominious: "They shall not lament for him . . . . he shall be buried with the burial of an ass, drawn and cast forth beyond the gates of Jerusalem" (*Jeremiah* 22/19).

Cattle, sheep and goats, mules and asses, all are familiar names, even if seldom seen by urban dwellers. Camels remain as exotic as elephants, yet their role in the Bible exceeds that of horses. Their frequent appearance in the pages of Holy Writ serves to remind us of the arid sandy nature of much of the lands of the Scriptures, for the camel is essentially the steed of the desert. Awkward in appearance, treacherous and unsentimental in nature, the camel is peculiarly adapted to packing heavy loads across arid sandy wastes. Five hundred pounds is a normal load for a long caravan trek, while a good camel can carry half a ton for a short distance. With the callous disregard of many eastern drivers for their animals it was not uncommon to overload the sturdy beast, and so we get our proverb, "It's the last straw that breaks the camel's back." Camels can go for three or four weeks, if need be, without water, but a careful driver tries to water them every third day, particularly if they have no access to green pasture. The broad tough elastic foot of the camel keeps it from sinking in the sand, and makes it surefooted on rocky hillsides. The Bible camel was the single hump variety.

One of the oldest "boy meets girl" stories in the world is in the 24th chapter of *Genesis,* and the part played by camels in this romance gives us an insight into their habits. "And Abraham was old, and well stricken in age . . . And Abraham said unto his eldest servant of his house, that ruled over all that he had . . . . swear by the Lord . . . . that thou shalt not take a wife unto my son of the daughters of the Canaanites, among whom I dwell: But thou shalt go unto my country, and to my kindred, and take a wife unto my son Isaac. And the servant said unto him, Peradventure the woman will not be willing to follow me unto this land; must I needs bring thy son again unto the land from whence thou camest? And Abraham said unto him, Beware thou that thou bring not my son thither again . . . . and if the woman will not be willing to follow thee, then thou shalt be clear from this my oath . . . . And the servant took ten camels of the camels of his master, and departed; for all the goods of his master were in his hand: and he arose, and went to Mesopotamia, unto the city of Nahor. And he made his camels to kneel down without the city by a well of water at the time of the evening, even the time that women go out to draw water. And he said, O Lord God . . . . behold, I stand here by the well of water; and the daughters of the men of the city come out to draw water: and let it come to pass, that the damsel to whom I shall say, Let down thy pitcher, I pray thee, that I may drink; and she shall say, Drink, and I will give thy camels drink also: let the same be she that thou hast appointed for thy servant Isaac . . . . and it came to pass, before he had done speaking, that, behold, Rebekah came out . . . . with her pitcher upon her shoulder.

"And the damsel was very fair to look upon, a virgin, neither had any man known her: and she went down to the well, and filled her pitcher, and came up. And the servant ran to meet her, and said, Let me, I pray thee, drink a little water of thy pitcher. And she said, Drink, my lord: and she hasted, and let down her pitcher upon her hand, and gave him drink. And when she had done giving him drink, she said, I will draw water for thy camels also, until they have done drinking. And she hasted, and emptied her pitcher into the trough, and ran again unto the well to draw water, and drew for all his camels. And the man wondering at her held his peace, to wit whether the Lord had made his journey prosperous or not. And it came to pass, as the camels had done drinking, that the man took a golden earring of half a shekel weight, and two bracelets for her hands of ten shekels weight of gold; and said . . . . is there room in they father's house for us to lodge in? . . . . and she said, We have both straw and provender enough, and room to lodge in . . . . and the damsel ran, and told them of her mother's house these things. And Rebekah had a brother . . . . Laban: and . . . . when he saw the earrings and bracelets upon his sister's hands, and when he heard the words of Rebekah . . . . that he came unto the man; and, behold, he stood by the camels at the well. And he said, Come in, thou blessed of the Lord: wherefore standest thou without? for I have prepared the house, and room for the camels. And the man came into the house: and he ungirded his camels, and gave straw and provender

[253]

for the camels, and water to wash his feet, and the men's feet that were with him. And there was set meat before him to eat."

Abraham's servant stated his mission, and related the sequence of events, then asked for a decision. "Then Laban and Bethuel answered and said, The thing proceedeth from the Lord: we cannot speak unto thee bad or good. Behold, Rebekah is before thee, take her, and go, and let her be thy master's son's wife, as the Lord hath spoken." The servant handed out valuable gifts all around, and the family decided, with or without ulterior motive, that they couldn't bear to part with Rebekah for at least ten days, but the envoy insisted on an immediate departure. So, "they called Rebekah, and said unto her, Wilt thou go with this man? And she said, I will go . . . . And Rebekah arose, and her damsels, and they rode upon the camels, and followed the man . . . . And Isaac went out to meditate in the field at the eventide: and he lifted up his eyes, and saw, and behold, the camels were coming. And Rebekah lifted up her eyes, and when she saw Isaac, she lighted off the camel. For she had said unto the servant, What man is this that walketh in the field to meet us? and the servant had said, It is my master: therefore she took a vail, and covered herself . . . . And Isaac brought her into his mother Sarah's tent, and took Rebekah, and she became his wife; and he loved her."

The camel was classified as unclean in the Mosaic law (*Leviticus* 11/4), and its flesh was prohibited as food. Evidently the prohibition did not extend to its milk, for when Jacob and his caravan entered the land of Canaan, he sent a gift of thirty milch camels to his estranged brother Esau, camels which had been raised in Rebekah's old homesite (*Genesis* 32/13-15).

Midian was famous camel-breeding territory, and when these nomads temporarily conquered the Israelites, "They came up with their cattle and their tents, and they came as grasshoppers for multitude; for both they and their camels were without number" (*Judges* 6/5). Eventually, Gideon overthrew the Midianites and personally slew their kings, Zebah and Zalmunna, "and took away the ornaments that were on their camels' necks" (8/21). A marginal note amplifies "ornaments" into "ornaments like the moon," while the Revised Version uses the word "crescents." Modern camel drivers still hang the traditional crescent round the necks of their beasts. The ones Gideon took were probably gold, for he asked his followers to give him the golden earrings of the vanquished enemy, and they complied, adding "the chains that were about their camels' necks" (8/26). The Hagarites, when defeated by the tribe of Reuben, lost fifty thousand camels to the victors. Job's herd of three thousand were captured by the Chaldeans (*Job* 1/17).

Like the mules, camels seem to have had their biblical zenith in the times of the patriarchs and the early kings. In the latter part of the Old Testament it is usually the camels of foreign nations which are referred to. *Ezekiel* in his chapter on the varied commerce of Tyre makes no mention of camels. The camel was essentially a pack animal, but breeding produced a lighter, swifter more delicate camel known as the dromedary. "Thou art a swift dromedary traversing her ways," says *Jeremiah* (2/23), while Isaiah (60/6) tells of "the dromedaries of Midian and Ephah." The dromedaries mentioned as belonging to Solomon in 1 *Kings* (4/28), and in *Esther* (8/10) as bearing royal messengers, are given the vaguer title of "swift steeds" in the Revised Version. It is likely that the four hundred Amalekites who escaped by camel from the slaughter of the rest of their band at the hands of David's guerillas were mounted on dromedaries (1 *Samuel* 30/17).

Camels make no personal appearance in the New Testament, yet Jesus' statement, "It is easier for a camel to go through the eye of a needle, than for a rich man to enter into the kingdom of God" (*Matthew* 19/24) is better known to Christians, even if disregarded, than all the herds and camel trains which roamed the deserts and caravan trails of the Old Testament. The other of the Master's camel references (*Matthew* 23/24) is correctly translated in the Revised Version: "Ye blind guides, which strain out the gnat and swallow the camel." The older version uses "strain at."

Nowadays a camelhair coat is a luxurious garment, a far cry from the harsh fabric of the old ascetics. John the Baptist "had his raiment of camel's hair" (*Matthew* 3/4). Its coarseness is implied in Jesus' allusion to the Baptist in *Matthew* (11/8): "But what went ye out for to see? a man clothed in soft raiment? Behold, they that wear soft clothing are in kings' houses." Hair clothing was the traditional garb of *bona fide* prophets and holy recluses. Speaking of false prophets, *Zechariah* (13/4) predicts, "Neither shall they wear a rough garment to deceive." A marginal note substitutes "garment of hair."

Oxen, insofar as they constitute bovine members of cattle herds, have been dealt with in the previous chapter. They will be found elsewhere in the book too, for whenever a plough furrowed the soil or a cart rumbled toward the threshing floor or the barn, a sturdy ox was usually in the shafts. A yoke of oxen was the heavy-duty draught team of the Bible. In the concluding paragraphs of this chapter will be summarized an account of some of the services and relations of the plodding ox to the men and women of old.

The Bible has more than one hundred and fifty references to oxen. No scriptural animal was held in such high regard, nor was as important to the agricultural processes of Palestine, as the ox. The Mosaic legislation provided for his well being: "Six days shalt thou do thy work, and on the seventh day thou shalt rest; that thine ox and thine ass may rest" (*Exodus* 23/12). The laborer was worthy of his hire, even if the laborer was but an animal, and the ox who helped thresh the wheat on the hot dusty corn floor was allowed to munch away, unhampered by a muzzle, as he dragged the threshing implement (*Deuteronomy* 25/4).

The Golden Calf was proscribed, but brass oxen supported the sacred altar of Solomon's great temple: "It stood upon twelve oxen, three looking toward the north, and three looking toward the west, and three looking toward the south, and three looking toward the east . . . . and all their hinder parts were inward" (2 *Chronicles* 4/4). When David brought the ark to Jerusalem in triumphant procession, oxen, doubtless well groomed and trapped for the occasion, hauled the new cart on which the ark rested (2 *Samuel* 6/6). As the God-fearing New England settlers left frontier stockades and headed westward into unknown and dangerous territory, they gained quiet confidence as they thumbed their Bibles and read of the earlier pioneers who "brought their offering before the Lord, six covered wagons, and twelve oxen" (*Numbers* 7/3).

After a brief preliminary flourish, *Isaiah* opens his long book with the homespun observation, "The ox knoweth his owner . . . but Israel doth not know." Oxen were prized and usually well cared for, for there was a friendly bond between man and beast. In *Proverbs* (14/4) Solomon chides the teamless farmer: "Where no oxen is, the crib is clean; but much increase is by the strength of the ox." Solomon's oxen were stall fed as well as pastured, as the account of his meat supply in 1 *Kings* (4/23) reveals: "Ten fat oxen, and twenty oxen out of the pastures." The choice steers were probably for the royal family, the rangier beasts for the staff. Yet the cares of state, and the bickerings of a thousand jealous glamor girls, sometimes spoiled the king's appetite for the choicest of steaks, and he yearned for the simple life; "Better is a dinner of herbs where love is, than a stalled ox and hatred therewith" (*Proverbs* 15/17). Jesus reminded his sanctimonious critics that every farmer put the welfare of his ox above strict sabbath observance (*Luke* 13/15; 14/5).

The number of oxen slaughtered for sacrifices, and on ceremonial occasions ordained by law or custom, must have added up to a stupendous total of animal life. Here and there in the Bible we find spiritually developed men trying to stem the bloody rite. David did his share of animal sacrifice, but in *Psalms* (69/30-31) he displays a more progressive attitude: "I will praise the name of God with a song, and will magnify him with thanksgiving. This also shall please the Lord better than an ox or bullock that hath horns and hoofs." *Isaiah*, in his first chapter, lashes out more severely at animal butchery in the name of religion. Jesus started His public career by driving the purse-swollen sellers of oxen, and their livestock, out of the temple precincts (*John* 2/14-15). However, the Jews were no different from their neighbors, for *Acts* (14/13) tells of the unexpected and unwanted tribute which Paul's mental healing ability called forth in Lystra, a city located about one hundred miles south of the modern Turkish capital of Ankara: "Then the priest of Jupiter, which was before their city, brought oxen and garlands unto the gates, and would have done sacrifice with the people."

Here and there, in the shadow of the jet plane and the supertractor, oxen still hold favored place as farm draught animals. The Province of Nova Scotia is one such stronghold.

CHAPTER 21

Poultry, and Pigs, and Bees

THOUGH THE Bible has lots of fowls, very few of them are of the domestic or farmyard variety. In ancient Egypt ducks and geese formed the subject of many drawings still extant, and the details of plucking, dressing and broiling are unmistakable. Ducks and geese are missing from the Bible, although archaeological research has uncovered mosaic tiling depicting these birds along with others, the relic antedating the Christian era by a couple of centuries. The word "fowl" is used to translate five Hebrew terms and two Greek ones; one of the former, which occurs only in the passage in 1 *Kings* (4/23) designates edible birds—"fatted fowl"—for Solomon's table. Gesenius considers that these were geese. *Nehemiah,* a meticulous historian, tells (5/17-18) of his state guests and their culinary requirements: "Moreover, there were at my table an hundred and fifty of the Jews and rulers, beside those that came unto us from among the heathen that are about us. Now that which was prepared for me daily was one ox and six choice sheep; also fowls were prepared for me." *Ezekiel* (44/31) commands, "The priests shall not eat of any thing that is dead of itself, or torn, whether it be fowl or beast."

In the New Testament we find the hen, her chickens, and the cock. Only a man who loved not alone his country, but the country life of his country, would display hopeless concern for a doomed city in the language Jesus used: "O Jerusalem, Jerusalem, thou that killest the prophets and stonest them that are sent unto thee, how often would I have gathered thy children together, even as a hen gathereth her chickens under her wings, and ye would not!" (*Matthew* 23/37). In a parallel passage in *Luke* (13/34) "brood" is used instead of "chickens." All four Gospels tell of the cock whose strident call plunged Peter into bitter remorse. Doves and pigeons are common in the Bible, being favored by the poorer classes who could not afford a more expensive flesh offering. Though flocks of wild pigeons were caught by fowlers, there is a passage in *Isaiah* (60/8) from which we infer that domesticated pigeons

[258]

were raised in dovecotes: "Who are these that fly as a cloud, and as the doves to their windows?"

There are several egg references, but all except two are to the hatching or inedible variety. Jesus, explaining the beneficence of God to those who call on Him, points out that mortal man does not refuse or mock the sincere requests of his children: "If he shall ask an egg, will he offer him a scorpion?" (*Luke* 11/12). From the previous context, a visual similarity between the genuine and the spurious seems indicated, so perhaps a coiled up scorpion may have resembled an egg. *Job* (6/6) asks, in a question which answers itself, "Is there any taste in the white of an egg?"

The Egyptians regarded the pig as unclean, and Moses maintained the same taboo in his instructions to the Israelites. "The swine, because it divideth the hoof, yet cheweth not the cud, it is unclean unto you: ye shall not eat of their flesh, nor touch their dead carcase" (*Deuteronomy* 14/8). No reason other than its being a non-ruminant is advanced against the use of the pig for food.

In later times the injunction was disobeyed, indeed insult was added to infringement by the offering of swine's flesh as sacrifices to idols, with the sacrifice ultimately eaten. In two places, (65/3-4: 66/17), *Isaiah* refers to this forbidden and idolatrous practice. "A people that provoketh me to anger continually to my face . . . . which eat swine's flesh, and broth of abominable things is in their vessels . . . . that sanctify themselves, and purify themselves in the gardens behind one tree in the midst, eating swine's flesh, and the abomination, and the mouse, shall be consumed together, saith the Lord."

The taboo on the pig was an Egyptian idea, copied by the Jews and later by the Mohammedans. The Babylonians and the Syrians had no such scruples, and when Jesus crossed the Sea of Galilee to Gadara in Syria he was in Gentile country where pork was esteemed and sold to the occupying Roman army as well as to the natives. Jesus, indoctrinated in the Mosaic law, probably felt as little compunction in outraging local opinion as Carrie Nation did in smashing whiskey bottles in a saloon. The tale of the Gadarene swine is repeated in *Matthew, Mark* and *Luke*.

Mark's version in his fifth chapter follows in condensed form. "And they came over unto the other side of the sea, into the country of the Gadarenes. And when he was come out of the ship, immediately there met him out of the tombs a man with an unclean spirit . . . . and no man could bind him, no, not with chains . . . . neither could any man tame him . . . . When he saw Jesus afar off, he . . . . cried with a loud voice . . . . I adjure thee by God, that thou torment me not. For he said unto him, Come out of the man, thou unclean spirit. And he asked him, What is thy name? And he answered, saying, My name is Legion, for we are many. And he besought him much that he would not send them away out of the country. Now there was nigh unto the mountains a great herd of swine feeding. And all the devils besought him, saying, Send us into the swine, that we may enter into them. And forthwith Jesus gave them leave. And the unclean spirits went out, and entered into the swine: and the herd ran violently down a steep place into the sea, (they were about two thousand) and were choked in the sea. And they that fed the swine fled, and told it in the city, and in the country. And they went out to see what it was that was done . . . . and they began to pray him to depart out of their coasts."

Swine also figure in the parable of the Prodigal Son (*Luke* 15/11-32). When the prodigal's money had been spent, and his fair-weather friends had deserted him, "He went and joined himself to a citizen of that country; and he sent him into his fields to feed swine. And he would fain have filled his belly with the husks (carob pods) that the swine did eat: and no man gave unto him." The Master must have observed the hoggish habits of swine, and He used them for the lesson of the famous proverb which remains as true as when it was uttered: "Give not that which is holy unto the dogs, neither cast ye your pearls before swine, lest they trample them under their feet, and turn again and rend you" (*Matthew* 7/6). Less well known is a somewhat similar observation of Solomon's: "As a jewel of gold in a swine's snout, so is a fair woman which is without discretion" (*Proverbs* 11/22).

Canaan was glowingly depicted as a land flowing with milk and honey. The Israelites got their milk the same way we do, by breeding, feeding, and milking dairy cattle, but the honey required no capital investment and little labor. Wild bees abounded, and so much honey was available that it became an important item of commerce, being exported from Judea to Tyre (*Ezekiel* 27/17). Twelve hundred years earlier, Jacob had sent a gift of Canaan honey to Egypt (*Genesis* 43/11).

There is no scriptural record of bees being domesticated or hived,

[260]

but archaeologists have discovered a number of large inverted jars, having a series of small openings, and they have been conjecturally tabulated as primitive bee hives. On the other hand, we read of honey being discovered in various natural receptacles, one such being the pin on which an interesting tale is hung. Saul, having defeated the Philistines, ordered all his followers to abstain from food until evening, in order that every moment might be devoted to pursuing and massacring the fleeing enemy. Jonathan, Saul's son, was absent when the command was promulgated, and when informed of it later he considered that it showed poor judgment, and he ignored it.

"And all they of the land came to a wood; and there was honey upon the ground. And when the people were come into the wood, behold, the honey dropped; but no man put his hand to his mouth: for the people feared the oath. But Jonathan heard not when his father charged the people with the oath: wherefore he put forth the end of the rod that was in his hand, and dipped it in an honeycomb, and put his hand to his mouth; and his eyes were enlightened. Then answered one of the people, and said, Thy father straitly charged the people with an oath, saying, Cursed be the man that eateth any food this day. And the people were faint. Then said Jonathan, My father hath troubled the land: see, I pray you, how mine eyes have been enlightened, because I tasted a little of this honey. How much more, if haply the people had eaten freely to-day of the spoil of their enemies which they found? for had there not been now a much greater slaughter among the Philistines?" (1 *Samuel* 14/25-30). This honey was apparently in the cleft of a tree, and the comb had been broken, permitting some of the honey to trickle down the bark to the ground. The phrase, "his eyes were enlightened," may be more correctly translated "his eyes shone," or "lit up."

Bees, then as now, did not take kindly to being robbed of their supplies gathered with so much labor, and sometimes the honey-seeker had to beat a hasty retreat. Moses probably spoke from experience in *Deuteronomy* (1/44): "And the Amorites, which dwelt in that mountain, came out against you, and chased you, as bees do." *Psalms* (118/12) tells of the same retaliation from angry bees: "Yea, they compassed me about .... they compassed me about like bees." A debated passage, connected with the bee, occurs in *Isaiah* (7/18-19): "The Lord shall hiss for the fly that is in the uttermost part of the rivers of Egypt, and for the bee that is in the land of Assyria. And they shall come, and shall rest all of them in the desolate valleys, and in the holes of the rocks, and upon all thorns, and upon all bushes." The Hebrew word translated "hiss" includes the sibilant *Hist!* or short sharp whistle demanding attention, and also the hiss of dislike or reprobation. Some authorities consider that the bees were enticed out of their hives with a hissing buzzing sound, while others claim that the word signifies an ordinary call or summons. The original, *sharaq,* is not onomatopoetic like our "hiss" or "hist" or "buzz." Deborah is Hebrew for "bee," a feminine name borne by two well known biblical women.

Solomon speaks of honey and the honeycomb in many passages. "My son, eat thou honey, because it is good; and the honeycomb, which is sweet to thy taste" (*Proverbs* 24/13) might be commended to publicity minded apiculturists, while "Pleasant words are as an honeycomb, sweet to the soul, and health to the bones" (16/24) is equally laudatory. Elsewhere, the philosopher-king observes that one can get too much of a good thing, even honey. "Hast thou found honey? eat so much as is sufficient for thee, lest thou be filled therewith, and vomit it" (*Proverbs* 25/16). This allusion is clearly to a wild honey cache. The cloying nature of honey is emphasized in "It is not good to eat much honey" (25/27), and "The full soul loatheth an honeycomb" (27/7). Here the unimaginative translator changed the literally accurate Hebrew into colorless English, for the correct rendering is "The full soul treadeth under foot (or: trampleth upon) an honeycomb," which confirms that the reference is to wild honey. Solomon waxes romantic as well as gastronomic over honey: "Thy lips, O my spouse, drop as the honeycomb: honey and milk are under thy tongue" (*Song of Solomon* 4/11), while in *Proverbs* (5/3) he warns against the more dangerous sweets of the siren: "For the lips of a strange woman drop as an honeycomb, and her mouth is smoother than oil." In more exalted mood, Solomon's father declared, "The judgments of the Lord are true and righteous altogether.... sweeter also than honey and the honeycomb" (*Psalms* 19/9-10).

One of Samson's legendary exploits, related in the 14th chapter of *Judges,* centers on a swarm of bees in an unusual hive. Samson had fallen in love with a Philistine woman, and, over his parents' objection, made up his mind to marry her. Masculine development of abnormal

[262]

muscular strength and physique has always fascinated a certain type of attractive woman, a fact which the bicep-building schools play up in their advertising layouts. Strong man Samson had a yen for Philistine pulchritude and kept returning there to burn his fingers, the Philistine corn, and finally and tragically, his eyes.

On this occasion, his mishaps lay in the unknown future, and he was blithely on his way to visit his fiancée when he encountered a lion. He killed the lion, but thought so little of the incident that he didn't mention it. He returned home and persuaded his parents to make the formal marriage arrangements, and accompanied by his father and mother set out for the home of his future bride. En route, "he turned aside to see the carcase of the lion: and, behold, there was a swarm of bees and honey in the carcase of the lion. And he took thereof in his hands, and went on eating, and came to his father and mother, and he gave them, and they did eat: but he told not them that he had taken the honey out of the carcase of the lion. So his father went down unto the woman: and Samson made there a feast; for so used the young men to do. And it came to pass, when they saw him, that they brought thirty companions to be with him. And Samson said unto them, I will now put forth a riddle unto you: if ye can certainly declare it me within the seven days of the feast, and find it out, then I will give you thirty sheets (margin: shirts) and thirty change of garments. But if ye cannot declare it me, then shall ye give me thirty sheets and thirty change of garments. And they said unto him, Put forth thy riddle, that we may hear it. And he said unto them, Out of the eater came forth meat, and out of the strong came forth sweetness. And they could not in three days expound the riddle. And it came to pass on the seventh day, that they said unto Samson's wife, Entice thy husband, that he may declare unto us the riddle, lest we burn thee and thy father's house with fire. Have ye called us to take that we have" (Hebrew: impoverish us?).

The intimidated bride, torn between the threat of the Philistines and her new husband's prestige, let the former loyalties sway her, and she wore down the infatuated Samson with the age old sob story, "You don't love me anymore or you would do what I ask." Finally, at the eleventh hour, "He told her, because she lay sore upon him: and she told the riddle to the children of her people. And the men of the city said unto him on the seventh day before the sun went down, What is sweeter than honey? and what is stronger than a lion? And he said unto them, If ye had not plowed with my heifer, ye had not found out my riddle."

However, the joke, or the tragedy, was on the Philistines, for our hero merely went down to the nearby township of Askelon and broke the necks of the first thirty well-dressed Philistines he met, "and took their spoil, and gave change of garments unto them which expounded the riddle. And his anger was kindled, and he went up to his father's house," deserting the faithless wife who was given to his erstwhile best man. Samson was unaware of this, and when he had cooled off the old attraction began to work, and he set out to make the peace with his estranged wife, bringing a goat kid along as a gift. When he discovered that she was now married to another man, his rage flared anew and he set fire to and destroyed the whole wheat harvest of the Philistines. The infuriated farmers "came up, and burnt her and her father with fire. And Samson said unto them, Though ye have done this, yet will I be avenged of you . . . . and he smote them hip and thigh with a great slaughter: and he went down and dwelt in the top of the rock Etam," probably very soured on life.

The Mosaic law (*Leviticus* 2/11) prohibited the use of honey in any holy offering, possibly because of its fermenting quality, or because it was one of the oblations tendered Baal. In the idol worship, evidently of a phallic nature, which *Ezekiel* (16/17-19) condemns, honey formed part of the sacrifice of sweet savor. The manna which fed the Israelites in the desert tasted "like wafers made with honey" (*Exodus* 16/31). This would imply the use of honey in a baking recipe, except for the fact that the word "made" is italicized, and is not in the original.

In the New Testament, *Matthew* (3/4) tells us that locusts and wild honey comprised the wilderness diet of John the Baptist. This use of the adjective "wild," repeated in a parallel passage in *Mark* (1/6) and not found elsewhere, may imply that honey from domestic hives was available in the time of Jesus. Honey formed part of the first meal eaten by the Master after His resurrection (*Luke* 24/41-43). "He said unto them, Have ye here any meat? And they gave him a piece of a broiled fish, and of an honeycomb. And he took it, and did eat before them." The incident took place in Jerusalem, and is related only in Luke's Gospel.

Index to Bible References

[265]

INDEX TO BIBLE REFERENCES

MATTHEW

2/1-2, 11: 148
2/13-5: 24
3/4: 106, 255, 264
3/12: 139
5/18: 200
6/28, 30: 95
6/30: 207
7/6: 260
7/16: 165
11/8: 255
11/29-30: 128
12/20: 117
13/-: 166
13/3-8: 129
13/7: 169
13/30: 132
16/2-3: 37
19/24: 255
20/-: 90
21/-: 90
21/1-8: 250
21/18-20: 73
21/33: 84, 167
23/23: 50
23/24: 255
23/27: 258
24/41: 141
25/31-46: 233
26/27-9: 91
27/29: 169
27/57-60: 47

MARK

1/6: 264
2/22: 92
4/8: 129
4/28: 107
5/-: 152
6/13: 78
12/1: 88
13/18: 118
15/23: 152

LUKE

5/39: 93

6/1-2: 193
6/44: 167
7/33-5: 90
8/3: 99
8/8: 129
9/62: 125
10/34: 78
11/12: 259
11/42: 50, 196
12/54-5: 37
13/6-9: 75
13/8: 29, 127
13/15: 257
13/34: 258
14/3: 153
14/5: 257
14/19: 128
14/34-5: 206
15/11-32: 260
15/16: 105
15/29: 239
16/15-7: 181
16/19-20: 116
16/31: 182
17/6: 76
17/7-9: 127
19/1-9: 75
19/12: 29
20/9: 29
22/31: 139
23/56: 145
24/1: 145
24/41-3: 264

JOHN

1/29: 223
1/45-50: 75
2/11: 90
2/14-5: 257
6/9-13: 111
10/-: 223
10/3: 249
10/11-4: 222
12/3: 153
12/13: 71
12/24: 107

15/1-6: 90
15/2: 210
18/1-2: 47
19/39: 68, 153
19/39-40: 145
19/41-2: 47
20/11-6: 48

ACTS

2/-: 168
2/13-5: 92
7/22-3: 178
7/30: 167
9/4-5: 128
14/13: 257
27/38: 113

ROMANS

11/13-24: 211
11/17: 79
14/2-3: 51
14/5: 208

1 CORIN-THIANS

3/1-2: 243
9/9-10: 193
15/-: 113

2 CORIN-THIANS

6/14-7: 191
12/7: 169

GALATIANS

4/10: 208

EPHESIANS

4/11: 223

1 THESSA-LONIANS

5/7: 92

HEBREWS

5/12-3: 243
6/7-8: 165
9/19: 230
11/37-8: 231
13/20: 223

JAMES

1/11: 95
5/14-5: 78

1 PETER

1/24: 95

3 JOHN

-/13: 160

REVELATION

1/13-4: 229
6/2-8: 247
6/6: 111
6/12: 231
6/13: 74
7/1-3: 57
7/9: 71
8/11: 54
9/7-9: 171
10/8-10: 159
11/1: 160
18/11-3: 149
18/12: 64
18/13: 114
18/22: 140
19/8: 117
21/15-6: 160
21/20: 103

Subject Index

Barn 108, 124, 132-3, 139-40, 166, 172, 256
Barnfloor 133
Bartholomew 75
Bashan 64
Bay (tree) 63
Bazaar 108
Bdellium 150
Beans 102, 114
Bear 222, 228
Beaten corn 108
Beating (agricultural) 136-7, 192
Bedouin 146, 213
Beer 26
Beeri 247
Beer-sheba 15, 32, 42, 57, 63, 216
Bees 76, Chapter 21
Beehive 260-1
Beetle 174
Beeves 224
Benjamin 240
Bethany 72
Bethel 65, 89, 165
Bethlehem 46, 49, 131, 184
Bezaleel 230
Binder 132
Binding house 228
Bio-dynamics 24
Bit 248
Bitter apple 104
Bitumen 157
Black cummin 112, 125
Black goat's hair 231
Blacksmith 122, 128
Blasting 176-7
Bleating 225
Blight 176
Blood 180-1
Boar 85, 167
Boaz 131, 135-6, 139, 184-7, 192
Bolled 111
Bone fertilizer 205
Bonfire 207
Boswellia 149
Botany 39, 45, 49-50, 96, 162
Bottles 92-3, 242
Bottomland 124
Bouillabaisse 54
Box (tree) 62
Bozrah 87
Bracelets 235

Bramble 58, 106, Chapter 15
Brass 30, 123, 136, 199
Brass oxen 256
Bray 142, 164
Bread 24, 26, 30, 42-3, 86, 101, 111, 114, 120, 131, 194-5, 204, 213, 240, 246
Bread corn 125, 246
Break clods 124-5
Bridle 248, 250
Briers 64, Chapter 15
Britain 107
British Museum 26
Bronze Age 102
Broadcast seed 125
Brood (chickens) 259
Broom 63, 106
Broth 259
Bubon galbanum 155
Buckthorn 167, 170
Bud 210
Bull (bullock) 206, 237, 240
Bulrushes 157, 159-60
Bundling 135
Burial 116, 145
Burnings 145
Burns, Robert 107
Burseraceae 149-50
Butchering 234, 241, 257
Butter 77, 101, 174, 213, 242-4
Buttonwood 75

C

Cabbage 22, 203
Caches 140
Cain 101, 120, 123, 212, 239
Calambac 68
Calamus 144, 146, 148, 153-4, 160
Calamus odoratus 154
Calendar 207-8
Calf 213, 234
Calf worship 232, 235-6, 256
Camel 20, 71, 147-8, 154, 212, 236, 238, Chapter 20
Camel hair 231, 255
Camel ornaments 254
Camphire 95, 97, 98, 146, 153-4

Canaan, pre-Israel 31
Cana of Galilee 91
Candlesticks 82, 98, 105
Cane 154, 160
Cankerworm Chapter 16
Caper 52, 106
Caraway 50
Carmel 32, 37, 89, 226-7
Carob pods 105, 260
Cart 125, 128, 133, 137, 256
Cart wheel 124-5, 135, 137, 205, 246
Carving 230
Cassia 144, 148, 151-4
Caterpillar 42, Chapter 16
Cattle 26-8, 71, 89, 109, 120, 127, 172, 182, 189, 193, 202, Chapter 19, 252, 254
Cattle rustling 193-4
Caves 140, 227-9
Cedar 58, 62, 64, 66, 229
Celcius 52
Celery 22
Census 240
Ceratonia siliqua 105
Cereal 101
Ceylon 67, 152
Chabatstseleth 97
Chaff 113, 138-9
Chaldea (Chaldeans) 25, 36, 83, 130, 141, 207, 246, 255
Charash 123
Chariot 171-2, 245-7, 252
Charits (Charuts) 136
Chartreuse 53
Chattle 212
Chebar 83
Cheese 122, 128, 244
Cherries 22
Chestnut 66, 81
Chian 65
Chickens 258
Chick pea 204
Chile 203
Chilion 186
China 26, 69, 99, 150, 152
Chisel 122, 128
Chrysanthemums 22
Chrysophrasus 103
Churchill 91
Churning 243
Cinnamomum cassia 152

SUBJECT INDEX

[278]

[279]